BASIC PRINCIPLES OF EDUCATION

Basic Principles of Education

Shashi Prabha Sharma

KANISHKA PUBLISHERS, DISTRIBUTORS
NEW DELHI-110 002

KANISHKA PUBLISHERS, DISTRIBUTORS
4697/5-21A, Ansari Road, Daryaganj
New Delhi -110 002
Phones : 2327 0497, 2328 8285
Fax : 011-2328 8285
E-mail : kanishka_publishing@yahoo.co.in

Basic Principles of Education

First Published: 2004
Edition: 2021

ISBN : 978-81-7391-695-0

PRINTED IN INDIA

Published by Madan Sachdeva for Kanishka Publishers, Distributors, 4697/5-21A, Ansari Road, Daryaganj, New Delhi-110 002, Typeset by Sunshine Graphics, Delhi, and Printed at Rajdhani Printers, Delhi.

Preface

Human beings need education because they are destined to be real man, not wild beasts, dull animals, and clumps of wood. Education is the differentia between man and animal because education cultivates an integrated life in a man, thus it is education that fashions and models man for society and therefore, education is essentially a vital human activity and considered as most rewarding investment.

Education is the foundation stone of nation's intellectual power which shapes the power profile of a nation in the community of world nations, thus, it is rightly said that progress of a country particularly of a democratic country depends upon the quality of its system of education and for this reason teaching is the noblest among all professions. It is because of this that Kothari Commission report starts with the remark, *"The destiny of India is being shaped in its classrooms"*.

Education as a composite discipline must confirm to the socio-economic, socio-political and socio-cultural conditions, therefore, principles of education encompassing all these aspects become a pre-requisite and thus arises the need to develop the thoughts and knowledge on these aspects in such a format as the present book at hand.

The present work captioned as Basic Principles of Education, among several books published in India, claims to be the most comprehensive. This book has been designed so as to make the students, scholars and teachers informed of the principles of education. The book presents a very systematic presentation of the subject matter in simple and lucid language drawing examples from the Indian Educational system. The book contains point analysis and description of the subject in Indian context and covers the syllabus of all the Indian universities on the subject.

The book in all contains 35 chapters out of which first 14 chapters are devoted to basic concepts such as Basic Elements' Forms of Education, Aims of Education, Theory and Practice of Education, Study of the Child, Classification of Agencies of Education, Family, Community, Religion, State, and School as Agencies of Education, Non-Formal Education and Educational Values. Because no other book contains all these aspects as they are written as per syllabus of some particular universities.

The remaining 21 chapters in the book contain pinpoint study of the principles of education because education must meet the socio-economic, socio-political and socio-cultural needs and conditions of the society and the nation, which in totality has not been done, to the best of my knowledge, by any other Indian author. The principles of education encompassed in 21 chapters of this book are related to—Curriculum Construction, Organising Curricular and Co-curricular Activities, Role and Responsibilities of Headmaster/Principal and Teacher and Authority of the Teacher, Principle of Assessing Students' Progress, Principles of Social Control, Social Values, Social Change, Cultural, Religious and Moral Values, Population Education and Socially Useful Productive Work, Principles of Nationalities, Emotional and Inter-cultural and National Integration Together with International Understanding. Principles of Democratic Polity, Modernization, Mass Education, Scientific Attitude and Vocational Education are also included in this book.

All these aspects of principles of education are vital and must be followed by educators and planners of Indian educational system in a democratic set-up which we have in India. Therefore, this book is of vital academic as well as national importance.

The subject matter contained in 35 chapters of this book, I trust, would fulfil the needs, requirements and expectations of the students, scholars and teachers of education of all the Indian universities.

Planned as a text book for the students and reference book for the scholars and teachers, this book is a critical constructive appraisal of the subject. While I have tried my best to make this book the best on the subject, the students, scholars, teachers and other general readers are the best judge of its merits.

The author is very grateful to the publisher for bringing out the book expeditiously.

Suggestions for improvement are, therefore, cordially invited, through the publisher.

Shashi Prabha Sharma

Contents

1

Meaning and Basic Elements of Education

To understand the principles of education, one must have a clear concept of the meaning, nature, basic elements and aims of education, which are being, briefly, discussed in the initial chapters of this book.

Introduction

The new born infant is a helpless human being. He has neither friends nor enemies. He is not aware of the social customs and traditions. He is not even keen to achieve any ideal or value. But as he grows older, he is influenced by the informal and formal agencies of education. He develops his physical, mental and emotional self and social feelings. By and by, he develops sense of responsibility like his elders. He solves the problems of life successfully.

Thus, education instills in the child a sense of maturity and responsibility. Education bestows immense benefits upon a person. A well educated person is known all over the region because he is able to meet the conflicting challenges.

Education culturises the individual and helps him to fulfil his needs. Education develops the individual like a flower which distributes its fragrance all over the environment. Thus, education is a conducive process which develops child's individuality in all its aspects—physical, mental, emotional and social.

With this all-round development, he becomes a responsible, dynamic, resourceful and enterprising citizen of strong good moral character who uses all his capacities to develop his own self, his society and his nation to the highest extent by contributing his best to national honour, national glory, national culture and national civilization of which he is an integral part.

On one hand, education develops personality of an individual in all fields and aspects making him intelligent, learned, bold, courageous and possessing strong good character, on the other hand, it contributes to growth and development of society. It is only through education that moral ideals and spiritual values, as aspiration of the nation and its cultural heritage is transferred from one generation to another for preservation, purification and sublimation into higher and higher achievements.

With the growth and development of individual, the society also develops to higher and higher levels of attainments. Thus, education is essential for the growth and development of individual as well as society. Therefore, there are few people who are not in some sense interested in education. Parents, teachers, school governors, ministers of religion, and politicians, all have the word frequently on their lips, and all may be supposed to use it with a more or less definite notion of its meaning.

But if there is such a thing as a theory of education—and at this point we can only take leave to assume its existence—one of its functions must be the critical examination of current notions, and the exposure of their short-comings. This is no superfluous task, for the smallest details of the educator's work are inevitably coloured by his general conception of its aim, and it is not too much to say that most of the defects of educational practice are due to the absence of any clearly conceived aim, or to the presence of a wrong one.

Importance of Education

A serious student of education is essentially concerned with the practice of education. It must, however, be remembered that practice pre-supposes a certain amount of theory. It has been rightly said that even the most practical and matter-of-fact educationist has some kind of a theory of education. A practical educator like Tagore or Gandhi, Rousseau or Dewey would arrange and classify his theoretical ideas whereas another (and there is a large majority of them) might leave behind a disjoined crowd of his ideas. One thing is definite and must not be overlooked. An attempt to formulate the theory of any activity which is to be practised for a length of time is of great help in deciding the worth of what is being practised.

Education is an important human activity. It was born with the birth of the human race and shall continue to function as long as the human race lives. The importance of education may be summed up as under:

1. *An essential human virtue.* Education is an essential human virtue. Man becomes 'man' through education. He is what education makes him. It has been rightly said that without education, man is a splended slave, a reasoning savage.
2. *A necessity for society.* Education is necessary for society. Education fashions and models man for society. Man cannot be conceived merely in terms of his biological existence. Education brings into focus the social aspect of man. Education signifies man's supreme position in socicty.
3. *Important for the integration of separate entities.* An individual is made up of different entities. Education brings about the integration of these separate entities.
4. *Gives significance of life.* Education teaches what man lives and struggles for. It cultivates an integrated life. By so doing, it gives significance of life.
5. *Educated men are superior.* Education is a sign of superiority. Aristotle wrote, "Educated men are as much superior to uneducated as the living are to the dead."
6. *Sign of freedom.* Education is a sign of freedom. Epictetus had declared, "Only the educated are free."
7. *A controlling grace.* Diogenes felt that "Education is a

controlling grace to the young, consolation to the old, wealth to the poor and ornament to the rich."

8. *Basis of good life.* Education is an essential basis of good life. A man becomes a human being in the real sense when he is transformed from primarily an animal being into a human being'.

In short education is an essential concomitant of all human societies. "What sculpture is to a block of marble, education is to the soul", says Addison.

Meaning of Education

To define any subject is the most difficult task for each and every scholar and more than it is to get universal acceptance for any definition. Hereunder an attempt is being made to define education for critical evaluation by the students and scholars:

Etymological Meaning of Education

The Latin word 'Educatum' means to train. 'E' means from inside and 'Duco' means to draw out, to lead out or to bring up. By combining the two, education comes to mean to draw from within. Education is a process which draws from within. Each child is born with some innate tendencies, capacities and inherent powers. Education draws these powers out and develop them to the full.

Latin words 'Educare' and 'Educere' mean to bring up, to lead out and to develop etc. In this way, the word education means to develop the inborn qualities of a child to the full.

Education, as we have seen, is bound up with human race. Its boundaries are as wide as those of life. Its implications are rich and varied. Just as it is difficult to squeeze life in a few words, in the same way it is difficult to give a single meaning or definition of education. Before we arrive at a comprehensive (though not all-inclusive) definition of education, let us understand the term in its derivative sense as follows:

In its derivative sense the term education may be understood as 'educare' or 'educere':

(a) *Educare.* Educare is a Latin word and it means 'to nourish', 'to bring up', 'to raise'. This means, educating a child means nourishing or bringing up the child according to certain ends or aims.

(b) *Educere.* Educere is also a Latin word and it means 'to lead out' or 'to draw out'. This means, educating a chid implies drawing out what is ingrained in the child or leading him out of darkness into light.

Above words establish that education is the process of development of humanity. To understand the nature and rate of progress, one must know the data of education as follows:

Data of Education

1. *The child.* The foremost data of education is the child. Each child has certain innate powers. His natural development is possible only according to these native endowments.

2. *Heredity.* Hereditarians believe that education of a child is predetermined by heredity. According to them, hereditary impressions influence a child from his infancy before any formal education begins.

These innate tendencies and qualities are the firm foundation for his education. These also delimit and define the highest achievements to be achieved by him. Thus, to hereditarians, education is development according to lines pre-determined and prelaid by the heredity of a child.

3. *Environment.* Another factor of education is environment. Every child is born in a family at a particular place and time. His upbringing also takes place in a specific environment. This environment is either controlled or uncontrolled. Both types of environment exert their influence upon the growing child in different ways. Controlled environment leads to controlled growth and uncontrolled environment promotes uncontrolled growth.

According to them, environment is a powerful factor which influences the development of child. One cannot escape its influence at any cost. The environmentalists hold that as the child gradually comes into contact with the physical and social environment, his innate tendencies flower out and his behaviour begins to change.

4. *Time.* During the process of development, specific activities are indulged by the child at specific times. To understand this process of development, one must have a clear understanding of the various stages of development. As different and specific tendencies sprout out of these various stages, education must correspond its plans and programmes to these budding capacities. Then only, the development of the child will be normal and natural. Any discord or imbalance will result in stunted growth or no growth at all.

Hence, education should correspond and suit the mental level of the child, otherwise it will create complexes and mar the development.

Both the hereditarians and the environmentalists assert one side of the truth. The two factors are not contradictory. They are mutually complementary and supplementary. Both work together to develop the child smoothly and in a balanced way. Both are essential for the proper development of a child.

Education in Narrow Sense

In its narrow sense school instruction is called education. In this process, the elders of society strive to attain predetermined aims during a specified time by providing pre-structured titbits of knowledge to children through set methods of teaching. The purpose is to achieve mental development of children entering school.

In this process, the teacher is the most important factor and the child is assigned a subsidiary role. The teacher is expected to instil ready made doses of knowledge in the child's mind. By this, the child cannot attain the wholesome development of his personality. Such knowledge strangles the natural development of the child and hence, is of no use to him for his actual future life.

Following opinions of some educationists represent the narrow meaning of education:

1. "In narrow sense, education may be taken to mean any consciously directed effort to develop and cultivate our powers."

—S.S. Mackenzi

2. "Education is a process in which and by which knowledge, character and behaviour of the young are shaped and moulded."

—*Prof. Drever*

3. "The influence of the environment on the individual with a view to producing a permanent change in his habits of behaviour, of thought and attitude."

—*G.H. Thompson*

Education in Analytical Sense

Following are the constituent fields of education:

1. *Not limited to knowledge imparted in schools.* Education can not be confined to the processes of giving knowledge to children in schools. Its programme goes on from birth till death. Everyone learns something or the other throughout life by various experiences and activities. All this is education.

2. *Education as the development of child's innate power.* Education is developing the native endowments of a child rather than something forced into the mind from outside. Addison has rightly remarked, "Education when it works upon noble mind, draws out to view every latent virtue and perfection which without such help are never able to make their appearance."

3. *Education as a dynamic process.* Education is not a static but a dynamic process which develops the child according to changing situation and times. It is a purposive activity always pursuing some aim of life.

4. *Education as a bipolar process.* In his book "Evolution of Educational Theory" Adams has interpreted education as a bipolar process. He analysed education as under:

(*i*) "It (Education) is a bipolar process in which one personality acts upon another in order to modify the development of the other."

(*ii*) "The process is not only a conscious one but a deliberate one. The educator has the clearly realised intention of modifying the development of the educand."

(*iii*) "The means by which the development of the educand

> is to be modified are two folds: *(a)* The direct application of the educator's personality to the personality of the educand, and *(b)* The use of knowledge in its various forms."

According to Adams, the bipolar education has two poles. At one end is the teacher and at the other is the child. Both are equally important in education. If the teacher instructs, the child follows. If the teacher gives, the child receives.

Thus, in the process of education there is interaction between the teacher and the child. The teacher tries to mould and modify the behaviour of the child so that the latter develops his personality to the full.

5. *Education as a tripolar process.* Like Adams, John Dewey also regards education as a process of development. But, while accepting the psychological view, Adams emphasizes the importance of teacher and the child, John Dewey emphasizes the sociological view point.

Hence, according to John Dewey, education has two aspects (1) Psychological, and (2) Sociological. He accepts the contention that education of the child should be according to his native endowments. He further asserts that the development of a child does not take place in a vacuum. It takes place in and through the society in which the teacher and the child both live.

It is the society which will determine the aims, contents and methods of teaching. In this way, the process of education contains three poles, namely (1) The teacher, (2) The child, and (3) The society. These three factors actively co-operate in the efficient and successful working of the educational process.

Education in Wider Sense

In its wider sense, education is not the communication of information by the teacher or the acquisition of knowledge by the child but the total development of the personality. Education consists of all those experiences which affect the individual from birth till death.

Thus, education is the process by which an individual freely develops his self according to his nature in a free and uncontrolled environment. It is a life-long process of growth and development. It is not confined to the limits of time, place and individual.

Any person who gives the child a new experience is a teacher and any place where this giving and receiving takes place may be termed as a school.

Thus, education is essentially a process of growth and development which goes on throughout the whole life. Rousseau developed his philosophy of naturalism keeping this wider concept of education in his view-point. Following eminent scholars interpret education in the wider context:

(1) "In the wider sense, it is a process that goes on throughout life, and is promoted by almost every experience in life." —*S.S. Mackcenzi*

(2) "By education, I mean the all round drawing out of the best in child and man—body, mind and soul." —*M.K. Gandhi*

(3) "Education in its widest sense includes all the influences which act upon an individual during his passage from cradle to the grave." —*Dumvile*

CONCEPT OF EDUCATION IN INDIA AND IN THE WEST

The system of education changes according to time and cultural conditions, therefore, hereunder we first mention Indian concepts of education:

Indian Concept of Education

Indian approach includes the spiritual aspect as a part of the development by education. In fact, Indian thinkers have placed special emphasis upon this. Yajnavalkya opined that only that is education which gives a sterling character to an individual and renders him useful for the world.

Shankaracharya said that education is that which leads to salvation. Even the more recent educationists have stressed the importance of the spiritual aspect.

In the words of A. S. Altekar, "Education has always been regarded in India as a source of illumination and power which transforms and ennobles our nature by the progressive and harmonious development of our physical, mental, intellectual and spiritual powers and faculties."

This spiritual tradition has been carried on by contemporary Indian philosophers of education in their integral approach, synthesis of idealism and pragmatism, rationalism and humanism, diversity in unity and harmony of the individual and society.

It was due to this emphasis on the spiritual meaning of education that Vivekanand said, "Religion is the inner most core of education."

In the words of Sri Aurobindo, "The child's education ought to be an outpouring of all that is best, most powerful, most intimate and living in his nature, the mould into which the man's action and development ought to run is that of his innate quality and power. He must acquire new things but he will acquire them best, most wholly on the basis of his own developed type and inborn force."

M.K. Gandhi expressed the same idea when he defined education by saying, "By education, I mean an all round drawing out of the best in child and man, body, mind and spirit. Literacy is not the end of education not even the beginning. It is one of the means whereby man and woman can be educated. Literacy in itself is no education."

Hereunder we mention view points of Indian educators very briefly for understanding the Indian concept of education.

Ancient Indian thinkers took an idealistic or spiritual view of education. Modern Indian thinkers have regarded education more from the practical point of view than the idealistic one.

(a) Ancient Thinkers

(i) In *Rigveda*, education has been understood as something which makes a man self-reliant and selfless'.

(ii) In *Upanishadas* education has been understood as something the end product of which is salvation (साविद्या या विमुक्तयें or साविद्या या वियोक्षधति प्रदा)

(iii) According to *Yajnavalkya*, 'Education is that which makes a man of good character and useful to the world'.

(*iv*) According to *Kautilya*, the great Indian statesman and law giver, 'Education means training for the country and love for the nation.'

(*v*) Shankracharya regards Education as 'the realization of the self.'

(b) *Modern Thinkers*

(*i*) According to *Swami Vivekanand*, 'Education is the manifestation of divine perfection already existing in man.'

By Education he meant drawing out the divine potential already existing in man.

(*ii*) According to *Swami Dayanada*, 'Education is a means for character formation and righteous living.'

(*iii*) According to *Gandhiji*, "By Education I mean an all-round drawing out of the best in child and man, body, mind and spirit." Gandhiji's definition includes the physical, intellectual and spiritual aspects of human personality.

(*iv*) According to *Gurudev Tagore*, 'Education is that which makes one's life in harmony with all existence and thus enables the mind to find the ultimate truth which gives us the wealth of inner light and love and gives significance to life.'

(*v*) According to *Aurobindo*, 'Education means helping the growing soul to draw out that is in itself.'

(*vi*) *Prof. Humayun Kabir* has defined Education as a "dynamic process which in its totality changes with the changing situations and developing circumstances."

(*vii*) *Dr. Zakir Hussain*, the late President of India, defined education as "the process of the individual mind, getting to its full possible development."

Western Concept of Education

Educational thinking, like every other branch of knowledge, started in the philosophical deliberation of the ancient Greek philosophers. Thus, the meaning of education in west is initially available in the works of Plato. It is interesting to note that thousand of years ago, Plato gave a meaning to education which is even now followed in the West with slight changes here and there. Western interpretation of the term Education has been changing from time to time. But fact remains that modern concept of education owes much to Western thinkers.

(a) Thinkers of the past

(i) According to *Plato,* "Education is the capacity to feel pleasure and pain at the right moment. It develops in the body and in the soul of the pupil all the beauty and all the perfection which he is capable of."

(ii) According to *Aristotle,* "Education is the creation of a sound mind in a sound body.... It develops man's faculty especially his mind so that he may be able to enjoy the contemplation of supreme truth, goodness and beauty of which perfect happiness essentially consists."

(iii) According to *Comenius,* "All who are born as human beings need education because they are destined to be real men, not wild beasts, dull animals, and clumps of wood."

(b) Modern Thinkers

(i) According to *Pestalozzi,* "Education is the natural, harmonious and progressive development of man's innate powers."

(ii) According to *Froebel,* "Education is unfoldment of what is already enfolded in the germ. It is the process through which the child makes internal and external."

(iii) According to *John Dewey,* "Education is the development of all those capacities in the individual which will enable him to control his environment and fulfil his possibilities."

(iv) According to *Raymont,* "Education is a process of development... from infancy to maturity, the process by which he adopts himself gradually in various ways of his physical and spiritual environment."

(v) According to *T.P. Nunn*, "Education is the complete development of the individuality of the child so that he can make an original contribution to human life according to the best of his capacity."

(vi) *Thompson* defines Education as "the influence of the environment on the individual with a view to producing a permanent change in his habits, behaviour, of thought and of attitude.

(vii) According to *John Adams*, "Education is conscious and deliberate process in which one personality acts upon another in order to modify the development of that other by the communication and manipulation of knowledge".

(viii) *Redden's* comprehensive definition of the term: The definition of Education as given by Redden is quite comprehensive. He states: "Education is the deliberate and systematic influence exerted by the mature person upon the immature, through instruction, discipline, and harmonious development of physical, intellectual, aesthetic, social and spiritual powers of the human being, according to individual and social needs and directed towards the union of the educated with his creator as the final end."

All the foregoing definitions have stated that education is the process of development. It, therefore, becomes necessary to discover what is implied in this development.

Although the ability to learn depends upon development, but development is not synonymous with education. Development means the gradual and continuous progress of mind and body. Through this development the child acquires the following elements:

1. Knowledge of the environment by which he is surrounded.
2. The necessary motor control to fulfil his individual needs.
3. Linguistic abilities to enable him to converse.
4. Some knowledge of individual and collective relationship.

The development of all these elements begins at home itself. The educator's task is to continue this process and to encourage it while the child is at school.

In fact, this process of development continues right through an individual's life time. Consequently, it is accepted that education in its general sense continues throughout a man's natural span of life. Even the successful teacher or educator himself remains a student throughout his life.

On the one hand, he teaches certain things to some people but at the same time he learns something from them. All successful educators experience that the development undergone by their thoughts, personalities and abilities would have been impossible otherwise. In much the same way, people other than the educator, teach and learn simultaneously.

Synthesized Concept of Education

It is clear from the above discussion of the meaning of education in West and India, ancient and modern that it may be synthesised since all these accept some common characteristics of education. The following points concerning the meaning of education emerge from a review of the meaning of education in the West and in India:

1. *A Life-long process.* Education according to most of the philosophers continues from birth to death. As Madam Paul Richard pointed out the education of man "should begin at his very birth and it is to continue the whole length of his life."

2. *Unfolding.* Education is a gradual unfolding. In his 'Allegory of the Cave', Plato observed that "the power and capacity of learning exists in the soul already, and just as the eye was unable to turn from darkness of light, without the whole body, so too, the instrument of knowledge can only, by the movement of the whole soul, be turned from the world of the becoming into that of being and learn by degrees to endure the sight of being and of the brightest and best of being or in other words of the good." It is in the same sense that Sri Aurobindo said, "The chief aim of education should be to help the growing soul to draw out that in itself which is best and make it perfect for a noble use."

3. Based on child psychology. Western thinkers unanimously agree that true education should be based on child psychology. This again has been accepted by Indian philosophers of education.

According to Sri Aurobindo, "Nothing can be taught to the mind which is not already concealed as potential knowledge in the unfolding soul of creature."

Educational theory must be based on sound psychology. As Sri Aurobindo points out, "The true basis of education is the study of the human mind, infant, adolescent and adult."

4. Individual as well as social. True education is individual as well as social. Plato brought out a scheme of education according to each individual's capacities to serve the society. Philosophers in the West have everywhere laid emphasis upon individual as well as social aims of education.

Contemporary Indian philosophers also exhibit this tendency. M.K. Gandhi said, "I value individual freedom, but you must not forget that man is essentially a social being. He has risen to his present status by learning to adjust his individuality to the requirements of social progress."

5. Total development. Thus, education by general agreement is a total development, physical, mental and spiritual, individual as well as social. This total development is the meaning of self-realisation. This synthesis of the different aspects of man's development is characteristic of not only idealism but also naturalism, pragmatism and realism. It is again the meaning of perfection, acclaimed as the aim of education by so many thinkers, it is also what is known as complete education. It is again the humanist meaning of education since man is a complex being several aspects of his personality all of which require full development.

According to Sri Aurobindo, education should help the individual to grow, "into a fullness of physical and vital energy and utmost breadth, depth and height of his emotional, his intellectual and his spiritual being."

The total development lays equal emphasis upon physical as well as spiritual growth. Without physical culture, mental training has been considered as one-sided.

In the words of Aldous Huxley, "Where the body is maladjusted and under strain, the mind's relations, sensory, emotional, intellectual, conative, with external reality are likely to be unsatisfactory." Education aims at an all-round and total perfection of the individual and society. Hence, physical culture should form an important part of the educational process. As Sri Aurobindo puts it, "If seeking is for a total perfection of the being, the physical part of it can not be left aside, for the body is the material basis, the body is the instrument which we have to use."

Similar quotations may be hunted from other philosophers of education in West and East. The total development involves character development, development of social virtues and individual skills. It includes all the various aims of education. It involves all the functions of education in human life such as development of natural abilities, character building, personality integration, preparation for adult life, control and sublimation of basic instincts, creation of useful citizens, development of a sense of community, progress of culture and civilization, social welfare, use of leisure and synthesis of national as well as international consciousness.

Nature of Education

Following points give clear concept of the nature of education.

(a) *Education is a process.* Any one act or single experience does not by itself make up education. Education is neither a mere serial aggregate of facts. It has an intrinsic continuity.

(b) *Education is an integrating process.* The function of education is to create integrated human beings. Only, such human beings are intelligent and capable of solving individual and collective problems.

(c) *Helps to discover lasting values.* Education should help us to discover lasting values. It should help us to break down our national and social barriers.

(d) *Life-long process.* Education is a life long process. It includes all influences which act upon an individual during his passage from the cradle to the grave.

(e) *Modification of behaviour.* Education is the modification of behaviour. It enlarges human experience and so it produces some change in one's behaviour which involves thinking, feeling and action.

(f) *Education is life.* John Dewey says that education is not preparation for life, it is life itself. Edward Thring says, "Education is the transmission of life by the living to the living'. A.N. Whitehead also supports this view when he says: "There is only one subject-matter of education and that is life in all its manifestation." Prof. T. Raymont is also of the view: "It is really life that educates. One is educated by one's vocation, by home life, by friendship, by marriage, by parenthood, by recreation, by travel, and so forth." In this sense it also includes self-culture.

In the Report of International Commission on the Development of Education (UNESCO), entitled Learning to be, the idea of life-long education has been developed as: "......... human beings keep on learning and training themselves throughout their lives, above all through the influence of the surrounding environment and through the experiences which mould their behaviour, their conceptions of life and the content of their knowledge."

We may conclude in the words of Dr. S. Radhakrishnan: "Education, to be complete, must be humane, it must include not only the training of the intellect but also the refinement of the heart and the discipline of the spirit."

Education—A Bi-Polar Process

Education is a bi-polar process in which one personality acts upon another in order to modify the development of that other. The process is conscious as well as deliberate one. The means by which the development of the educand is to be modified are two-fold: *(a)* the direct application of the educator's personality to the personality of the educand, and *(b)* use of knowledge in the various forms. This is the view of John Adams.

In this sense, education becomes a shared activity. The child as well as the teacher both become active participants in the teaching-learning process. Ross observes in this context, "Like a magnet, education must have two poles."

Education—A Tripolar Process

According to John Dewey, education is a tripolar process. It has three important ingredients:

(1) The teacher,
(2) The learner, and
(3) The curriculum.

1. *The teacher.* In ancient times, the teacher had the main role to play while the learner's role was subsidiary. In modern time, the role has been reversed. Though the place of teacher has now become secondary, yet his responsibility has increased because a teacher is not only an important factor in the educational environment of the learner, he is also a builder of the whole educational environment which is very comprehensive and all inclusive.

In the process of education, a teacher's role is two fold. Firstly, being the important factor of the educational environment, he influences the personality of the learner through his own magnetic personality. Secondly, as a builder of the educational environment, he provides suitable experiences to the learner to develop and use fully his skills and capacities to achieve the good of his ownself and the welfare of his society, of which he is an integral part.

Besides, by his own attitudes and behaviour, the teacher builds the character of learners and infuses in them respect for moral and spiritual values. This is only possible when the teacher is himself a man of strong moral character. He must be well aware of the modern strategies, tactics and techniques of teaching. He should be capable of using them to the best of his knowledge to make teaching learning most effective.

Thus, to develop the learner as well as the society, a teacher is a very important factor in the educational process of today.

2. *The learner.* According to psychological findings and democratic feeling, education starts from the child. Thus, education has become child-centred today.

Adams was the first educationist to point out this truth by his remark, "The teacher teaches Latin to John." John is more important than Latin. Modern educationists are unanimous about the importance of child in the educational process.

Education should develop the personality of the learner according to his interests, inclinations, abilities, and capacities. Everything concerning education is now child-centred.

Aims, curriculum and methods keep the child at the centre of their formulation and planning of educational programmes. No teacher can be successful in his activities, if he fails to understand the learner with which he is to deal.

To make teaching-learning normal, natural and effective the teacher should not be the master of content only but also know fully well the stages of child development and their characteristics.

3. *Curriculum.* The essential link between the teacher and the child is the curriculum. It serves as a vehicle for the realisation of educational aims. The teacher uses the items of curriculum according to modern methods of teaching to educate children to realise the predetermined aims of education. In the wider sense, curriculum means all the experiences and activities from which a child learns something or the other.

The teacher and the child both co-operate in building and formulating experiences conducive to learning. Curriculum is structured according to the ever growing needs of children and changing demands of dynamic society. This is the difference between the curriculum of despotic as well as democratic countries. In the former type, all activities are rigid, predetermined and fully controlled by the state, while in the latter pattern, there is flexibility, freedom and adjustment.

The modern concept of education takes into consideration the social setting in which the interaction between the educator and the educand takes place. Thus, education is a three-dimensional process. The view that education is a tri-polar process was given by John Dewey. In Dewey's own words, "All education proceeds by the participation of the individual in the social consciousness of the race." He believed that any system of education devoid of its social significance is incomplete.

Social Environment
↓ ↓
Educator ⇄ Educand
↑ ↑
Social Environment

In a democratic society, every activity 'should' develop out of the real needs of the group. Education must cater to the individual as well as the social needs. Child's instincts, urges, impulses and tendencies have to be directed towards the socially desirable channels. This is possible when the child participates in the social situation and there is interaction involving the educator, the educand and the social environment.

True Definition of Education

The different meanings and definitions of education as given in this chapter lead us to the conclusion that education should have a comprehensive definition.

Thus, education may be defined as a purposive, conscious or unconscious psychological, sociological, scientific and philosophical process which brings about the development of the individual to the fullest extent and also the maximum development of society in such a way that both enjoy maximum happiness and prosperity.

In short, education is the development of individual according to his needs and demands of society, of which he is an integral part.

T. Raymont has rightly remarked, "Education is that process of development in which consists the passage of human being from infancy to maturity, the process whereby he adapts himself gradually in various ways to his physical, social and spiritual environment".

Modern Concept of Education

To understand the modern concept of education, one has to make a comparative study of the old and modern concepts. Following are the differences between the old and the new concepts:

1. *Meaning of education.* Education is derived from the Latin word 'Educatum' which means to draw out, to foster growth and to develop. Hence, the modern concept of education seeks to develop the inherent capacities of a child in the social environment. In the old concept, education was taken to mean as a process to thrust ready made titbits of knowledge into the mind of a child as if it was an empty vessel.

The old concept has exploded under the weight of psychological researches and democratic values. The mind is a dynamic self-adjusting and self-learning force needing proper guidance for wholesome growth and development. Modern education seeks to develop the mind according to its own inherent capacities in a social environment.

2. *Aims of education.* Ancient education emphasized scholarship and mental development. It kept an indifferent attitude towards other aspects of personality. Acquiring more and more knowledge was regarded as the prime aim.

On the contrary, modern educationists lay equal stress upon other aspects of development viz., physical, mental, emotional and social. Thus, the aim of modern education is to develop individuality to the full and attain social efficiency and dynamism.

3. *Curriculum.* In the old curriculum, only subjects promoting mental development were included and emphasized. Thus, old curriculum got rigid and stratified. It was confined mostly to classroom activities and experiences.

Modern curriculum is flexible, varied and progressive in the sense that it tries to meet the needs of the developing child as well as demands of ever changing modern society.

4. *Methods of teaching.* As the methods emphasized cramming and stimulated rote memorization education was a lifeless, dull and drab process.

Modern methods condemn rote memorization and promote the adoption of lively and effective methods like play-way, learning by doing, learning by experience etc. These methods stimulate motivation, interest and attention.

5. *Discipline.* Old concept of discipline emphasized the use of rod and punishments to enforce obedience and discipline

in children. This concept of enforced discipline through repression has now been given up. The modern concept is self-discipline leading to natural obedience.

6. *Examination.* The old method of essay type examination encouraged cramming and rote memorization. Modern techniques evaluate as well as examine. These include objective tests, progress reports, cumulative records, interviews and practical performances.

7. *Agencies of education.* According to old beliefs, school was the only agency for the education of children. According to modern views all formal and informal agencies are harnessed to the task of education.

8. *Teacher.* Old education put the teacher at the top of the educational process. In modern times a teacher is considered as a friend, philosopher and guide.

9. *Child.* According to old concept, the child was a mere passive recipient of whatever the teacher instructed. Modern education is child centred. The entire educational process is to cater to his needs and develop him according to his nature. He is to interact actively with the teacher and his class mates to achieve effective learning promoting his own development and the development of the society of which he is an integral part.

10. *School.* According to old concept, school served as a shop for selling knowledge. Everything was pre-planned in advance. Teachers were concerned with the input and bothered little about output. Modern concept of education regards school a miniature of society laying emphasis more on output in comparison with input.

11. *Education as a discipline.* In ancient times, education meant only training of something for some aim. Modern education is a separate discipline of deep study, investigation, and research. It is a very important process of human development in all fields of human activities. It has its own distinct special features and factors to promote it as a vital formative process.

The following chart clarifies the modern concept of education:

Serial Number	*Aspects of Education*	*Old Concept of Education*	*Modern concept of Education*
1.	Meaning	Instruction	Development
2.	Aims	Knowledge	(1) Development of total personality (2) Social efficiency
3.	Curriculum	Subject-Centred	Activity-centred social efficiency
4.	Methods	Rote Memorization	Learning by doing, project etc.
5.	Discipline	Rigid, repressionistic	Self-discipline
6.	Examination	Essay type tests	Objective type tests, evaluation
7.	Agencies	Formal (School)	Formal and informal both.
8.	Teacher	Instructor	Friend, Philosopher and guide
9.	Child	Passive recipient	Active, dynamic
10.	School	Teaching shops	Miniature of society

QUESTIONS FOR ANSWER

1. Define education and explain its scope.
2. Explain the various aspects of education according to modern concept of education.
3. "Education has been defined and interpreted in many ways, but these definitions are mostly complementary rather than contradictory." Explain this statement with suitable examples.
4. Define education as a process and a system and explain why it is necessary to educate the human being?
5. What do you mean by education? Differentiate between wider and narrower meaning of education.
6. "Education is the process of Human Resources Development." Discuss this statement in the light of nature and scope of education.
7. "A system of education is a response to the changing needs of the society it serves." Critically discuss the above statement, giving examples.
8. 'Education is a bi-polar or tri-polar process'. Discuss.
9. "Education is preparation for life through life experience". Discuss the functions of education in the light of above statement.
10. Write a note on Indian concept of education.
11. Write a note on Western concept of education.

2

Forms of Education

Generally instructions imparted in schools and colleges are considered as education, but in true sense education is 'very' complex process hence, hereunder we will try to focus on various forms of education.

Education is a comprehensive concept which comprehends the knowledge obtained through various other means, in addition to the formal education provided in colleges. The average individual interprets the term in the sense of college education, which is obviously different from the education obtained from the other sources. Educationists have distinguished between the various types of education in order to remove this confusion. Briefly, education is of the following kinds:

1. *General education.* As is evident from the name itself, general education is the minimal education required by an individual to satisfy all his various needs. It aims at developing the general qualities of the child, so that its personality can develop and it can become capable of adjusting to its environment.

It also enables him to earn his livelihood and to behave properly, in accordance with his age. It is generally believed that this general education continues upto the eighth class. All modern states make general education compulsory for all children, and in many cases it is provided free of charge.

2. *Specific education.* General education which is outlined above, is a supplement to specific education, which, as is

evident trains the child to pursue some specific profession or job. The modern age is a period of specialization.

As long as an individual cannot perform some particular task better than any other person, he will find it difficult to make a place for himself in society. It is for this reason that nowadays individuals are given vocational guidance in order to help them to take up professions for which their abilities are best suited.

General education is more liberal while specific education is comparatively narrow. It is not so closely connected with the development of the person's general personality and character. This is the task of general education. Specific education is spread over a long period of time and is often centred in specialized institutions such as medical colleges, engineering colleges, technical institutes, etc.

In each case, the aim is to make the individual proficient in a particular skill, be it curing sick people, designing or repairing machines, growing crops or anything else. Besides, specific education is also often more expensive than general education. Specific education, on the contrary, can be really profitable only if the individual possesses mental and physical qualities commensurate with that profession. Specific education plays a very important role in a nation's development because it provides specially trained personnel in every field who can serve society and enhance the welfare of the nation.

3. *Formal education.* In another classification, education is divided into the formal and the informal. The former comprehends education as it is provided in educational institutions according to a particular pattern. In the school, the educator educates the educands according to programme aiming at particular, goal. He follows a pre-determined syllabus. It has following merits:

(i) *Planned with a particular end in view.* Formal education is planned with a particular end in view. It is given in school, college and similar other institutions which are established with the purpose. In this way it is direct schooling, instruction and tuition.

(ii) *Limited to a specific period.* Formal education is limited to a specific period or stage. It is provided according to certain set rules and regulations. It is in the form of systematic, planned and guided instruction.

(iii) Well defined and systematic curriculum. Formal education has a well-defined and systematic curriculum. This curriculum is based on certain aims and objectives. These aims are in conformity with the needs of the society and the state.

(iv) Given by specially qualified teachers. Formal education is given by specially qualified teachers. They are supposed to be efficient in the art of instruction.

(v) Includes activities outside the class-room. In modern progressive schools, the process of education is not merely restricted to the four walls of the class-room. There are more activities outside the class-room than inside it.

(vi) Observes strict discipline. Formal education observes strict discipline. The pupil and the teacher are both aware of the fact and engage themselves in the process of education.

It may, however, be mentioned that any process of teaching which involves supervision, instruction, set plan, definite aims and principles, amounts to formal education.

Because of its completely of formal nature, formal education often fails to touch certain aspects of one's personality and leaves it completely undeveloped. At times, it can also become so detached from reality that it hinders rather than helps the educand in satisfying his needs.

This fact can be seen in the case of the contemporary pattern of formal education in India. It would not be inaccurate to state that, in India, the more formal education a person receives after a certain stage, the more useless he becomes in facing the problems of real life. His adjustment deteriorates instead of improving.

4. *Informal education.* Informal education complements the formal education outlined above, without which formal education remains incomplete. Education of this kind has no specific time or place at which it is provided. Even the educator is not fixed. All fixed syllabi, rules, formalities are absent from it.

Education of this kind is the education one receives while playing in field, talking to family members in the house, roaming around somewhere, in fact, everywhere. This kind of education never comes to an end, and it teaches the individual more than he can ever learn through his formal education.

A child learns many things when he comes in contact with new people. He discovers many new worlds when he goes to new places. This education that he receives cannot be evaluated as formal education can. Its merits are:-

(i) *Incidental and spontaneous.* Informal education is incidental and spontaneous. There is no conscious effort involved in it. Courtesies, gentleness etc. learnt in a market place or in a hotel or in one's sitting room amount to informal education.

(ii) *Not pre-planned nor deliberate.* Informal education is an educative activity which is neither pre-planned nor deliberate. The child learns many habits, manners and patterns while living with others or moving in different spheres like home, society, groups etc.

(iii) *Not imparted by any specialised agency.* Unlike formal education, informal education is not imparted by any specialised agency such as school or college.

(iv) *No prescribed time-table curriculum.* Informal education is not given according to any fixed time-table or through formal means of education. There is no set curriculum required. Informal education consists in experiences and actual living in the family or community.

(v) *May be negative education also.* Informal education may take to negative direction also. Instances are not rare when one learns stealing, or some other forms of misbehaviour from the experiences which the child may casually have in the street, in the market, in the cinema hall or in some other such place.

In the words of an expert, Informal Education is "the process by which a person imbibes attitudes, develops skills, cultivates values and acquires knowledge, without there being any organisation or system about it. This would include the deliberate attempts of parents and elders in the family and community to help the young ones grow and adapt themselves to the environment. Informal Education would also include all incidental learning that takes place while at work or at play and during travels—as well as spontaneous learning through films, radio and, television."

5. Direct education. In another classification, education is divided into the direct and indirect classes. Direct education is the equivalent of formal education and specific education. In its form of education, the educator and the educand are in direct contact whence education on a specific subject is disseminated.

Its chief advantage lies in the material learnt by the educand more by the example of the educator's personality and character than by the formal material he seeks to impart. It is for this reason that direct education was very much in vogue in India in the past. The student lived with the teacher and learnt various skills and sciences.

Direct education becomes difficult when the number of students becomes very large, or education itself becomes very mechanical and purely vocational. It then loses the advantages of the direct contact between the educator and the educand.

If the pattern of direct education is to be maintained, then the number of teachers must be very large, for one teacher can establish rapport only with a small number of educands. Once the value of direct education was realized, educationists stressed the importance of limiting the size of a class.

6. Indirect education. Direct education was efficacious and practicable in the past when the population was not too large and life had not become as complex as it is today. With the present increase in population, it is no longer possible to provide direct education to all the people. In the past, this kind of education was popular also because of the comparative primitive forms of communication. Such modern developments as the printing press, radio, television, etc., have made it possible to communicate the ideas of the greatest thinkers to those people who have never come into direct contact with the thinkers themselves. For this reason, in the present context, indirect education has come to acquire greater significance than direct education.

Many universities have undertaken to conduct correspondence courses, which are a fine example of indirect education. In this form of education, the subject of a lecture is printed and posted to the student. The student is required to answer certain questions sent along with the lecture. These answers are sent by him to the university where they are evaluated and returned to the student with the appropriate guidance. As this kind of indirect education offers a better and more practical adjustment to the circumstances of a very large number of individuals, it is becoming increasingly popular, particularly in the west.

All the books that are written by the greatest thinkers and read by a vast audience are an excellent example of its indirect education. It cannot be denied that irrespective of the abilities of the educator, he cannot provide complete education to the educand without turning to books for assistance.

For this reason the scope and field of indirect education is increasing steadily. In the last few years, teaching through the medium of radio and television is becoming more popular and reaching a higher level of sophistication. In India, the All India Radio regularly broadcasts lectures and programmes on musical education, cultural education and the like. By this many millions of individuals gain some kind of education.

7. *Individual education.* Education is also classified into the individual and the collective groups. Many of the modern educational psychologists have stressed the importance of individual difference between people and suggested that the educator should pay individual attention to each educand, remove his difficulties and, if necessary, modify the syllabi and teaching programme to suit the specific abilities and traits of the educand.

Scientifically considered, this advice is very good, and if arrangements can be made to provide individual education at this level, nothing could be better. Kindergarten, Montessori and Project methods, all of which are modern methods of child education, attempt to provide the highest degree of individual attention possible.

But where education is to be provided to a very large number of individuals, the most expensive kind of education yet devised since one educator can pay attention to the specific needs of only a very small number of students. The experiment conducted by Rabindra Nath succeeded as an experiment, but if it is accepted as a pattern for large scale education, it would be completely impractical. That is why arrangements are made for collective education, although the value of individual education can be clearly visualized.

8. Collective education. Collective education is provided to a group of individuals collected at one place. Formal education is often also collective education. Keeping in mind the obvious advantages of individual education, efforts are made to restrict the size of the group of educands. The very meaning of education would be lost if the educator lost all contact with the educands, if they are in too large a number.

This form of education is comparatively economical of time and money because one single educator can teach a large number of educands. In view of the present size of the population, and the possibilities of its growing further, collective education is the only practicable answer to the need for universal education.

9. Conscious education. Education is also divided into the conscious and the unconscious kind. The conscious kind of education is the education which is provided with a full knowledge of the objectives to be achieved through it. College education is of this kind. It is intended to fulfil certain pre-determined objectives. Conscious education is arranged for the child by his parents and by the state, but the child deliberately receives conscious education.

10. Unconscious education. An individual does not learn all the things he actually knows consciously. Many of the important facts that a child learns are absorbed unconsciously from his natural and social environment which surrounds him. This kind of education is informal and since it supplements the education received consciously, neither can be said to be more or less important than the other.

Of the various classifications listed above, the division into the formal and informal classes is the most common. All the other classifications are based on some specific approaches to education, although most of them resemble each other. For example, formal education is also collective education.

This classification of education into different kinds has been made by different educationists according to their individual standpoint. A study of each one of these can help to throw much light on the vast field of education and on the various aspects of it. In every classification, both the kinds described, supplement each other because the process of education is many sided and synthesizing. It takes place at all times and places, but it does not remain the same in every circumstance. It has a multiplicity of forms, means, quantity and quality. It is imbibed both consciously and unconsciously by the individual.

Non-Formal Education

In July, 1979, the Central Board of Secondary Education, New Delhi started the Open School—the first of its kind in the country. It is an institution set up to bring the flexibility and openness in the educational system and to extend educational opportunities to the weaker and disadvantaged sections of the society. The main objectives of the Open School are the following:

1. To offer a parallel non-formal system as an alternative to a formal schooling.
2. To provide the opportunity of education to out-of-school learners, school drop-outs, working adults, housewives and learners from disavantaged section of society living in remote areas of the country.
3. To offer bridge/preparatory courses for enabling learners to take up secondary level courses.
4. To offer Secondary, Senior Secondary, Technical Vocational and Life-enrichment courses through distance teaching methods.
5. To promote an open distance-learning system of education through research, publication and information dissemination.

This is an example of non-formal education.

Non-formal education is an arrangement wherein flexibility is the key-word. Such a system is an open one with regards to various aspects of education, i.e., admissions, curriculum, place of instruction, mode of instruction and the time and duration of instruction. Various examples of such a system are the Open School and Open University, Open Learning and the Correspondence Courses.

Definitions of Non-Formal Education

Non-formal education includes adult education, continuing education and on the job education, etc. Philip Coombs talked about it in 1968. However, until 1970 it had not been defined. Non-formal education is a new concept for an ancient phenomenon. Some of its definitions are as follows:

1. *Coombs and Ahmed (1974).* "Any organized, systematic, educational activity carried on outside the framework of the formal system to provide selected types of learning to particular sub-groups in the population, adults as well as children."

2. *La Bella (1975).* Non-formal education refers to "organized out-of-school educational programmes designed to provide specific target population."

3. *Illich and Freire.* "Non-formal education is anti-formal education."

4. *Moti Lal Sharma.* "In brief, one could say that non-formal education is an active, critical dialectical educational programme which aims at helping people to learn, to help themselves, to place them in consciously critical confrontation with their problems. To develop integrated authentic human beings who can contribute to the development of the society is the aim of Non-formal education. In this not only the individuals but also the total social system learns, adding up to a true learning society."

Non-formal education is the "missing ingredient" in accelerated social and economic development schemes that do not work. Therefore, it has its own valid claim to reality. It is deliberate, planned, staffed, financially supported life formal education. It is functional, unrestricted as to time and place and in general responsive to needs like informal education. It is much more responsive to needs and change.

Thus, it is more effective tool for rural development. It unlocks the doors of development plans. According to Malcolm A. Adiseshiah, "Non-formal education should be marketable and vocationalised. It should lay emphasis on the self-learning pattern." According to H.S.S. Lawrence, "Non-formal education system was not rival to the formal educational system but it was complementary to the latter. The common ingredients in both should be identified and an integrated system evolved."

Features of Non-Formal Education

Non-formal education is one of the recent concepts getting into use. Indian involvement in non-formal education has increased as a result of our interest in making education a life-long affair rather than a matter of formal schooling.

(i) *Derived from the expression 'formal education'.* The expression 'non-formal' in non-formal education has been derived from the expression 'formal' in formal education by using the prefix non-

(ii) *Outside the realm of formal Education.* Unlike informal education which is unstructured, spontaneous and without formality, non-formal education would be structured and planned, but outside the realm of formal education. "Any organised, systematic educational activity, carried outside the framework of the established formal system, whether operating separately or as an important feature of some broader activity, that is intended to serve identifiable learning clienteles and learning objectives."

(iii) *Conscious and deliberate.* Non-formal education is consciously and deliberately organised and systematically implemented.

(iv) *To be organised for a homogeneous group.* Non-formal education should be organised for a homogeneous group. Such a group has to be identified in terms of their learning needs.

(v) *Serving the need of the identified group.* Non-formal education should be programmed to serve the needs of the identified group. This will necessitate flexibility in design of the curriculum and the scheme of evaluation.

Non-Formal Education and Adult Education

Explaining the difference between non-formal and adult education, writes Anil Bordia, "The New Non-Formal Education Plan differs from previous adult education programmes, in that it provides for adequate administrative and resource support and emphasizes need-based curricula and teaching and learning materials; but it is unique in emphasizing evaluation at all stages on a continuing basis. All training programmes and teaching and learning materials are to be pre-tested and also subjected to impact studies."

Nature of Non-Formal Education

After the World War II, in the post colonial period new nations, one after another, scrambled for expanded and improved formal education. By the late sixties, there was a growing uneasiness that expansion in the facilities in formal education was not the whole answer. The traditional two-fold categorisation of education into formal and informal education leaves a big gap.

Studies by Philip Coombs and other revealed that as societies developed a third kind of education emerged which could be labelled as non-formal education. This non-formal education accounts for much of the highly functional, development and short-term related needs of a rapidly changing society.

Advantages of Non-Formal Education

To sum up, non-formal education is needed on account of the following advantages:

1. Universalisation or primary education.
2. Eradication of adult literacy.
3. Meeting the omissions of formal education.
4. Meeting the enormous and imperative challenges of democratic setup.
5. Enabling the pupils to learn and earn.
6. Enabling those students to study who had to discontinue formal education owing to pecuniary and other circumstances.

7. Enabling the students in geographically remote areas to get education because the formal education can not be within their easy reach.
8. Enabling individuals to refresh and update their knowledge.
9. Rectifying the educational imbalance between those who live in villages and those who live in towns.
10. Providing educational facilities to social and economically neglected sectors of society.

Objectives of Non-Formal Education

Following are the three sets of objectives of non-formal education:

(i) The immediate objective is the removal of illiteracy
(ii) The middle-range objective is the application of new knowledge to resolve economic, cultural and social problems.
(iii) The long-range objective is to provide for life-long education.

Types of Non-Formal Education Programmes

1. Adult Functional Literacy Programmes
2. Correspondence Courses
3. Open School Studies
4. Satellite Instructional Television Programme
5. Programme for drop-outs in the age group 6-14.

Persons' Benefits by Non-Formal Education

Non-formal education is particularly useful for the following categories of persons.

1. *People of all ages.* Those who never had the opportunity to follow any formal education programme.

2. *Students.* Those who are not in position to complete primary, middle or secondary school.

3. *Learners.* Learners of different stages of education who feel the need for deeper and more comprehensive knowledge in a subject of particular interest.

4. Labourers. Both in urban and rural areas young workers, small farmers, landless labourers, small entrepreneurs, etc., who need up-to-date knowledge related to their jobs particularly related to latest technological improvements.

5. Educated unemployed. Unemployed educated persons of various age groups whose no-relevant education needs to be made more relevant in order to increase their chances of employment.

6. Graduates, professionals, intellectuals. Those who need a refreshment or orientation to make themselves up-to-date in their knowledge.

7. Other persons. Those who require programmes for personal satisfaction like recreation, leisure time activities, cultural or artistic programmes, etc.

Agencies of Non-Formal Education

The various agencies for organising programmes for non-formal education are as follow:

1. Institutions for formal education.
2. Special agencies for non-formal education such as Nehru Yuvak Kendras, training centres in factories, public libraries, centres of correspondence education, etc.
3. Voluntary non-governmental organisation like club and societies.
4. Radio and television.

Non-formal education is one of the modes of education, others are formal and informal. Therefore, non-formal education ought to be perceived and designed in coordination with formal and informal systems. It will prove an insufficient and an ineffective mechanism for solving the complex problems or for achieving concrete goals, if organised in isolation.

Again, it must not be limited to the imparting of basic skills only. It must be designed as an integrated system in the context of the total socio-economic environment. To make it effective in modern societal context, a more integrated community based programme of innovation and change is needed to which various forms of education may contribute.

This requires filling the gaps between the learning systems and the community needs.

One should try to avert the danger of education being isolated from the subject matter of life experience. Hence, one of the weightiest problems with which the philosophy of education has to cope with is the method of keeping a proper balance between the informal, the formal and non-formal, the

Formal v/s Non-Formal Education

Formal Education	*Non-formal Education*
1. Limited to a period of being taught.	1. Life-long and not limited to any period of being taught.
2. Generally not integrated with work.	2. Integrated with work.
3. Has fixed points of entry and exit.	3. Has flexible points of entry, exit, re-entry and re-exit. In fact, it continues throughout the life span of the individual.
4. Has fixed curriculum.	4. Has a diversified and varied curriculum.
5. In it the 'giver' dominates and the 'receiver' is rather passive.	5. A process of sharing, exploring, analysing and judging together.
6. Geared to knowledge acquisition.	6. A process of enabling the individual understand his needs, the environmental situation and mutual relationships.
7. Fosters an uncritical obedience.	7. An open-end process of education which develops self-reliant awareness.
8. Works within a fixed social change.	8. Anticipates and prepares for change.
9. Associated with traditional schooling—schooling confined to a school or a college, etc.	9. Not confined to any educational set-up.
10. Rigid with regard to various aspects of education, i.e., admissions, curriculum, place of instruction, mode of instruction, the time and duration of instruction.	10. Very flexible in regard to various aspects of education.

incidental and the international modes of education. It may be remembered that one should try to incorporate the virtues of informal education as far as he can and also to keep away the dangers of too much formal education.

Functional Side of Education

The functional side of education has been discussed by various thinkers. In "Democracy and Education", John Dewey has discussed at length the functions of education. However, Prof. N. L. Jacks has observed: "As a whole, there is plenty of work for education to do; its prime task is to transfer the original evil into acquired goods." Thus the true function of education is to cultivate the true significance of life through integrated growth.

1. *Education is all one with growth.* John Dewey is of the view that integrated growth of the individual lies at the heart of the business of education. In his own words : "Since growth is the characteristic of life, education is all one with growing". He further says: "Our net conclusion is that life is development, and that developing, growing is life. Translated into its educational process, this means that:

(i) the educational process has no end beyond itself; it is its own end;

(ii) the educational process is one of the continual reorganising, reconstructing, transforming."

Let us not forget that there may be right growth or wrong growth; abnormal growth or normal growth. Both the teachers and parents must take proper safeguards to ensure growth in the right manner. It must lead to the formation of habits involving educative skills, definiteness of interests and specific objects of observation and thought. "Growth must be towards an ideal human character." (H.H. Horne).

2 *Education is the continuous reconstruction and re-organisation of experiences.* John Dewey believes that "Education is the process of living through a 'continuous reconstruction of experiences". A close analysis of this view will make the point clear.

The *a priori* assumption is: the child has own experiences: Education reconstructs or reorganises these experiences, refines them and gives them meaning. The reconstruction or reorganisation of experiences adds to the further refinement of experiences. The two together develop the ability in the child to control and direct the subsequent experiences.

There are three focal points which must be kept in mind. These are:

(i) Inheritance. Every new generation inherits experiences of the past generation.

(ii) Participation. Every new generation participates in the experience of the race. The superfluous elements of the cultural heritage are eliminated and the essential ingredients are preserved.

(iii) Contribution. We not only participate but also contribute to the experiences of the race by transmitting those experiences.

The three focal points—inheritance, participation and contribution—rolled into one constitute the process of continuous reconstruction and re-organisation of experiences. According to John Dewey, educative experiences further direct the subsequent experiences. They help us in anticipating certain situations and consequences. We, therefore, plan our future experiences in such a way that we secure their "beneficial consequences and avert the undesirable ones."

3. Education is direction. Educating the child means directing the child properly. Direction is fixation of the activity into a proper response by elimination of unnecessary and confusing movements. In the words of Prof. V. R. Taneja, "Educative process is nothing but directing the children to have worthy interests in the various phases of life."

Direction includes 'guidance' as well as 'control'. This is the natural way of educating the child—'to kindle and restrain', as Wordsworth puts it.

Both the teacher and the parent have a special role to play. At home, the parents should appear as a model. At school, the teacher must set an example and inspire the child, through personal and impersonal methods to move in the right direction. Compulsion, threats and coercion must be avoided. Direction must be towards certain social and personal standards and ideals and these should be known to the teacher.

Child-Centred Education

Child-centred education is the modern approach to the educative process. This approach is one of the significant outcomes of researches in the field of educational psychology, especially the concept of individual differences. It is now an admitted fact that no two individuals are perfectly alike. Every human child is a novel experiment in the hands of nature. A modern educator who swears by modern techniques of teaching must understand the significant role the child is going to play in the educative process.

What is Child-Centredness?

The concept of child-centredness implies that child occupies the central place in the educational process. The old concept of education emphasized the importance of teachers, whereas the modern concept of education gives the pride of place to the child. The child is now considered to be the centre of the educative process. It is now rightly believed that the child is full of potentialities, and the teacher is obliged to use such methods of teaching which will help in the development of those potentialities. Not only this, every child differs in his innate capacities. So, the teacher must adapt his methods of teaching to suit the individual differences of children. This means that a teacher cannot employ a particular method of teaching without taking into consideration the needs and requirements of children. Moreover, all the progressive educationists such as Roussean, Frockel, Montesson, Gandhi and many others have advocated freedom for the child. They have stressed that the teaching process be based on the capacities and requirements of children.

Child—the Nucleus

It is a simple fact that it is the child who is the nucleus of the whole thing. It is the child who is to be educated. The teacher and all other agencies of education are really means to educate the child. The central place in the educational process should, naturally, go to the child.

The Teacher is Important, Too

It must be mentioned here that it is in a special sense that we say that child is the centre of educational process. That in no way minimises the importance of the teacher. In a way, the teacher's importance has rather increased, his functions have become varied and complex. He must study the child psychologically, which means assessing and measuring the innate capacities of children, a stupendous task in itself. Then, the teacher has to use his ingenuity to adopt his methods of teaching to suit individual differences. The teacher, in fact, is indispensable, and his responsibilities have really increased. Instead of transmitting knowledge only, his function now is to develop the entire personality of the child. The concept of child centredness merely implies the awakening of the educators to the educational requirements of children. It should not lead us to believe that the importance of the teacher has been in any way minimised.

QUESTIONS FOR ANSWER

1. Define 'Formal Education' and write a note on its merits.
2. Distinguish between 'Direct' and 'Indirect' education.
3. Define 'Individual' and 'Collective' education.
4. Define 'Non-Formal' education and write a note on its basic features.
5. Distinguish between 'Formal' and 'Non-Formal' education.

3

Aims of Education

The comprehensive meaning of education, its nature, its modern concept and forms of education etc. as discussed in previous chapters of this book have laid solid foundation, which will enable the readers to study and understand the aims of education easily. The nature of the ideals which education should seek to realise may be termed as educational aims. Hereunder we will briefly discuss the aims of education.

Importance of Educational Aims

The process of education has all along been discussed in terms of its aims. The importance of aims in Education has been emphasised by scholars, philosophers and educators through all ages. Education must have aims as "activity with an aim is all one with acting intelligently". This means a system of education which is not clear about its aims or which works towards undesirable ends is bound to fail. According to Riulin, "Education is purposeful and ethical activity, hence it is unthinkable without aims." It has been rightly observed by B.D. Bhatia that "without the knowledge of aims, education is like a sailor who does not know his goal or his destination and the child is like a rudderless vessel which will be drifted along somewhere ashore".

Education at different stages is geared to different aims. Primary, secondary, university and adult education—each stage has its own specific aim. Again, different types of education—

humanistic, scientific, technical, art, commercial etc.—each has its own aim. However, education as a whole may broadly be conceived in terms of the general purpose of 'man-making.'

Educational aims are important for the following reasons:

1. *Aims give direction to the activity.* Education is a planned activity. The activity is planned with certain ends in view. The aim as a foreseen end gives direction to the activity of education.

2. *Aims help in acting intelligently.* 'Activity with an aim," says John Dewey, "is all one with acting intelligently". Thus by keeping thc aim in view, one knows what one is doing and why one is doing it. This saves waste of time and effort.

3. *Aims are necessary to assess the outcomes of the educative process.* In this sense, aims help in measuring the success and failure of work done in school.

4. *Necessary for efficient school administration.* Aims are necessary for efficient school management. They help in proper selection of teachers, proper curriculum planning, proper equipment of library, desirable planning of curricular and co-curricular activities, etc.

5. *Useful for parents and general public.* Aims are useful for parents in the sense that they put check on their undue criticism of the school system. The society reviews and appreciates the work of the school in terms of aims. In a democratic society, this assumes much greater importance.

6. *Acting with meaning.* Highlighting the importance of educational aims, John Dewey says: ".........to have an aim is to act with meaning, not like an automatic machine : it is to do something and perceive the meaning of things in the light of that intent.

7. *Aims give continuity and significance to education.* Education is a process. It is a continuous process. Any one act or single experience does not by itself constitute education. It is neither a mere serial aggregate of facts. Education has an intrinsic continuity. "It is the aim that gives continuity and significance to the series of events and experiences that make up what we call education.

In short, aims are potential seeds from which grows the plant of a well-defined educational policy.

Factors Determining Educational Aims

Aims of education cannot be just "pulled out of a hat". A large number of factors contribute to the determining of educational aims. These factors touch every phase of human life that *was*, that *is*, or that *will* be. The following factors usually determine aims of education.

1. *Views about the nature of reality*. Aims of education have direct relationship with the prevailing philosophy of life. The philosophy of life at a certain time is influenced by the views of eminent thinkers and schools of philosophy. According to *idealistic view*, the aim of education should be self-realisation or unfolding of what is potential in the child. According to *naturalistic viewpoint*, self-expression or self-gratification should be the aim of education. The *pragmatists* think that education should aim at enabling the individual "to control his environment and fulfil his possibilities."

2. *Views about Human Nature*. Educational aims have often been decided keeping in view one or the other element which comprises human nature. Idealists regard 'unfolding the divine in child and man' as the aim. To naturalists, the aim of education is 'self-expression.'

3. *Political ideologies and Individual-State Relationship*. Political ideologies influence aims of education. Under a totalitarian system, the aims of education will be much different from those under a democratic political system. Under the former, the system of education becomes stereotyped and education takes the form of indoctrination. School and text-books must promote the ideology of the State. Under the latter (democratic), the individual enjoys freedom and free play. The goal of education is the good man who is to be educated for a life of freedom. Education aims at developing the full personality of each individual, irrespective of caste, creed, class or religion.

4. *Socio-Economic Problems*. Socio-economic problems of a country also determine the aims of education. For example, the Indian Education Commission (1964-66) put emphasis on 'increasing productivity' as one of the national objectives of education.

5. *Exploration of Knowledge.* Exploration of knowledge is a potent factor in determining aims of education. With the advancement of scientific and technical knowledge, education all over the world has become science-oriented.

Nature of Educational Aims

1. *Core of a workable philosophy.* The aims of education are the core of a workable philosophy of education. Without philosophy, an educator could not have aims and without aims he could not have a practical philosophy. Aims are the frame of reference of his philosophy.

2. *An integral part of the educative process.* Aims are an integral part of the fabric of education. Aims enable an individual to continue his education. From this point of view, an aim is not an end; it is only a means to an end.

3. *Both within and without the educative process.* According to Prof. Ward G. Reader: "Education finds its aims both within and without the educative process. It must keep in mind the interests and the abilities of the pupil and prepare him to share in democratic living both now and when he becomes an adult."

Important Aims of Education

Since education is a 'man making' process and man is a social being therefore, there are many aims of education. Though some of the aims, such as individual versus social aim, may look contrary to each other but in real truth they are complimentary to each other. Hereunder, some of the most important aims of education are being discussed for the benefit of the scholars:

1. Individual Aim of Education

"Individuality is the ideal of life," thus observed Sir Percy Nunn, and added that "a scheme of education is ultimately to be valued by its success in fostering the highest degree of individual excellence". Exalting the 'individual development' as the aim of education Sir Percy Nunn observes "that nothing good enters into the human world except in and through the free activities of individual men and women, and that educational practice must be shaped to accord with that truth." His belief in this aim is based upon the fact that individual is an architect of his own fate. He is responsible for his own destiny. Education, therefore, must cater for the complete development of an individual.

The concept of individual development is based on the socio-political philosophy that social institutions, such as the family, the church, the school and the state exist only for believing and improving the life of the individual. The individual is the end and these social institutions are the means. Therefore, they justify their existence only if they are conducive to the promotion of the individual's welfare. The society, the state, and in fact all the social and political institutions exist and work for the welfare of the individual. Therefore, the aim of education should be the fullest possible development of the individual. The school as one of the important social institutions exists for the educand, and not the educand for the school. Therefore, the school should offer an environment and atmosphere which is conducive to the development of each and every student. Rousseau, the father of the philosophy of Naturalism and a great educationist, is the greatest supporter of individual aim in education.

Education should aim at the training and development of the individual. Only a well-trained and properly educated individual can understand his rights in the society and his obligations to his community. It is, therefore, that maximum opportunities should be made available for realising his physical, moral, intellectual, and spiritual possibilities, unhindered by environment and unhampered by society. It is only this type of individual that makes a good citizen.

G. Thompson's view based on Biological belief. The *biologists* believe that every individual is different from others. Every child is a new and a unique product and a new experiment with life. Prof. G. Thompson says, "Education is for the individual, its function being to enable the individual to survive and live out its complete life. Education is imparted to preserve the individual life. Community exists for the individual not the individual for the community. Therefore, individual and not society should be the centre of all educational efforts and activities".

Rousseau's Naturalistic View. The *Naturalists* like Rousseau hold that "the central aim of education is the autonomous development of the individual." According to Rousseau, "Every thing is good as it comes from the hands of the Author of Nature, but everything degenerates in the hands of man. God makes all things good; man meddles with them and they become evil." He believes that man and citizen cannot be trained simultaneously, we have to make our choice between the two.

Modern View of Psychologists. The *Psychologists* are of the opinion that education is an individual process. No two children are identical in intellectual capacity and other dispositions. Therefore, a rigid and uniform curriculum for all the children is not justified. The process of education should be individualised.

There is a great force and truth in the individual aim of education. But, it must be noted that individual aim, in its extreme form, is not desirable. The social aim has its justification too. After all, society is an organisation which is made by the individuals for their own betterment and well-being. To live and adjust efficiently in the Society, the individual must also be properly socialised. Therefore, the claims of society also should not be ignored; and therefore, the extreme form of individualism should be avoided even for the well-being of the individual himself.

Criticism of the Individual Aim. The Individual Aim of education has been criticised on the following points:

Isolated-individual—a figment of imagination. "An isolated individual," as T. Raymont says, "is only a figment of imagination." In fact, says he, "we cannot conceive of an individual living and developing in isolation from society."

Every individual is a social being. "As a social being," opines Dr. Dewey "he is a citizen, growing and thinking in a vast complex of interactions and relations." So, an educational activity that does not swear by the social end, consequently fails even to serve the individual.

Inherently defective. In the extreme form, the idea of absolute freedom to the individual may take the form of unchecked 'self-expression' or 'self-assertion'. This sort of unchecked 'self-expression' will ridicule all social conventions or moral laws which form the bases of society's regulated life. Even Sir Percy Nunn, the greatest champion of individual aim, believes that "Individuality develops only in a social atmosphere where it can feed on common interests and common activities."

Against spiritual nature of man. The critics of individual aim believe that the individual, left to himself, is an animal, selfish and undisciplined.

Individual must be made fit for society. Rusk informs us that the aim of education is not development of individuality but the enrichment of personality. Education must lift him from the level of a reasoning savage. It must give him character, moral and aesthetic sense and thus make him fit to live in society. An enriched and exalted personality is the one that thinks not only for itself but also thinks for others.

The basis of individual's greatness is social. The great contributors to the progress of human civilization did not work in a vacuum. The fact remains that their greatness was due to their assimilation of the rich heritage of thought, wisdom and action evolved and preserved by others in society. They worked against some social background. Hence the very basis of their great achievements was social.

Adverse effect on politics and economy of a country. The unwarranted claim of the individual may adversely affect the politics and economy of a country. The 18th and 19th century emphasis on the political independence of an individual led to the education of the individual and for the individual. It also led to laissez-faire i.e., a free hand to exploit the material wealth for personal advantage.

2. *Social Aim of Education*

The supporters of social aim of education believe that society or state alone is real, and the individual is only a means, and therefore, must always work for the welfare and progress of the society or the state. They, therefore, hold that an individual should be educated for the good of society. The interests of society are supreme; and the position of the individual is always subordinated to that of the state. The supporters of social aim cannot think of an individual living and developing in isolation from society. As Raymont says, "The isolated individual is a figment of the imagination." As long as human beings are living in society, there will be some subordination of individuality to public or social needs of society.

State-Idealised Super-human Entity. The social aim, in its extreme form, regards the state as "idealised super-human entity, over and above the individual." The state or society alone is the reality, and the individual is only "a throb in the social pulse." They believe that "Individuality is of no value, and personality a meaningless term apart from the social environment in which they are developed and made manifest." Therefore, the function of education according to the social aim is to work consistently for the welfare of the state, subordinating the welfare of the individual to that of the state. Hence the state is to control and direct every affair in life including education which is but a means of shaping its citizens into a certain mould. The state has the right to mould and shape the individual, so as to suit its own purposes and progress. It uses education as the most convenient means for preparing individuals to play different roles in society. The curriculum as well as the methods of education are also the complete monopoly of the state and the individual has no choice to develop his powers and capacities in his own way. He is only to obey what the authorities dictate. His needs, urges and nature are completely ignored.

Education through Social Control. The exponents of this school of thought believe in imparting education through social control, and their emphasis in the educational process is on strict discipline and obedience. In the end, it is the state which determines the field where the services of the individual are most needed, and not where he can do his best according to his own ability and aptitude. The state is supreme to dictate what shall be taught and how shall be taught. Discipline is its watchword, willing acceptance of authority is the method, and obedience is the rule.

Criticism of the Social Aim of Education. This is certainly very one-sided view. First, social aim in its extreme form can never be accepted, as it reduces the individual to a mere non-entity. Secondly, the extreme notion of the all-powerful state or society ignores the legitimate needs, desires and interests of the individual, and suppresses his creative power. Thirdly, it tries to make the individual only a tool of the government, and demands unquestioning, obedience and loyalty from the individual. Fourthly, this is against all concepts of education and individual development. Therefore, social aim in its extreme form can never be justified and therefore, can never be accepted.

3. *Synthesis of Individual and Social Aim of Education*

The question of Individual vs. Social Aim of education has been widely considered and debated. Very often individual and social aims of education have been regarded as opposed to each other. But in the final analysis, it will be seen that development of individuality assumes meaning only in a social setting. It has been rightly observed.

"Schools of every type fulfil their purpose in so far as they foster the free growth of individuality, helping every boy and girl to achieve the highest degree of individual development of which he or she is capable in and through the life of a society."

Conclusion. In the end, we say that in a truly democratic society, the true aim of education cannot be other than the highest development of the individual as a member of the society. The most practical approach would be to let education burn the individual flame, feeding it with the oil of society. Let the light of this flame illumine the social horizon, shedding away all the prevailing darkness.

4. *Knowledge as an Aim of Education*

Importance. Knowledge has almost been widely accepted as the aim of education since the time of Sophists, 400 B.C. Knowledge is a powerful agent for intellectual satisfaction. The present civilization has come to pass through the dissemination of knowledge through the medium of education.

Socrates has also said that "one who had true knowledge could not be other than virtuous." So, education cannot but have knowledge as its important aim.

Sometimes it is contended that knowledge is misused. It is true to some extent. But in that case, the fault does not lie in having knowledge as an aim of education. In fact, knowledge has helped man to overcome the forces of nature and thus satisfy human wants. "If mean men are unwilling and stupid men unable to use knowledge for the best interests of society, the fault is not with knowledge. The cure for folly and ignorance is not less knowledge but more."

Knowledge as an aim of education is accepted on the following merits:

(a) *Instrument of education.* Knowledge is an instrument of education. It is a link between the teacher, the pupil and the social environment.

(b) *Essential for adjustment.* Knowledge is essential for adjustment to and mastery of environment. Healthy adjustment is possible only when the individual possesses knowledge of the same.

(c) *Essential for growth of society.* Prof. D.I.O, Conner says that knowledge is essential for the continuity and growth of society. Human society as it stands today is much different from that of the old stone age. This is because education has propagated social heritage comprising a knowledge of facts, skills and ways of behaviour.

(d) *Basis of moral behaviour.* Knowledge is the basis of moral behaviour. Education is the modification of behaviour. So knowledge is an important aim of education. In the teachings of world's greatest philosophers and teachers, we find such slogans as 'know thyself', 'knowledge is virtue'.

(e) *Mental food, a potential power.* Knowledge is mental food. It is a potential power. It is knowledge that makes human mind a thinking agent.

(f) *Means of human happiness.* Knowledge is a means of never-ending happiness. Knowledge has helped man overcome disease and misery, superstition and imaginary fear.

(g) *Valuable asset.* Knowledge is man's valuable asset. It is an essential means of promoting human welfare.

Criticism. Education should not aim at knowledge for knowledge sake. Knowledge as an exclusive aim of education is narrow and not worthy of all human aspirations. It has been rightly said by Prof. Whitehead: "A merely well-informed person is the most useless bore on God's earth." Gandhiji has also pointed out: "Man is neither mere intellect, nor the gross animal body, nor head, nor soul alone. A proper and harmonious contribution of all the three is required for the making of the whole and constitutes the true economics of education."

5. *Livelihood Fallacy or Vocational Aim of Education*

Importance. The vocational aim of education is the direct outcome of industrial and scientific advancement. Vocationalisation of education is an important slogan of modern democratic education. Without a proper emphasis on vocational aspect of education, those who merely go to school, suffer all their lives. The vocational aim of education is important from the following points of view:

1. *Balances individual capacity with social service*. In the words of John Dewey, "Education with vocational aim will balance the distinctive capacity of the individual with social service." Such a balance will lead to the learner's social efficiency.

2. *Balances economic and industrial progress*. Vocational Education strikes a balance between economic and industrial progress. It prepares students for a useful life and useful occupation. In the words of Gandhiji, "True education ought to be a kind of insurance against unemployment."

3. *Reduces emphasis on verbalism*. Vocational aim of education will reduce the impact of verbalism and mere intellectual domination. Modern educators have advocated the idea of vocational education. Rousseau preferred workshops to giving verbal education. In our country, Gandhiji introduced some craft and manual work as a part of his Basic Education.

4. *A purposeful activity*. Education with a vocational bias becomes a purposeful activity. All purposeful activities lead to efficiency. Kilpatrick also gives maximum importance to purposefulness in a project. Indian Education Commission

(1964-66) recommended 'Work Experience' as the basis of all education and emphasised the science and technology oriented education.

5. *Suitable for persons with lower intelligence.* Vocational training is also suitable for the persons with lower intelligence.

Criticism. On account of its utilitarian value, the vocational aim of education may be over-emphasised. It may be reduced to just "bread and butter" aim. In this sense the vocational aim is a narrow aim of education. Man does not live by bread alone. In the words of Prof. V.R. Taneja, "Education when reduced to vocational education does not exercise that inspiring and elevating influence which leads to rich and fuller life."

The vocational aim cannot be ignored either. Education minus emphasis on the individual's vocational efficiency is just verbose and an exercise in intellectual arithmetic. We may conclude by saying that "a liberal education, which is divorced from vocational education which is not supplemented by a programme of liberal education is bound to be mechanical."

6. *Character-Building Aim of Education*

Importance. The one essential aim of education is character-building. Education consists in the cultivation of certain human values and development of attitudes and habits which constitute the character of a person. Gandhiji gave top priority to character education. By this he meant that the purpose of education is to develop courage, strength and virtue. Raymont also says that the teacher's ultimate concern is to cultivate strength and purity of character.

Great thinkers have highlighted the character-building aim of education.

- *(i)* According to John Dewey, "The establishing of character is a *comprehensive aim of school education.*
- *(ii)* According to Swami Vivekananda, "*We want that education by which character is formed,* strength of mind is increased, the intellect is expanded and by which one can stand on one's own feet."
- *(iii)* On being asked 'What could be your goal in education'? Gandhiji replied: "Character building. I

would try to develop courage, strength, virtue, the ability to forget oneself in working towards great aims." Gandhiji believed that "a man of character wills loftily and honestly as well as effectively."

(iv) Various Commissions on Indian Education have laid down that building of character is one of the most important aims of Indian education.

(v) Education for character is the need of the hour in India today. The need is to build men and women of sound character and integrity. There is the crisis of character as well as the crisis of courage. Pt. Nehru had once said: "Hang every corrupt person by the first lamp-post." Do we have the courage of character to say so or do so?

How to educate for character? To impart character education is a crucial problem. Teachers must set a stage for such education. If they are to understand and influence young people, they must be persons not only of superior character themselves but intelligent, gifted, capable, and creative. "Such persons can teach excellence in the best way through the example of what they themselves are." Merely asking the students to become moral beings carries no weight. It can be better done through activities like morning assemblies, mass prayers, talks by eminent persons and by actually living in the situations. The whole school environment should be made congenial and effective. Above all, parents and different agencies can save the society and the nation from mass moral degeneration.

Conclusion. In our institutions, presently, the intellectual aspect is dominant, physical aspect plays second fiddle to the former, and the moral aspect is totally neglected. Education in the fullest sense of the term takes care of the physical, intellectuals and moral development of the individual. Moral life cannot grow in a vacuum. Morality has social reference. Hence, in the school curriculum, place must be given to principles of moral education.

7. *'Complete Living' as an Aim of Education*

This aim has been formulated and brilliantly expounded by

Herbert Spencer. Education, according to this great thinker, should acquaint us with the laws and ways of complete living. Complete living 'implies living one's life to the full in its various aspects. An individual's personality has innumerable aspects, which clamour for development and expression. Every aspect of one's personality should find expression through various types of activities and experiences. This means that the aim of education should be to provide to the pupils with varied types of experiences so that every aspect of their personality may be so developed, that they can participate successfully in each and every phase of their lives.

Role of Education

1. *First,* education should enable man to know the art of self-preservation.

2. *Secondly,* education should enable one to earn his living and secure the necessities of life. Man cannot live merely on air and water, education should be such as will equip the child to get a job, to make him efficient to earn his living.

3. *Thirdly,* education should impart knowledge about bearing and rearing children who carry the message of the previous generation. Only thus can it ensure survival.

4. *Fourthly,* education for complete living aims at preparing the pupils to perform well, social and political responsibilities.

5. *Lastly,* education must prepare one to utilise one's leisure well by enjoying the refinements of culture, art, literature and the like. This will promote physical and mental health.

Criticism. The 'complete living' aim of education has been criticised on many grounds.

- *(i)* There is no sense in giving an arbitrary division of the requirement of life once for all.
- *(ii)* Self-preservation is not a high ideal. Had it been so, our Indian Jawans would not fight the Chinese, knowing well that death is the result.
- *(iii)* There is too much stress on science.
- *(iv)* There is too much stress on biological existence.

8. *Harmonious Development as an Aim of Education*

Importance. Education cannot be regarded as an activity with a single aim. To bring one aspect of the learner's personality into focus is to render education lop-sided and incomplete. It is to answer this charge that a comprehensive aim of education, enveloping all the recognised aspects of one's personality is often suggested. It is the harmonious development of personality which education should aim at.

Education should Produce a Well-balanced Personality. A human child is blessed with a number of powers and capabilities. Development of all these powers of the child should be harmonious in order to produce a well-balanced-personality.

Supported by all Progressive Educationists. Harmonious development of personality as the true aim of education has been supported by all progressive educationists.

(i) *Rousseau* was the first modern educator who conceived education as "the process of development into an enjoyable, rational, harmoniously balanced, useful and hence, natural life."

(ii) *Pestalozi* was the greatest champion of the harmonious development aim. He says in Educational Writings: "The aim of instruction is, and can be nothing but the development of the human nature by the harmonious cultivation of its power and talents and promotion of manliness of life." He further says: "The sole aim of education is the harmonious development of the faculties and dispositions which make up personality." In other words, Pestalozzi emphasised the development of 3 H's instead of 3 R's—Head, Heart and Hand—as the essence of true education.

(iii) *Gandhi's view.* Gandhiji believed that the whole man is the subject of education. He said: "By education I mean an all-round drawing out of the best in child and man—body, mind and spirit."

Limitations. The idea of the harmonious development as an aim of education is, no doubt, comprehensive and all inclusive. However, it has the following limitations:

1. *Vague.* The term harmonious development is vague. It is not clear. What standard of development of various capacities would be ideally harmonious? Again, harmonious development will mean producing men who are jacks of all trades but masters of none. We are living in an age of specialisation. Due margin has to be allowed to develop the best in man for which he is best fitted.

2. *Educational Limitation.* Harmonious development may mean putting equal stress on intellectual, emotional, aesthetic and moral side of human nature. If that is so, one may again ask: What type of curriculum is needed? How much weightage on each subject in the curriculum is to be given? How is the whole scheme to be put through? Of course, Pestalozzi and Gandhi agree on the point that the development of Head, Heart, and Hand constitutes the true meaning of 'harmonious development.' None of these is to be developed independent of the other.

Conclusion. The above discussion leads us to conclude that 'harmonious development' as an aim of education is fairly convincing though it has its limitations as regards the meaning of the term itself. Education cannot afford to neglect any aspect of human personality—knowledge, vocational, moral, aesthetic, and religious. But, the true meaning of 'harmonious development' does not consist in making an athlete-cum-scholar-cum-artist-cum-saint-cum-everything. Its true meaning lies in development of that aspect or specific ability, whether artistic or scientific, which is more powerful than the others, to the fullest extent. However, education must provide for the development of other abilities to the reasonable limits.

9. *Democratic Aim of Education*

Education should aim at teaching and inculcating democratic values in the children. Democratic values imply respect for the individuality of each and every person, provision for free expression and fearless airing of differences of opinion, and cooperative and collective decision-making. Some of the important values or principles of democracy are *(i)* Respect for individuality, *(ii)* Equality, *(iii)* Toleration, *(iv)* Cooperative living,

(v) Faith in change through persuasion. The function of education is to inculcate these values in the pupils.

According to University Education Commission : "Education is the great instrument of social emancipation by which democracy establishes, maintains and protects the spirit of equality among its members." Education therefore, must work for inculcating democratic values in the students. According to Ross, "Schools ought to stress the duties and responsibilities of individual citizens. Everywhere there should be a spirit of teamwork, the emphasis should always be laid on community. The true function of a school in a democracy therefore, is to provide for the enrichment of individual life. It is a prepared environment in which he may best blossom". Thus, schools should aim at producing such individuals who are social, disciplined, creative and adaptable. They should discover the inherent worth of each individual pupil and try to develop and utilize it to serve the best interests of both the individual and the society.

To achieve these aims, the schools must be run on democratic lines. The teacher as well as the head of the school must function in a democratic way. Thus, it should function as a democratic community mutually discussing educational matters, exchanging views in a cordial atmosphere, and arriving at collective decisions. The school should act as a Community Centre where democratic ideals are not only taught theoretically but acted upon practically. This will inculcate democratic values in the pupils, so essential for the citizens of a democratic country like India.

10. School Masters Fallacy as an Aim of Education

If, however, the too anxious parent or the short-sighted economist is apt to entertain a one-sided ideal, no less so is the schoolmaster. His characteristic fallacy, for which, however, he is not primarily responsible, is that of identifying education with learning, and of regarding the acquisition of knowledge, or, more crudely still, success in examinations, as the proper aim of the school. This of course is another "idol of the cave". We need not insist at length upon the truism that mere learning, even if it goes along with a well-disciplined intellect, may leave a person deficient in qualities which everyone would place higher in the scale of values, and which the educator has it in his power to foster. Nevertheless, it is a truism which bears repetition only too well, because, through force of circumstances, an inadequate ideal lingers in practice even when no one would attempt to defend it on rational grounds.

11. *Formulation of Theories as an Aim of Education*

Herbert Spencer, for instance, has defined education as "a preparation for complete living' a definition which, though it does not carry us far, we may well accept, without binding ourselves to all the conclusions to which it leads its author. Others have sought to provide us with a better conception of education by pointing out that its aims are manifold, including the harmonious cultivation of the physical, intellectual, aesthetic and moral sides of human nature. In one respect this statement is suggestive: it warns us distinctly against partial and one-sided aims. It tells us that we must so train the young as to make it unlikely that we shall tend to foster by nurture types of character that are one-sided by nature—the irresolute man of reflection, such as Shakespeare has exemplified in Hamlet; or the rash and unreflecting man of action, of whom history and common experience furnish instances numerous enough; or the soul that seeks complete satisfaction in the aesthetic life, like that portrayed by Tennyson in *The Palace of Art*; or the mere animal in human form, like the young man of whom Addison says that "he had a great stock of health but nothing else; and if it were a man's business only to live, there would not be a more accomplished young fellow in the whole country."

12. *Morality the Ultimate Aim of Education*

The reply is not far to seek. The cloud of witnesses known as educational reformers, or at least those of them whose work is proving permanent and beneficent, declare in effect that the child is essentially and above all a "behaving organism"; that the teacher's ultimate concern is to cultivate, not wealth of muscle, nor fullness of knowledge, nor refinement of feeling but strength and purity of character: and that in its influence upon the pupil's habitual motives to conduct all education that is worth the name finds its real meaning and value. In other words, 'the ethical aim is supreme. By this we do not mean that other aims are unimportant, but that they are safely pursued only when they are regarded as subordinate to the highest aim—the one thing in education that cannot possibly be overdone. We lay it down, then, not as a mere pious opinion, but as a statement to be taken in sober earnest, and to be applied unflinchingly in practice, that the ultimate aim of education—that from which the significance of all proximate aims proceeds—the formation of character.

13. Ethical Aim of Education

We could no doubt formulate the aims of education more neatly if ethical theorists had composed their differences. Those differences are of the speculative sort, turning upon the ultimate meanings of such terms as "right" and "obligation". Meantime, men have to live; and upon the educator is laid the task of helping them to live rightly. Whatever may be the ultimate meaning of right living, it is enough for the educator to keep in view the moral order he finds around him. The highest mortality of his place and period serves as his working ideal; and that morality takes specific shape in the virtues that are most prized by the best members of the community. The most enlightened parents desire that their children should be trained to habits of industry, self-control, perseverance, truthfulness, and the like; and the teacher who practically recognises such training as the main function of the school has no obligation laid upon him to trouble himself about the problems of ethical theory. One may say so much, without denying that the study of ethics will tend to illumine the teacher's judgment upon all matters relating to the highest ends of his calling.

14. Patriotism as an Aim of Education

By the making of citizens we must not be understood to mean the inculcation of a narrow and selfish patriotism. This warning is necessary, because it seems only too possible to take a parochial view even of a great empire. The waving of national flags and the singing of national anthems, though quite proper in their way, stand for a very small part of what we mean by trying to make good citizens. What is really meant is that the spiritual inheritance of a British or an American or a German child is predominantly British or American or German, and that in that inheritance he must on the whole find salvation. When for example, we speak for training a boy to conduct himself as gentleman, we refer implicitly, in this country, to the conduct of an English gentleman. Even conscience—the feeling of uneasiness that comes of violating a moral principle—is to a great extent the voice of the "tribal self". And if national ideals are a governing factor in the direct fashioning of character, no less are they operative in the determination of curricula. That the national culture should form the basis of instruction has generally been recognised an axiom in regard to the primary school, and is becoming more and more recognised in the sphere of higher education. "It is our duty," said William II of Germany, on an occasion which was epoch-making for the higher schools of his country, "to educate men to become young Germans, and not young Greeks and Romans. We must relinquish the basis which has lasted for centuries, the old monastic education of the Middle Ages. We must make German the basis, and German composition must be the centre round which everything turns." We may accept this declaration, without accepting the false patriotism that inspired it. The national culture must be the basis of all school instruction, but there must be no narrowing of the educated man's outlook and sympathies. The national greatness, if it exists, must be understood and appreciated, but there must be no exploitation of the people by privileged classes, who identify their own interests with those of the State.

Aims of Education in Democratic India

In conformity to our national heritage and national values alongwith cherished national goals our educational system must aim at as discussed below:

1. Development of Democratic Citizenship. It is a challenging responsibility with education to carefully train every citizen for democratic citizenship. Such a training involves development of multi-sided qualities.

(a) *Capacity for clear thinking.* A democratic citizen should have the understanding and the intellectual integrity to distinguish truth from falsehood and facts from propaganda. Education should train the young scholar to reject fanaticism and prejudices.

(b) *Receptivity to new ideas.* Education must aim at broadening the intellectual horizon of young scholars. It must enable them to accept the inflow of new ideas that can help in strengthening democratic forces.

(c) *Clearness in speech as well as in writing.* Education must develop the quality of clearness in speech as well as in the writing. This quality is essential for successful living in democracy which is based not on force but on free discussion and persuasion.

(d) *True Patriotism.* Education in a democracy must foster the development of a sense of true patriotism. True patriotism involves three things:

 (i) A sense of appreciation of the social and cultural achievements of one's country.

 (ii) A readiness to recognise its weaknesses frankly and to work hard to overcome them.

 (iii) An earnest desire to serve one's country to the best of one's ability by subordinating individual interests to broader national interests.

2. *Improvement of Vocational Efficiency.* Education must aim at increasing the productive or vocational efficiency of young students. In order to achieve this aim, there should be much greater emphasis on crafts and productive work. Diversification of courses should be introduced at the secondary stage so that a large number of students may take up agricultural, technical, commercial or other practical courses which will train their varied aptitudes. This will also enable them to take up vocational pursuits at the end of the secondary school course.

3. *Development of Personality.* Education should develop literary, artistic and cultural interests of the students. These are necessary for self-expression and for the full development of human personality. For this purpose subjects like art, craft, music, dancing etc. should be included in the scheme of studies.

4. *Education for Leadership.* In order to make democracy function successfully, it is essential to inculcate the qualities of leadership in our youth. Education should train the youth to provide leadership in the social, political, industrial and cultural fields.

Kothari Education Commission and Educational Objectives. In its Report which appeared in 1966, the Kothari Education Commission observed that education must become a powerful instrument of social, economic and cultural transformation. For this purpose, the Commission suggested the following objectives of education:

1. Increasing productivity.
2. Social and national integration.
3. Accelerating the process of modernisation.
4. Developing social, moral and spiritual values.

(1) Education for Increasing Productivity. The Commission suggested that education must be related to productivity to increase national income. In order to create a link between education and productivity, the following programme has been suggested by the Commission:

(i) Science Education. In order to enhance productivity, science education "must become an integral part of school education, and ultimately some study of science should become a part of all courses in the humanities and social sciences at the university stage." This will develop understanding of basic principles, problem-solving attitude, promote the ability of apply these principles to problems of life and to encourage the spirit of enquiry and experimentation.

(ii) Work Experience. According to the Commission, work experience implies participation in productive work in school, in the home, in a workshop, on a farm, in a factory or in any other productive situation. In the programme of relating education to life productivity, this work-experience must be introduced as an integral part of all education, general and vocational.

(iii) 'Forward Look' in Work Experience. Every attempt should be made to link work experience to technology and

industrialisation, including agriculture. The education of a student is not held to be complete unless he participates in some type of work-experience in real life conditions. It is in this way that education can pay high dividends. This 'forward look' in work experience is important for a country which has embarked on a programme of industrialisation.

(iv) *Vocationalisation of Secondary Education.* Every attempt should be made to give a vocational bias to secondary education and to increase the emphasis on agricultural and technological education at the university stage. This will surely bring education into closer relationship with productivity. This is of special significance in the Indian education where education has so far been training the youth for the so called white-collar professions.

(2) *Education for Social and National Integration.* According to the Commission, social and national integration is an important objective of a national system of education. The Commission has suggested the following steps for strengthening the nation through education:

(a) *The Common School System*: In the opinion of the Commission, "If our educational system is to become a powerful instrument of national development in general and social and national integration in particular, we must march towards the goal of a common school system of public education:

— which will be open to all children irrespective of caste, creed, community, religion or social status;
— where access to good education will depend, not on wealth or class, but on talent;
— which will maintain adequate standards in all schools and provide at least a reasonable proportion of quality instruction;
— in which no tuition fee will be charged; and
— which would meet the needs of the average parent."

This system should effectively be implemented in a phased programme spread over 20 years.

(b) *Social and National Service.* The Commission felt that the existing educational system increases the sad gulf between the educated and the uneducated classes, between the intelligents and the masses. In order to eliminate this evil, the Commission, recommends that "Some form of social and national service should be made obligatory for all students and should form an integral part of education at all stages. This can become an instrument to build character, improve discipline, inculcate faith in the dignity of manual labour and develop a sense of social responsibility." The Commission has suggested the following two main forms in which such service can be organised:

(i) Encouraging and enabling students to participate in community living on the school or college campus; and

(ii) Providing opportunities of participation in programmes of community development and national service.

(c) *Evaluation of Language Policy.* The development of a proper language policy can also assist in social and national integration.

(d) *Promoting National Consciousness.* According to the Commission, education must aim at promoting national consciousness by:

(i) Promoting understanding and re-evaluation of our cultural heritage;

(ii) Creating a strong faith in future;

(iii) Developing international understanding;

(iv) Inculcating Democratic Values. The educational programme in schools and colleges should be designed to inculcate democratic values.

(3) *Education for Modernisation.* The present century has seen great advancement in scientific and technical knowledge as a result of exploration of knowledge. While the rest of the world is marching ahead in every field of human activity India

cannot go limping behind. In order that India should keep pace with modernisation, the Commission has made the following suggestions:

(i) Education should awaken curiosity, develop proper interests, attitudes, and build up such essential skills as independent study and capacity to think and judge for oneself.

(ii) Education should create adequate and competent intelligentsia to meet the needs of the day.

(4) *Education for Social, Moral and Spiritual Values.* The national system of education should emphasise the cultivation of fundamental social, moral and spiritual values. For this purpose the Commission has suggested the following steps:

(a) The Central and State Governments should adopt measures to introduce education in moral, social and spiritual values in all institutions under their control. This should be done on the lines recommended by the University Education Commission and Committee on Religious and Moral Instruction. The privately managed institutions should also follow on the same steps.

(b) In order to develop social, moral and religious values, some periods should be provided in the time-table. Instruction of this type should be given by general teachers.

(c) The University Departments of Comparative Religions should show special concern about this aspect of education.

(d) It is necessary to promote a tolerant study of all religions so that its citizens can understand one another better and live together amicably.

QUESTIONS FOR ANSWER

1. Why is it necessary to have educational aims? How far do you agree that "Acting with an aim is all one with acting intelligently."
2. Discuss the factors which determine educational aims. How far are they true to Indian situation?
3. In search for the right man in society relationship, some stress the importance of the individual, others value adaptation of the

self to the demands of others. What is your attitude in regard to these views?

4. What are the rival claims of individual and social aims in education? How far is it possible to strike a balance between them?
5. What do you understand by social and individual aims of education? Is it possible to strike a balance between the two? Explain in detail.
6. What should be the aims of education in democratic India? What are the views of Indian Education Commission (1964-66) in this regard?
7. Examine critically the aims and objectives of education as suggested by the Kothari Education Commission (1966). How far do they meet the needs of a national system of education?

4

Education—Theory and Practice

To some education is "art" and to some it is "science", therefore this chapter is devoted to this controversy and conclude that education is an "applied science".

Introduction

The question whether there is, or indeed can be, a science education truly so called, has given rise to not a little controversy. Before passing on to more purely pedagogic topics, it may be well, therefore, to endeavour to clear away the dust of that controversy by inquiring in what sense the pairs of correlative terms "science" and "art", "theory" and "practice" so commonly used with reference to education, are approximately so used; and what is the relation between the two aspects of education supposed to be connoted by these terms.

Science and Art

If we think of any branch of human knowledge which by universal consent is ranked among the sciences, we find that it consists of a connected and systematised body of truth, possessing generality of form, employing a more or less settled terminology, and pursued for its own sake, without special reference to any ulterior practical end.

Thus the geometer, the chemist, the physiologist, the geologist, and the psychologist, as such, seek to build up systems of truth, not necessarily with any thought of the uses to which the results of their investigations may possibly be put by the engineer, the manufacturer, the physician, the mining expert, and the teacher, respectively.

If, on the other hand, we think of those branches of investigation which no one would refuse to place among the arts—agriculture, mining, and navigation, for example—we find that each of them, while it may also possess a systematic body of doctrine and a technical terminology, pursues some aim other than knowledge, that its primary object is, not to know, but to do or to effect something. The distinction, though not a very sharp one is sufficiently clear.

Using the terms science and art, then, in these broadly contrasted senses, it is quite obvious that education is an art and not a science. Some of the arts, however, have been brought to such a degree of system and generality, that they are often spoken of as sciences; but in this case we must distinguish between the pure sciences, which pursue knowledge, for its own sake, and the applied sciences, which correspond to certain of the arts as we have defined them.

The arts we have named, as well as medicine, surgery, and all others which are grounded on scientific principles, may thus be alternatively described as applied sciences. Assuming that the study of education offers a systematic and logically coherent body of doctrine. We may call education an applied science.

Theory and Practice

We come now to the terms theory and practice. Some of the pure science—e.g., biology, chemistry, and physics—have a theoretical and a practical side, the former comprising a systematic account of the facts and generalisations with which the science is conversant, whilst the latter involves that quickness of eye, steadiness of hand, and skill in the manipulation of materials, upon which the advancement of science so largely depends.

The arts or applied sciences also have their theoretical and practical sides; but, of course, with this difference, that, whereas in the pure sciences the practice exists for the sake of the theory, in the applied sciences the theory exists for the sake of the practice.

The complete pursuit of any of the arts implies, then, two things; first a systematic body of knowledge, drawn largely from the appropriate sciences, and constituting the theory of the art; and, secondly, those elements of skill and empirical tact which constitute the practice of the art. Applying this distinction to the problem before us, we may speak provisionally of a theory and a practice of the art of education.

It is true that the term "practice" is ambiguous. We have reserved it here to denote the actual work of the teacher in the school. We are aware that books are written, syllabuses devised, and examination papers composed on "the practice of education" as distinguished from the "theory". But no one who has tried his hand at these things will deny that the distinction is hard to maintain, the fact being that the whole subject, so far as it aims at systematic thought and exposition, is rightly named theory. The real distinction is that some parts of the theory lay stress on general aspects, and others on special details.

Practice Precedes Theory

In the first place it is well known that in the pursuit of any art, theory waits upon practice. Men tilled the ground and sailed the seas and practised the healing art, before they worked out anything that deserved to be called a theory of the art of agriculture, of navigation, and of medicine. Now if this is true of the arts that correspond to the most primitive of instincts, those relating to immediately self-preservation, much more should we expect it to be true of the more elusive and less obviously necessary art of education. So it happens that we enter upon the twentieth century without having achieved a complete and coherent account of the aims and means of education. Partly owing to the fact that teaching was so long regarded as an incidental function of the clerical profession, and partly owing to a certain national obtuseness in realising the importance of the subject, our progress in the practice of education cannot be called astonishing; and the progress of theory is therefore slow.

Education Indebted to Psychology

It is not to be expected that a satisfactory theory of any art can be expounded, when the pure sciences upon which it depends are in an unsettled state. Now there is no study which has made more striking advance in recent times than psychology, the very science to which education stands specially inedible. The psychology of earlier days was vitiated by the assumption that the mind is endowed with a number of independent "faculties memory, imagination, reasoning, and the like each susceptible of and requiring separate culture.

This error is of course no longer committed by the competent psychologist. Indeed he has tended to go to the other extreme of abandoning the useful word "faculty" altogether. On the other hand, the mistakes of the faculty-psychology are still frequent in works on education. "One is constantly coming across disquisitions," wrote Dr. James Ward, "on the training of the senses, the training of the memory, the training of the imagination; of the faculties of conception, abstraction, judgment and so on.

Dr. John Dewey, referring to "the modern conception of mind as essentially a process—a process of growth, not a fixed thing," he says: "According to the older view, mind was mind, and that was the whole story. Mind was the same throughout, because fitted out with the same assortment of faculties whether in child or adult. If any difference was made it was simply that some of these ready-made faculties—such as memory—came into play at an earlier time, while others, such as judging and inferring, made their appearance only after the child, through memorising drills, had been reduced to complete dependence upon the thought of others.

But even if we are careful to ensure the soundness of our psychology, we may easily go wrong in applying it to educational problems. The attempt has often been made, for example, to construct model curricula, based on the proposition that the business of instruction is to supply an all-round mental gymnastic.

And that psychology can furnish no adequate guidance in the framing of curricula is only part of the larger truth that it cannot decide any question relating to the aims of education.

Psychology does undoubtedly furnish us with valuable hints when we come to inquire by what methods our aims may best be realised.

What these aims shall be, however, depends upon our ideals of life and conduct, and not upon anything that psychology professes to teach us. Instead of appealing to psychology we must inquire what knowledge on the whole is of most worth, and what are those virtues of mind and heart which are most valued in the community in which we live, and which constitute the moral atmosphere breathed by its best members.

The attempt to found a theory of education upon psychology alone has led to another result which can only tend to bring that theory into disrepute. It has been the fashion to compose, for the benefit of young teachers, books which are in effect systematic treatises upon elementary psychology, interspersed with a regular series of pedagogic comments and applications.

The result has been disastrous in a twofold sense. First, the natural order of procedure has been inverted. A theory of education must start from its own premises, and must pursue its own course by its own methods, calling to its assistance psychology, physiology, ethics, "pedology", and the rest, whenever their help is wanted. Otherwise the student is never led to face systematically the fundamental problems of education. There may come a time, for example, when the results obtained by the cultivator of experimental psychology will be sufficiently assured and important to find a place in any systematic attempt to furnish guidance to the young teacher. But that time has hardly yet arrived, and, even if it had, the approach to the problems in question should be from the educational rather than from the psychological side.

It is no doubt an advantage that the teacher should, on the analogy of other professions, begin by mastering the really relevant portions of certain sciences. Having done so, he should go forward to an independent study of the theory of his art. Only so can the problems of education be seen in their true perspective, and only so can the conditions upon which their solution depends be fully grasped.

Good teaching like the efficient practice of any other art, is a function of many variables, of which the study of principles and methods is only one. That study, if properly pursued, should indeed guard the young teacher from many pitfalls. It should save him from becoming a blind imitator either of his own past self or of other people; it should enable him to improve upon traditional practice; if should render his own experience a thousand times more fruitful, by enabling him to bring it continually to the test of principles; and it should raise his occupation to the dignity of a real profession; which it can never be so long as he works on a merely imitative and empirical level.

But none of these results can be accomplished if he be seriously lacking in the other qualities that go to the making of a teacher; if, for example, he be comparatively ignorant of what he professes to teach, or if he possesses only in a low degree those personal gifts which are important to a teacher.

And so it may easily happen that one who has studied the theory of education with the utmost care and with considerable insight may turn out a signal failure as a practical teacher; just as it may happen that one who prides himself upon never having read a book on teaching may attain all but the highest success, through the possession of a quick and ready sympathy with children and their ways of thinking, a winning manner, a fund of enthusiasm for his vocation, and instincts which really enable him unconsciously to construct a very serviceable theory of his own.

It is manifestly unfair to estimate the worth of educational theory by reference to extreme examples .such as these. Good teaching has been done without a knowledge of theory and bad teaching has been done with it; but these are facts which should cause no surprise to one who rightly apprehends the relation between theory and practice.

Theory and practice are not opposed, but complementary; not different things, but different sides of the same thing, each meaningless without reference to the other. A good practical teacher must have a theory behind his practice, whether implicit or explicit; and a same theorist must have constant regard to existing circumstances.

There are two extremes to be avoided; that of the mere theorist, who spins fine webs of doctrine that collapse on contact with the hard facts of experience; and that of the mere empiricist, or rule-of-thumb practitioner, who seeks no rational basis for this practice.

But the mere theorist and the mere empiricist are both mere consequences of one-sided views. Experience which has not been reflected upon is only a treadmill round whose value may easily be exaggerated; whereas theory which is not the result of reflection upon actual practice must be received with extreme caution.

"The history of education," wrote the late Prof. Sidgwick, "is the battleground and burial-ground of impracticable theories; and one who studies it is soon taught to abate his constructive self-confidence, and to endeavour humbly to learn the lessons and harmonise the results of experience." To which we may add that the attempt to "harmonise the results of experience" is precisely what we mean by sane theorising, and precisely what Sidgwick brilliantly exemplified in his essay on *"The Theory of Classical Education"*. "Sound practice is sound theory unconscious of itself; sound theory is merely sound practice conscious of itself."

Lastly we are bound to acknowledge the danger that in teaching, as in other departments of practice theoretical the attitude of mind may become habitual as to induce a dreaminess or an impatience of the facts of the concrete situation, which are alike fatal to efficiency when one is fairly at the work.

The practical schemes of the apostolic Pestalozzi were not successful; and in his less happy moods he is said to have banged the doors upon disappointing classes, and on one occasion to have thrown his boots at an offending colleague. The moral is not, however, to be drawn too hastily; it lies, not against theory as such, but against its untimely obtrusion.

The "day-dreams of a schoolmaster" may indeed be sometimes fruitful of results; but on the whole it is certainly undesirable that he should be occupied in the hours of school with thoughts of the ultimate meaning and issue of his labours. He should rather trust, when amongst his pupils, to the afterglow of his periods of private illumination. In this way he may find that even the apparently trifling details of his procedure may be carried out so as to further the supreme purpose of education.

QUESTIONS FOR ANSWER

1. Justify that Education is an "Applied Science"?
2. "Education is indebted to psychology." Justify.

5

The Study or Knowledge of Children

Mr. R.H. Quick, the great educator of his time has rightly observed: That every child should be educated, that the education of girls is as essential to social well-being as that of boys, that the state should assume the supervision of its schools, and that instruction is not a mere affair of books,—all these truths had been pressed home by the reformers of previous centuries, though only in modern times have they become living forces in the progress of mankind. The most important item in the programme of "the new education"—the one that implies many of the rest—is that the educator should keep in view not only what sort of person he wishes the child to become in later life, but also what manner of person the child is, here and now.

This creed is, in a sense, at least as old as Plato. The Republic, in which he discusses education as part of the larger question of the welfare of society, contains as elaborate account of "the main elements of that human nature for which, as he conceived, it was the function of education to provide nurture. For him, the study of the being to be educated is an essential part of the study of education.

He believed that neither a State nor an individual can undertake to educate in a systematic way, unless they start with some idea, not only of what they wish to teach, but also of the living being to whom the matter to be taught is relative, and upon which the given character is to be impressed.

In modern times we find first strong plea for the study of the child in the pages of Rousseau. "I wish," says Rousseau, "that some discreet person would give us a treatise on the art of observing children—an art which would be of immense value to us, but of which fathers and schoolmasters have not as yet learnt the very first rudiments."

The year of the publication of *Emile* and *Le Contrat Social* found Pestalozzi, a young student at Zurich, in warm sympathy with the party which opposed the public condemnation of Rousseau's writings; and this early influence is traceable, in his ardent belief that an important factor in education had hitherto been insufficiently considered—the child himself. If the traditional idea of education, as a process of filling the mind with knowledge, was to give place to that of developing an organism, then the laws of development must be ascertained and adhered to.

With equal enthusiasm, and with greater philosophic insight, Froebel taught that each period of life is to be regarded, not simply as a means to something beyond, but also as an end in itself; that "the boy has not become a boy, nor has the youth become a youth, by reaching a certain age, but only by having lived through childhood, and, further on, through boyhood, true to the requirements of his mind, his feelings, and his body;" and that "similarly, adult man has not become an adult man by reaching a certain age, but only by faithfully satisfying the requirements of his childhood, boyhood, and youth".

As a plea for the greater consideration of the child, it would not be easy to match, even from the professed literature of pedagogy, the following passage from the pen of the late Mr. Lecky: "There is such a thing as looking forward too rigidly and too exclusively to the future—to a future that may never arrive. This is the great fault of the over-educationist, who makes early life a burden and a toil, and also of those who try to impose on youth the tastes and pleasures of the man....Many a parent, standing by the coffin of his child, has felt with bitterness how much of the measure of enjoyment that short life might have known has been cut off by an injudicious education. And even if adult life is attained, the evils of an unhappy childhood are seldom wholly compensated.... An early overstrain of our powers often leaves behind it lasting distortion of weakness, and a sad childhood introduces into the character elements of morbidness and bitterness that will not disappear".

Besides the practical motives which we have considered above, there remains to be noted the theoretical interest which has led men of science also to investigate different phases of child life.

The science of physiology has added immensely to our general knowledge of the child's physical growth and, what is of especial value, of the effects of mental effort upon the developing nervous system.

This is fortunate, not only because accurate knowledge of the facts of child life is thus extended, but also because there is need of introducing the truly scientific spirit into these investigations.

Methods of Child-Study

The teacher ought to concern himself with the pupil to be instructed and trained as well as with the instruments of instruction and the object of training, and postponing for the moment the question how far the teacher as such need be acquainted with the somewhat alarming mass of material which is being accumulated by students of childhood, and with the laborious methods by which that material is collected and sifted, let us take note of the chief heads under which these may be grouped.

The first method is that of making careful records of individual children, either of a comprehensive character or with reference to some special line of development. Such records, while deeply interesting to those immediately concerned, and very suggestive to others, must clearly be used with caution.

We must be on our guard against arguing from the special to the general case. Among the most noteworthy of them are Darwin's *Biographical Sketch of an Infant*, Preyer's *Mind of a Child*, Sully's *Extracts from a Father's Dairy* and Miss Shinn's *Notes on the Development of a Child*.

Accounts of observations upon children sometimes assume a statistical form, and a great deal of enthusiastic labour has been expanded upon this sort of investigation. We may at once put aside as irrelevant to our purpose all those results which do not bear upon the practical business we have in hand.

The results of Dr. Stanley Hall's investigations regarding "The Contents of Children's Minds on entering School," are suggestive to those who teach young children. Even, however, where statistical inquiries bear facts and figures that it is both a blunder and a crime to goad the half-fed and scantily clad children to be found in some of our primary schools into the same degree of mental activity as that displayed by their more fortunate fellows, and to require the weaklier pupils in our higher schools to perform tasks at home which keep them busy till bed-time. Therefore, only interpreted material, that which reveals principles or suggests lines of growth to which the educator has to adapt himself, can be of much practical avail."

Periods of Development

It is necessary, however, at this point, to trace in brief outline the course of the normal child's development through the period, longer or shorter, of his attendance at school. In tracing this development, we must, for the sake of clearness, divide school life into periods, but it will at once be understood that such a division must be more or less artificial, and must depend largely upon the point of view. The periods fixed upon would probably differ according as the division is based upon the child's physical, intellectual, linguistic, artistic, or moral progress.

On this understanding we may conveniently adopt the following divisions: (1) the first three years, the period of babyhood; (2) to the end of the seventh year, the period which may be called descriptively that of early childhood; (3) to the tenth or eleventh year, the period of later childhood; (4) to the fourteenth year, the period of boyhood or girlhood; and (5) from the fourteenth year onwards, the period of adolescence.

The earliest period (First 3 years) has received much attention from competent observers, because of its deep interest, and its importance for psychology and biology. The teacher is not called upon to study it minutely, but it would be a great mistake if any teacher, especially a teacher of young children, neglected it entirely; just as it is a mistake when a teacher of adolescence takes no account of the ways of younger boys and girls.

The most obvious thing that strikes one about these earliest years is a marvellous progress made in command of the bodily organs, sensory and motor.

The long task of intellectually grasping the world around him, of comparing, classifying, and generalising, begins during this period. Armed with a few heads of classification, the child boldly attacks the objects that present themselves; at first every man is "daddy," every large quadruped a "gee-gee" or a "moo-moo," and snowflakes are butterflies.

The control of bodily movements which has been acquired in the earlier period enables the child (3-7) years to go still further afield for objects of investigation, and under wise guidance his native curiosity will be busily employed in the observation of the simpler phenomena of nature. His curiosity, coupled with his growing skill in the use of the mother-tongue, also prompts him to an incessant questioning of his elders, so much so that this has been marked off as the questioning age.

The words "what" and "why" are continually on his tongue. "What is this?" "What is it called?" "Why is this so?" "Who made this?" These the verbal forms assumed by the child's thirst for facts and causes.

The distinction between work and play between the free spontaneous activity that seeks no end beyond itself, and the pursuit of a required end, imposed by external authority or by an internal sense of duty—has not yet been brought home to him.

The distinction gradually makes itself felt, as the processes of washing, dressing, tidying up, and going to school, take on the form of duties, but in the main this is the period of play. So strong is the dramatic instinct at this age that some children appear to spend a large portion of their waking life in playing parts, imitating their elders, and provoking "the years to bring the inevitable yoke." Not only dolls and other toys, but also the things appertaining to adult life, are pressed into this service.

The lively imagination shows itself, too, in the child's appreciation of stories whether of the possible or the impossible sort, and in his greater or less aptitude for inventing stories of his own. His retentive power becomes stronger, and some of his impressions work themselves into connections so firm as to become permanent.

He makes progress in his intellectual construction to the world. He is more apt to discern differences amid broad similarities. He has imbibed some degree of respect for authority, he has begun to form habits of obedience, and he has learned to control to some extent the more violent and antisocial of the emotions, such as anger.

In the next stage (7-10 years) child's physical development proceeds apace; he continues to add about two inches to his stature annually; his brain has completed about four-fifths of its growth, and he enters upon the period of secondary dentition. He leaves the Kindergarten or infant school, and, being now ripe for a clearer distinction between work and play, he goes to school in earnest, though under wise arrangements the step will not be taken abruptly.

His interests hitherto have been of the native and spontaneous sort, but he must now use these as stepping-stones to the acquired interests of civilised life; in particular, the symbols of language, of number, and of musical expression call for mastery, and usually prove somewhat formidable tasks. In acquiring such arts as reading, writing, and ciphering, he is helped, however, by his growing power to fix his attention on the thing in hand, and to resist the attractions of the various objects that assail his senses.

This means, in the language of psychology, that the primitive form of attention which is captured at once by objects that strike the senses is giving place in some degree to appreceptive attention, which is yielded to things that connect themselves with what we already know, and which implies ability to adopt the reflective attitude towards a proposed problem. Again, the child becomes still more retentive of impressions, so that what is now learnt is more apt to become part of his permanent mental stock.

It is sometimes said that memory is now at its best, but this is true only in the sense that physiological retentiveness is possibly stronger now than before or after; the adult makes up for this by the logical and other connections of his ideas. The fight of fancy begins to be less unbridled, for, though the child may still revel in fairy tales, lie is more apt to require verisimilitude in the stories that he hears.

With this intellectual advance there will go also, in normal cases, distinct progress on the moral side. The average child of eight or nine has learnt lessons of self-control, he is no longer the creature of impulse and caprice. He can take care of himself in the street, and go to school alone. He no longer follows authority so blindly as before. His moral progress is rather by way of free imitation of his elders, and thus the example of parent and teacher is more than ever important.

As in the sphere of thought his ideas are of the pictorial rather than of the abstract order, so in the sphere of morals he works by the concrete embodiment of virtuous conduct, and not by abstract ideas of virtue. His better moral judgments are determined by loyalty to a person rather than to a principle. It is to the people around him, and to the heroes of story and romance, that he first looks for guidance.

We come now to the period of boyhood (11-14 years) and girlhood. Physical growth proceeds almost as before, but whereas in the previous period boys grow a little faster than girls, the position is now reversed; girls at this age grow on the average more rapidly than boys, and for the two or three years following the twelfth year are actually taller and heavier, the difference being due to a check in the growth of boys, and to a considerable acceleration in the growth of girls.

On the mental side, perhaps the most striking thing about this period is the more important part played by forms and symbols in the extension of the boy's interests. He can now read fluently, thinking while he reads and reading while he thinks; and so the printed page, as well as the sensible object and the picture, becomes a source of knowledge and of pleasure.

Similarly, if in the preceding period his mind has been stored, by means of pictures and models, with concrete geographical notions, he is now able "to translate the mute symbols of a map into fresh-coloured images of mountain ranges and broad plains, of snow-capped peaks and deep valleys, of rivers and lakes and the boundless ocean, of villages and cities."

He is now at home, too, with the symbols of number; the system of numeration and notation, the common arithmetical tables, and the fundamental processes of arithmetic have become part of his permanent mental store. His greater power of abstraction, and the consequent freedom of many of his ideas from actual sense-impressions, is seen too in his ability to think of words as such, to understand their relations, and to appreciate the meaning and use of grammatical forms.

This increasing power of abstraction, and diminishing dependence upon his actual surroundings, are seen too in the widening range of his sympathies, and in the subjects of his moral judgments. Gradually, amid his wider intercourse with his fellows, and with the characters of literature and history, there has grown up a stock of universal rules of conduct—of the types, this sort of action is wrong, that sort is right.

It is an instructive fact that, though the years from eleven or twelve to sixteen or seventeen are years of rapid growth, and usually of strenuous exertion, whether at school or elsewhere, the body seems to be at its best for resisting disease and death, and death-rate being at its lowest at the age of fourteen.

But besides this increase in height and weight, the momentous changes incident to the passage from childhood to youth (14-18 years) now take place; the larynx enlarges, the vocal cords are elongated, the voice is modified, and there are probably equally important changes in the brain, since the shape of the head alters.

The higher mental processes become more fully developed, so that the abstractions of mathematics, logic, science, and language, and the more reflective forms of literature, now begin to be comprehended. The youth or maiden begins to live to a great extent in the future rather than in the present.

The mind becomes filled with hopes and dreams, passions and cravings. Social and ethical interests begin to dominate; political or religious zeal sometimes becomes the mainspring of action; and in the course of the period religious doubts often obtrude themselves.

The great increase in physical and mental energy shows itself in the waves of emotional vitality that now appear; indeed, one of the chief aims of those who aspire to guide youths through this stormy period should be to turn these tempestuous emotions into proper channels. It becomes more than ever important that education should not be the mere storing up of knowledge, but that it should provide outlets to action.

This is the time for athletic games, gymnastic exercises, manual training, and work in the laboratory. Now or never is the time, too, for opening out any intellectual and aesthetic interests that are to become permanent incentives to right conduct. "An undue tendency to introspection must be checked by allurements to action," and "exaggerated ambition and unreflecting activity must be checked by allurements to serious studies."

The above details about the child's development are general, yet individual variations are not against norms of individual's development.

Temperament

It would be a great help to teachers, as to all others who have to work upon human material, if there existed a developed science of individual character. Psychology has made great headway in the analysis and synthesis of the constituent elements of every mind, but little or nothing of scientific value has yet been done towards enabling us to classify and explain the peculiar mental constitution of the individual person. Failing this, we have to rely chiefly upon our general observation, and upon such facility as we possess in shrewdly estimating the characters of children.

Everyone knows, for example, the common distinction between the "quick" and the "slow" child. The one soon learns his lesson, but is apt to forget it easily; the other learns slowly but more surely. The one is alert and vivacious; the other perhaps comparatively heavy and dull.

The one judges and decides hastily; the other more guardedly and, on the whole, more soundly. The one is usually lacking in perseverance; the other is more tenancious of purpose. The one is quick-tempered but generous-hearted and forgiving; the other is low to anger but sometimes not of great mercy.

The one is more attractive and popular character; other wins his way to favour less easily, but often "wears" better. The one lives largely in the present; the other's thoughts are often directed to the future. If the one fails, it is because he needs more strength; if the other fails, it is because he needs more time.

These are of course very broad contrasts, and they hold only of extreme instances of the two types. Still, everyone who has had experience of life, whether amongst children or adults, will readily recall examples that answer fairly well to the above descriptions. We might go on to introduce an additional distinction.

Mental processes, besides being quick or slow, may be stronger or weak; and on this basis a fourfold classification has been suggested, which answers to the traditional four temperaments. The choleric temperament (quick and strong) is energetic, impetuous, and chiefly concerned with out-ward events; the melancholic (slow and strong) is sentimental, with a marked tendency to introspection and suspended judgment; the sanguine (quick and weak) is ardent, impressionable, and unsteady; the phlegmatic (slow and weak) combines tardiness with quiet persistence.

Mentally Deficient Child

The only point that calls for attention here is that there is no hard and fast line to be drawn between the normal and the abnormal, and so it is worthwhile taking note of the classes into which the latter are usually divided. At the bottom of the scale we have idiots—those unfortunates who passes no mental assets, who are incapable even of the direct self-preservation and require as much supervision as a child of six months.

Next to these come imbeciles, who are capable of direct but not of indirect self-preservation. A member of this class would, for example, get out of bodily danger, but could not be brought to earn a living, at least without permanent help and supervision.

The third class comprises those who may be expected, as a result of careful training, to earn a livelihood at some mechanical occupation, but who cannot be taught with profit in the ordinary primary school. These are technically known as defective or feeble-minded children.

The fourth class includes children who, though extremely dull and backward, can be taught profitably, though perhaps at considerable inconvenience, along with normal children.

Both for their own sake and for the well-being of society, the first two classes should be cared for in special institutions. In the case of children belonging to the third class has recently received considerable attention.

They are taught in small separate groups, great stress being placed upon manual employments. Many of them, under careful training, are able eventually to take their place in the ordinary school, though not with scholars of their own age; and many others become able at least to follow successfully some occupation in which considerable intelligence and skill are not called for.

Recall Your Childhood to Study Child

Since we cannot transplant ourselves within the child's own consciousness and examine the workings of his mind directly. The "giftie" to see others as we "see ourself" is a still more impossible one than that for which the poet sighed. There is only one child who can in any sense be observed directly, namely, one's own past self; and he can be observed only so far and so accurately as memory happens to serve one.

But our recollections of our own childhood are fragmentary, uncertain, and inevitably coloured by subsequent experience. Still, various ways suggest themselves by which our efforts at recall may be helped out; and the value of such efforts, to one who aspires to a complete understanding of the children committed to his care, can hardly be questioned, since one of the chief secrets of good teaching is the power to place oneself at the pupil's point of view.

So the young teacher is counselled to form as faithful picture as he can of his own childhood—of its events, and of his ways of thinking and feeling about them.

He will perhaps get assistance from parents and other relatives, from nurses and teachers, from old letters, and from other sources that will suggest themselves. He may be fortunate enough still to possess old exercise books and other similar records of his past; and he will do well to read over again some of the books that most impressed him in his juvenile years. The attempt so to reconstruct one's own childhood will be found no less interesting than profitable.

QUESTIONS FOR ANSWER

1. "For effective education the most important aspect is the study of the child". Justify.
2. "Development Child should form the basis of his education". Justify.
3. Write a note on the 'Periods of development' of the child.

6

Classification of Agencies of Education

Education is a "man making" process and its duration starts from the day the child is conceived by the mother till the day he leaves this world, therefore, in one way or the other various institutions, agencies, situations etc. have their impact in educating him. The right use of these agencies is the fundamental basic principle of education in personal, social and national context.

What is an Agency of Education?

Education is of paramount importance for the progress of society. It is one of the major forces behind the social and cultural life of a community. The experiences, traditions, customs, thoughts, and values of one generation are passed on to the succeeding generation through education. In this process certain individuals, certain groups, certain institutions play their role and transmit the rich cultural and social heritage to new generation. All these and other similar sources may be called "Agencies of Education".

In simple words, we may say that agencies of education are those sources, places or institutions which exercise an educational influence on the child.

Agencies of education are the specialised and non-specialised institutions which society has developed to carry out the function of education.

Classification of Education of Agencies

Agencies of Education may be classified as:

(a) Formal and Informal Agencies
(b) Active and Passive Agencies

(a) Formal and Informal Agencies of Education. Certain agencies are developed with the specific and exclusive objective of imparting education. College, University etc. are such agencies. These are called formal agencies of education. The aims and the programmes of work of these agencies is pre-planned. The place of functioning and the time for which they must function are also decided in advance.

There are certain other agencies the specific and exclusive function of which is not to impart education; but, their educative influence cannot be ignored. The family, the community, the peer group, professional organisations etc., are some such agencies. These are called informal agencies of education. The children receive a lot of education through these agencies without making much of conscious and deliberate effort. These agencies diffuse and transmit culture and knowledge from one generation to another in informal, unorganised manner.

(b) Active and Passive Agencies of Education. Agencies of education may also be classified as active and passive agencies.

The *active agencies* of education are 'active' and play a prominent role in imparting education. These agencies play their role through the interaction of persons involved in the educative process. The school is an active agency of education since the teachers and the pupils interact on each other. The family is an active agency of education as parents and children interact on each other. Education in case of active agencies is a two-way process. Besides the school and the family, other active agencies are the church, the state, the youth groups etc.

The *passive agencies* of education are those agencies which influence the learner but are not themselves influenced in return. In their case, education is a one-way process. The educational radio, educational television, the press, the theatre, the library are some of the important passive agencies of education. However, these agencies are subject to overall public opinion and public control.

Relative Role of Educational Agencies. Different agencies of education have a relative róle to play. A child first comes into contact with his family and the family or the home influences the child more than any other agency does. From the family, the child steps into neighbourhood environment. There he is influenced by the peer group. Inside the home, he is influenced by the radio, the television, the press and individuals who keep visiting the family. When he starts going to school, it becomes the major agency of education for the child although a number of other agencies also keep playing their parallel role.

The modern concept of education is life-long education. The educative process does not stop with the completion of mere schooling of formal instruction in schools and colleges. True education begins when formal education ends. In other words, different agencies of education play complementary as well as supplementary roles.

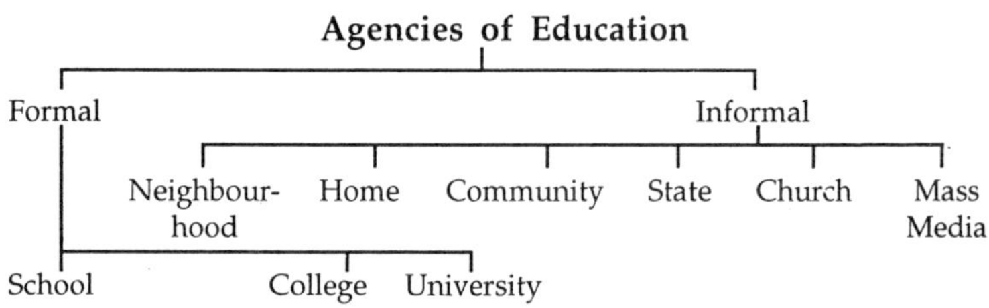

or

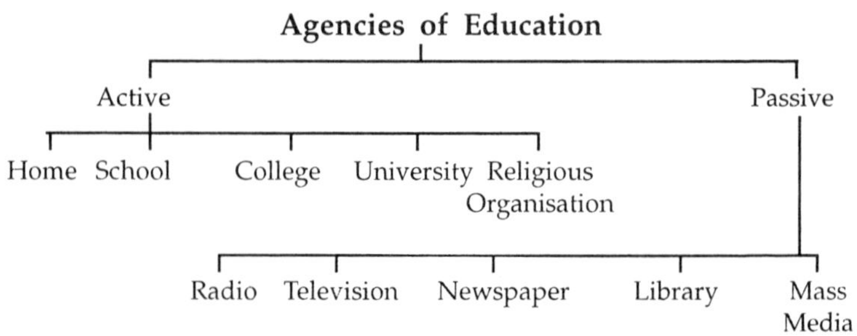

Third Classification of All the Agencies of Education

1	2	3	4
Formal	Informal	Commercial	Non-Commercial
(1) School	(1) The Family	(1) Radio	(1) Sports Club
(2) Religious institutions	(2) General Games	(2) T.V.	(2) Social Welfare Centres
(3) Library	(3) The State	(3) Cinema	(3) Dramatic Clubs
(4) Museum	(4) The Community or Society	(4) Clubs	(4) Scouting and guiding
(5) Zoo		(5) Theatres	(5) Youth Welfare Clubs
(6) Art Gallaries		(6) Newspaper	(6) Adult education Centres
(7) Organised games		(7) The Press	
(8) Educational programmes			

The above classification has been prescribed by Brown. Let us discuss it in some detail as under:

(1) Formal Agencies—Brown's formal agencies, described above, give pre-planned ready made tit-bits of knowledge to the child in such a way that he becomes conscious of the past history, wisdom of ages and cultural values of the race. In this way his character is formed.

(2) Informal Agencies—These agencies inculcate in children the desired human qualities and moral values. Through these agencies children learn various theories, principles of conduct and behaviour. Thus these agencies bring about the socialization of the child and imbue him with a sense of duty and responsibility.

(3) Commercial Agencies—According to Brown, these agencies give various kinds of knowledge, discoveries, inventions and achievements of human race. Through these agencies children acquire knowledge about the culture, beliefs and activities of different sections of human society. For example—newspapers and magazines prepare children to be sympathetic with regard to social happenings and activities

going on not only in their own country but also throughout the whole world by communicating them most up-to-date information. Thus, through these agencies, the child develops social attitudes and receives all kinds of social education and experiences.

(4) Non-Commercial Agencies—Brown is of opinion that non-Commercial agencies come into being for social good. They are not linked with any Commercial motive. For example—sports, educational tours, debates, scouting, girl guiding, youth forums, welfare activities and other programmes are all for the social good and character formation of children. In short, non-commercial agencies of education create the sense of dynamic citizenship and social service.

The above discussion regarding all the three classifications clearly signifies that the first classification is most to the point. In other words, formal and informal agencies of education are all embracing whereas the other two classifications may also be grouped under this one.

(1) Formal Agencies

Meaning of Formal Agencies—Under this category we list those institutions which impart definite and ready made titbits of knowledge in a specified time under a controlled and structured environment. Here the teachers are definite and the objectives to be achieved are specific. Such instructions are established by society with the purpose of directly providing the accumulated knowledge in specific dozes under a pre-planned programme. To be more clear, education imparted by formal agencies is limited and specific. Such type of education has its own merits, because the experiences are structured and learning gained can be measured and evaluated. Not only this, stages of progress are also pre-decided and well marked.

Merits of Formal Agencies—Everything is definite and specific about the objectives, learning experiences, desired behavioural changes together with measuring and evaluation techniques. Time limit prescribed leads to effective planning, organization, leading and controlling. John Dewey has rightly remarked—"Without formal education, it is not possible to transmit all the resources and achievements of a complex society. It also opens a way to a kind of experience which would not be accessible to the young, if they are left to pick up their training in informal association with others."

Demerits of Formal Agencies—Education imparted by formal agencies is often merely bookish, theoretical and artificial devoid of realities of life and society. It is planned under rigid conditions and strict discipline which makes the whole environment dead and lifeless. It emphasizes interpretations on words and phrases and often neglects the real spirit underlying the content. Lastly it promotes rote memorization , mechanical rendering and does not inculcate thoughts, understanding and insight into the minds of educands. John Dewey has rightly remarked- "Formal education easily becomes remote and dead, abstract and bookish. What accumulated knowledge exists in low grade societies is at least put into practice. But in advanced culture much which has to be learnt is stored in symbols. It is far from translation into familiar acts. There is the standing danger that the material of formal education will be merely the subject matter of schools isolated from the subject matter of life experience."

(2) Informal Agencies

Meaning of Informal Agencies—Informal agencies of education are those institutions which influence the child indirectly. Therefore they are often termed as indirect agencies also. The objectives of these agencies are wider and more comprehensive than mere educational objectives. In these agencies nothing is pre-planned and rigid. Experiences gained through these agencies are neither controlled nor rigidly structured. Everything is free and natural. The teachers and strategies, tactics and technologies used by them to impart knowledge are not fixed in advance. Education through these agencies, is imbibed incidently and naturally by the student's own initiative and efforts. There are no set places or locations for imparting education. The family, religious ceremonies, community, social gathering and newspapers are some of the important informal agencies of education.

Merits of Informal Agencies—Education imparted through informal agencies is natural and incidental. It is imparted in a free atmosphere without any rigid control and direction. It leads to initiative, self planning, self picking and self choosing. It stimulates the curiosity and interest in children and avoids external force and stern discipline. Hence the formation of character is quite smooth and natural. John Dewey has rightly remarked—"The child is informally educated by living with others and the very process of living together educates. It enlarges and enlightens experience, it stimulates and enriches imagination, it creates responsibility, accuracy and vividness of statement and thought."

Demerits of Informal Agencies—(1) Informal agencies often impart vague knowledge. (2) The accumulated knowledge of the race can not be imparted through informal agencies alone. (3) Duration and time limits are greatly essential in the preparation of citizens who are to lead their own lives

Difference Between Formal and Informal Agencies

Formal Agencies	*Informal Agencies*
(School, Religion, Museum, Zoo, Planned entertainment, Organizations and Library etc.	(Family, Community Centres, State, T.V., Radio, General games and sports, Market place and Fairs etc.).
(1) Controlled environment.	(1) Free and uncontrolled environment.
(2) Pre-planned achievement of narrow ends.	(2) No pre-planned scheme nor pre-determined aim and objectives.
(3) Direct education.	(3) Indirect education.
(4) Place and duration of work are fixed.	(4) Neither fixed locations nor fixed duration of time.
(5) Guided and supervised by definite persons.	(5) No definite persons guide and supervise these.
(6) Curriculum, time table and techniques are definite.	(6) No limitation of curriculum, time table or techniques.
(7) Their work is time bound.	(7) No such limits of duration and dozes of work.
(8) After prescribed work examinations are conducted and certificates, diplomas and degrees awarded.	(8) It is life long education. No certificate, diploma or degree is awarded.
(9) Planned scheme and programmes of education.	(9) No planning is often wastage of energy and time.

successfully and guide the destiny of their nation. No planning is often no education. (4) Much time and energy is wasted in random experience. (5) At the same time skills and techniques also can not be developed through informal education. (6) Sometimes children may go astray and develop harmful attitudes and habits which bring harm to the individual as well as to the society.

Balance Between Formal and Informal Agencies of Education

The truth is that none of the above discussed agencies is complete in itself. Each gives a certain type of education which is only a part of the whole. In reality both the agencies of education are mutually complementary and supplementary for the complete and wholesome development of personality. Thus both the agencies should co-operate in educating the child. There must be a balance of working by both the agencies for the total development of the child. No one is to be neglected as both complete the desired development.

QUESTIONS FOR ANSWER

1. What do you understand by agencies of education? Distinguish between formal and informal agencies of education.
2. Write a brief note on commercial and non-commercial agencies of education.

7

The Family (An Active and Informal Agency of Education)

Introduction

The immense importance of the home scarcely needs to be emphasised. Two children may attend the same school, may come under the influence of the same teacher and the same organisation, may pursue the same studies and perform the same exercises; and yet may differ *toto caelo* as regards their general knowledge, their interests, their speech, their bearing, and their moral tone, according to the homes they come from. In some ways the school is almost helpless when the influence of the home is on the wrong side. During the earliest and most impressionable years, the family is the child's entire social environment; and though his social circle widens when he goes to school and begins to form outside friendships, yet the family remains for some years the largest and most central portion of the circle. Under average circumstances, and still more when the conditions are wisely ordered, the home is the soil in which spring up those virtues of which sympathy is the common characteristic. It is there that the warmest and most intimate affections flourish. It is there that the child learns the difference between generosity and meanness, considerateness and selfishness, justice and injustice, truth and falsehood, industry and idleness: and it is there that his habitual leaning to the one or the other of these is first determined. It is there, too, that he learns to speak, acquires a full or a scanty vocabulary, and, corresponding therewith, a wide or narrow range of common ideas.

Importance

"The family is the oldest human group and the basic one. While the particular forms of family structure may and does vary from society to society, the central foci of family activities everywhere are child-bearing and initial induction of the child into the culture of a given society—in short, socialization."

—*Young & Mack*

Meaning and Definition of Family

Meaning of Family—The family is the oldest, basic and fundamental unit of human society. It consists of the husband, wife, children together with all the young and old dependents. They are related to one another in one way or the other. In some old societies even servants were included in the family. Thus family may be regarded as a small social group consisting of a few related persons. In our country, the picture of a family is more or less the same.

Definition of Family

To make the meaning of family more clear we are giving some important definitions given by some well known persons as under:

(1) "The family is a group defined by sex relationship sufficiently precise and enduring to provide for the procreation and upbringing of children." —*Mac Iver & Page*

(2) "By family we mean a system of relationship existing between parents and children." —*Clare*

(3) "A family is a group of persons united by the ties of marriage, blood or adoption constituting a single household interacting and in intercommunication with each other in their respective social role of husband and wife, mother and father, son and daughter, brother and sister creating and maintaining a common culture." —*Burgess & Locke*

The above definitions make it clear that a family consists of interrelated persons who interact with one another in different ways. Not only this, each family has its own distinct habits of clothing, eating, thinking, talking and living. These are the items of that family's culture. This culture has to be preserved and transmitted by each family from generation to generation.

Chief Characteristics of Family

The following are the chief characteristics of family:

(1) Universality—A family is found in all corners of the world. There is no human society which does not have a family of one kind or the other.

(2) Limited Size—The number of the members of a family is limited. It can not be increased or decreased arbitrarily. In other words, the concept of family denotes a few members.

(3) Centre of Social Organisation—A family is the smallest unit of society. Numerous families constitute a society. Thus society and its structure is based upon these small units.

(4) Innate Tendencies as Basis of Family—Innate tendencies born out of the sexual relations of husband and wife are essentially the foundations of a family. Such tendencies are mainly innate and inborn.

(5) Constructive Influence—The family exerts the most formative and powerful influence on the development of a child's personality. In other words, it is the family which imprints permanent and indelible impressions upon the growing child.

(6) Responsibility—Each member of family shares the responsibility of maintaining the family in one way or the other. Generally adults have greater responsibility than the minors.

(7) Cradle of Social Values—A family is the cradle of all social values. It is the set up of the family which inculcates socially desirable values and high qualities of character in its members who ultimately become useful and dynamic citizens devoted to national service and international understanding.

(8) Permanent Institution—Family is a permanent institution, because its basis and relationship is permanent. Its members may depart or live apart, their association or living together

may be temporary for some reason or the other but the basic relationship remains permanent.

Impact of Industrialization on Joint Family

The eighteenth century industrialization led to progressive decline of joint family system. Employment opportunities and prospects separated the members of a joint family with the result that young ones were neglected by the adults. The following were the main results when joint families began to disintegrate:

(1) Size of the Family—Joint families progressively disintegrated into small fragments and units of two or three persons only. Family planning programmes and complexity of multiplied needs have further reduced the size of the family.

(2) Effect on Traditional Vocations—A small modern family can not satisfy the diverse needs of the child. His physical, mental, emotional and vocational development has gone beyond the powers and capacities of the small sized individual family. Hence other institutions have come to the forefront to satisfy these needs. Day by day new institutions are being established either by the community or by the state to meet the diverse developmental needs of children.

(3) Decay of Family Power—In old times the head of the family—be a man or a woman, had a control over the young ones. But today that family discipline and control is gradually decreasing on account of democratic processes, urge for freedom and initiative by the young ones. In short, the family power has decayed whereas the concepts of equality and freedom have permeated in the innermost chambers of the family.

(4) Changed Morality Concept—In old times family traditions and social customs held their sway over the lives of all the members of a family. Marriage had inviolable sanctity and duty. Each member was very conscious and sensitive of moral values prevalent in his family. But today the picture is just the reverse. We see that under the stress of modernity and march of democracy all moral and sacred concepts are being torn asunder.

(5) Control of the State—The state has now entered into the sacred precincts of family. The moral, religious and social life of the individual have come under the control and guidance

of the state. We see that even the family welfare also is now planned, guided and controlled by the State and the family has to conform and obey.

Importance of Family in the Education of the Child

The infant begins his life under the fostering affection and care of his parents and other near and dear ones who are associated with his family. As he grows, he receives the first lesson of life in his family and tries to imbibe the habits, ideals and patterns of behaviour of his family members. In this way, the family continues to influence him throughout his life. To be more clear, it may be said that in addition to other facilities the child gets three important helps from the family. They are—(l) Affection, (2) Protection, and (3) Socialization. For the upbringing of the child, there is no better institution than his family. All the members of family act and react and this process of give and take teaches many things to the child. In short, each member of family has an important role to influence the personality of the child. The family activities and necessities of intercommunication make the child fit to equip himself with a working vocabulary. He receives the first lesson of speech in the family. Gradually this vocabulary increases as he grows and gets more and more education.

During the first six years of life the child lives freely under the fostering affection and care of his parents and other relations. The patterns of behaviour of adults, their habits and attitudes teach him many things. A congenial environment in a family develops his personality wholesomely whereas the stresses, strains and evil activities of a broken family mar his development. Thus the foundation of a child's future life is laid up in the family. In later life, it becomes very difficult, if not impossible, for him to demolish or reconstruct these foundations.

The family meets the various needs of the child. He is subjected to various experiences—good or bad, pleasant or painful and he gains from both. It is the duty of each and every member of the family to pay due respect to the individuality of the child and foster in him a sense of belongingness and responsibility towards his own self and others. Because each family has its own culture and set up quite distinct from the other, therefore no two children are the same neither at the beginning nor during development or as a growing up adult citizen. Raymont is right when he says—"Two children may attend the same school, may come under the influence of same teacher and the same organization, may pursue the same studies and perform the same exercises, and yet may differ *toto caelo* as regards their general knowledge, their interests, their speech, their bearing and their moral tone, according to the homes they come from."

Different Views on the Importance of Family in the Education of the Child

As discussed above, a child gets his first lesson in the family. The impressions gained and the family environment are indelible and remain for the whole life. A number of educationists have spoken very highly about the role of family in the education of a child. We are giving some of their opinions as under:

(1) "Education begins at birth and the proper nurse is the mother". —*Rousseau*

(2) "Home—a centre of love and affection—is the best place and the first school of the child." —*Pestalozzi*

(3) "Mothers are the ideal teachers and informal education given by home is most effective and natural." —*Froebel*

(4) "Child learns the first lesson of citizenship between the kiss of mother and the care of father." —*Mazini*

(5) "The home is the soil in which spring up those virtues of which 'sympathy' is the common characteristic. It is there that the warmest and most intimate affection flourish. It is there that the child learns the difference between generosity and meanness, considerateness and selfishness, justice and injustice, truth and falsehood, industry and idleness. It is there that his habitual learning of the one or the other of these is first determined. —*T. Raymont*

Madam Montessori is so much a devotee of home education that she named her schools as 'Children's House.'

An atmosphere of neatness, love and affection pervades in all these 'Children's Houses.'

The opinions of all the above mentioned educationists clearly reveal the importance and value of home or family in the education and development of the child. The great men of India as well as of other countries, one and all learnt the early lessons of greatness from their mothers or from others in the family. How right is Prof K.G. Saiyidain when he says—"The education of man depends on the environments that he enjoys. If these environments are based on good customs and traditions of the family, they will spread beneficial influence on his ideas and development and his education will be useful not only to him but to the whole community."

Functions of Family as an Agency of Education

The theories of education that have won general attention lay varying degrees of emphasis upon the function of home life in a child's upbringing. The ancient Greeks, in accordance with their low conception of the position of women, made little of the place of family life in the training of the young. John Locke, writing with the children of the wealthy in view, and mindful of his own unhappy school days, declares roundly in favour of home education, under a private tutor, as opposed to that given in public schools. Rousseau, with small faith in the family under the conditions of modern civilization, begins by assuming that Emile is an orphan, and that his tutor is charged with parental responsibilities and succeeds to parental rights. But Pestalozzi, with infinitely truer insight, regarded the home as the one indispensable factor in the young child's training, and the mother as the fount and source of all true education; indeed, one of the rewards of the reader who ploughs through the good old man's incoherent pages, is the occasional perusal of passages in which this cardinal doctrine is passionately preached.

Important functions of the family as an agency of education are as follows:

(1) *Physical Development*—To develop the child physically is first function of family. Parents and other members of the family are always careful about the health and well-being of

the child. For this purposes useful physical experiences, exercises and other activities are provided to the child. In other words, regular physical exercises, habits of cleanliness and vigorous living is fostered in the child. Not only this, wholesome food containing all the ingredients of a balanced diet is also provided to the child to achieve his maximum physical development.

(2) Mental Development—Mental development of the child is the second important function of family. By mental development we mean the development of mental powers namely, thinking, feeling, reasoning, discrimination, judgement and memory. To develop these powers parents provide adequate opportunities and experiences to the child. In comparison with poor families well-to-do families are able to provide better opportunities and experiences for their children to receive better education.

(3) Emotional Development—The influence of family greatly affects the emotional development of the child. Home environment, its upkeep, sanitation and decoration all influence the emotional growth of the child. Amity and good fellow-feeling in the members of a family affect the emotional make up of the child and develop in him healthy and positive emotions namely sympathy, courage, affection and love etc. On the contrary, disunity and maladjustment in a broken home or family develop in the child negative emotions namely, fear, anger, jealousy, and worry etc.

(4) Social Development—Home is the first social environment in the education of the child. Russell says, "Home gives the child the experience of effective and of a small community in which he is important. He has also the experience of relationship with people of both the sexes and different ages, and of the multifarious business of adult life". Thus it is in the family that the child gets his first social relationships, in which and through which he acquires and ogranises his experiences. It is in infancy that he acquires many of the social partners, habits, manners and attitudes which determine his future adjustment. Again it is in the home that he learns how to speak, talk, eat, wear clothes, live neatly and greet others respectfully. Thus, family is the first and most important social

agency which plays an important role in the socialization of the child.

(5) Economic Functions—Family is a well knit economic unit. Real economic socialism prevails in the family because the golden rule of socialism, "From each according to capacity and to each according to needs' prevails here. The child enjoys complete economic security and all his economic needs are fulfilled by the parents, which helps to provide a secure atmosphere for the overall development of the child. The child can study and acquire any type of training because he is not to worry about the expenses. Thus, the family provides the children with full economic security and freedom from economic worries. This is essential and helpful for a balanced personality of the child.

Family also acts as a medium for transmitting vocational knowledge and technical skill to children. In this way, children are prepared for future life. This is specially true in the case of primitive and rural vocations, like agriculture, carpentry etc. Thus the family helps the children in a large number of ways.

(6) Transmission of Culture—Though it is the duty of school to preserve, transmit and develop the culture of the race. But it does not mean that family, as an agency of education, has nothing to do in this connection. As a matter of fact, each society has its own culture. That culture is still practised in families. In schools, culture is taught whereas in families it is caught. It is why Hindu culture is alive in Hindu families and Muslim culture is fresh in Muslim families. In short, the child of particular family imbibes the culture of his family consciously or unconsciously.

(7) Development of Language—The child learns his mother tongue in a natural way in his family. Schools only reform it and add to the vocabulary. We observe that children belonging to educated and cultured families pronounce the words correctly in comparison with those who come out from backward and illiterate families. Schools are able to reform very little in such cases.

(8) Development of Interests and Habits—Good or bad habits and interests of a child spring up and develop in the family in which he lives. These good or bad habits and interests form the character of the child. If parents and other members

of the family are unmindful and indifferent towards the activities of their child, he develops such bad habits and interests that plague him all through his life and do great harm to his family members also. Therefore parents should be ever vigilant to know the activities of their children otherwise their children and they themselves shall have to suffer in the long run. We observe that the parents who are indifferent and careless about their children, the latter are getting more indisciplined, work-shirkers, careless and mischievous in schools.

(9) Development of Morality and Character—A family develops moral and ethical values in the child. These values lead to the formation of habit and attitudes which build character, the backbone of life. Other institutions can only help in this connection. Thus it is the family alone which originates and fosters these values in the early childhood. A child learns these values through imitation. As he grows older, he learns the desired moral and social values through insight. In, family is a cradle where character of the child takes roots upto the age of six years. Other institutions only develop it further.

(10) Development of Innate Tendencies—Congenial and conducive environment of the family brings out and develops the innate tendencies of the child. If these tendencies do not have a natural outlet, they turn into complexes and the child becomes maladjusted. Mention may here be made that the unfoldment of innate tendencies begins in the family and is evident during early childhood. Parents and other members of the family should be very careful about this and provide all facilities to the child for his self assertion and proper development.

(11) Development of Individuality—Though other institutions are also responsible to see that the child develops his individuality on proper lines, yet this development starts in the family. The seeds begin to sprout out during early childhood in the environment of the family. The responsibility of parents is utmost here and for this they are ever vigilant and considerate in this respect.

(12) Teaches the Basic Functions of Living—It is in the home that the child learns the basic functions of living. For example,

the child learns to speak, act, dress and pick up many good things or habits imitating the other members of the family. It is in this atmosphere that the child's whole personality grows and develops. Thus if development of a balanced personality is an objective of a good system of education, then home is the most effective educational agency.

(13) Basis of Personality—The infancy and the early childhood periods are the most impressionable years of a child's life. The broad basis of personality are laid down during this period. The family helps the children to form sound basis of personality, which proves to be very helpful for the future education of children.

(14) Vocational Education—The family also provides vocational education to the children who wish to adopt the trade and occupation of their father. The girls, on the other hand, learn to do the role of housewives by helping their mothers at home and by learning from them. This training and education proves very useful to them in their later life.

(15) Self-Confidence and Positive Outlook—The secure atmosphere of the family provides self-confidence and develops a positive outlook of life in the children which helps to develop a confident and well-balanced personality. Love, affection and security are the basic psychological needs of children, which are amply fulfilled by the family. A well knit family provides the right type of atmosphere for the growth and development of children, on which a sound edifice of future education of children is to be built.

Co-operation Between Parents and Teachers

We conclude, then, that even where parents are able and willing to provide for the instruction of their children in the home, it will still be best in general to send them to school. The division of responsibility between the home and the school must by no means be taken to imply a rigid separation of the two. It is, of course, true that the school (at least the day school) is mainly responsible for instruction, and only in a less important degree for the direct formation of character; whereas parents are chiefly responsible for specifically moral discipline, and only in a slight degree for instruction. The wise parent and teacher will, however, seek to understand each other's aims, and to second each other's efforts, so that the child's education will form an organic whole. Nothing can be more demoralising to the child than lack of unity and harmony between his home life and his school life. The teacher on his side should understand how immensely his own immediate aims are furthered by the whole-hearted sympathy of parents; and intelligent parents should on their side try to understand the inevitable limitations of the school and should use their superior knowledge of the child's individual capacity and tastes to supply what few schools, if any, can give.

QUESTIONS FOR ANSWER

1. What is family? Enumerate the chief elements and characteristics of the family.
2. Discuss the functions of a family.
3. Discuss the importance of family. How can it be made an effective agency of education?

8

The Community (An Active and Informal Agency of Education)

The community, alike family, have a great influence upon the child because the child comes in contact with his relations and members of neighbourhood families at a very early stage. Therefore, impact of the community on the growth and development of the child is almost equal to that of the family.

Importance of Community

Community is an important informal and active agency of education. Just as the family and the school have a great influence upon the child, much in the same way the community also modifies the behaviour of child through social contacts, group activities and group dynamics in such a way that he begins to participate in all the desirable activities of the community of which he is an integral part. It is why we still hear the saying that children of a community develop as the adults of that community wish them to become. In fact, the child does not develop in the environment of his family alone, the environment of the community also moulds and modifies the behaviour of the child according to its ideas, ideals and goals. It is the miracle of community environment alone in which the child develops his innate and inherent tendencies according to his nature and learns his language, and standard of living. In brief, the community environment exerts its impressions upon the developing children in all perceptible and imperceptible ways. Since each community has its own culture, we find a great difference in the culture and behaviour patterns of children belonging to different communities. A. Yeoger has rightly remarked—Since man by nature is a social being, he has learnt through the years that the personality as well as group activities can be best developed through community."

Meaning and Definition of Community

Generally community indicates a group of people living together on a geographical piece of land having common ways of working and common ideals to achieve Thus community may be a number of people living together in the neighbourhood sharing common ways of living and common experiences. The essential ingredients are a piece of land, a group of people living more or less a common life having a common spirit of work with common aims and common ideals. A community may be big or small in size. Generally the size of the community is related to the cultural, economic and political commonness of its members. In this sense a village, a town, a city, a nation and the whole world may be called a community.

Definition of Community

To make the meaning of community more clear, we are giving some definitions below:

(1) "A community may be thought of as the total organization of social life within a limited area."

—*Ogburn & NimKoff*

(2) "A community is the smallest territorial group that can embrass all aspects of social life." —*K. Davis*

(3) "By community is to be understood a group of social beings living a common life including all the infinite variety and complexity of relations which result from common life or constitute it." —*Ginsberg*

Community as an Agency of Education

Community is a dynamic form of organisation for the betterment and progress of its members. It is an informal type of agency of education as it is not formed with the express-purpose of providing education to its members. But as it is an organised body, its members have to follow certain rules and regulations made and adopted by its members collectively. The living together under a social organisation, and observing certain rules and regulations requires a particular way of thinking and living. Thus, every member has to adjust himself properly in society. This educates the individual members of the society in such a way that they are in a position to adjust themselves in society, as well as promote the well-being of the whole of the society. We may conclude by saying that society as an agency of education provides general and liberal education in the socialization of its individual members.

Every community has its various needs and glaring problems. When these needs are met and problems solved, the standard of community rises higher and higher. This progress goes on gradually and continually. On the contrary, a community which is unable to provide right type of education to its members, it remains cramped up and stagnant with the result that its progress is blocked and stunted. Therefore each community tries to plan its progress and development by providing purposeful and effective education to its members especially children. In other words, a community tries to mould education according to its social, economic and political needs or aspirations. This is an ongoing and continuing process. The school run by a community is therefore called a miniature of society. In short, the community, as an agency of education, influences its children both formally and informally.

"A community cannot expect something for nothing. If it wishes its young people to serve their community well, it must provide whatever educational advantages are needed by the young people, individually and collectively, to prepare themselves for that service." —*Crow and Crow*

Community's Educational Influence

Each community influences the education of the child formally as well as informally. We are discussing below the informal influences of community upon children:

Influence on Physical Development—Though the family and the school exert a potent influence on the physical developments of a child, yet the effect of the community environment also cannot be underestimated. The community organises local bodies which look after the sanitation of the localities. These local bodies also, often, build parks, gardens and provide gymnasiums. The children of the community make use of these facilities to the full. They get fresh light and air and do all sorts of physical exercises to build their physique and to keep them healthy. These local bodies run hospitals and dispensaries to keep children healthy and free from diseases and also teach them the general rules of health and sanitation. In this way, the facilities provided by local bodies greatly influence the health and physical development of children.

Influence on Character and Moral Development—Though family exerts a very powerful influence upon the character formation and imbibing of moral values by children, yet the community of which the family is a small unit also influences the character and moral development to a very great extent. If the environment of the community is bad, its effect on children will be bad and if it is good and wholesome, the influence will be positive and gainful. It may be noted over here that the influence of community in this connection comes after the influence of family. But there may be causes where the community casts its evil shadow on the whole family and the result of this influence can be well imagined.

Influence on Mental Development—The enlightened communities, often, organise reading rooms and libraries for use by the children and adults. Some communities organise exhibitions, symposiums and conferences on various subjects also. This provides healthy entertainment to children and also helps in their mental development.

Influence on Social Development—The community organises fairs, festivals, social conferences and many other religious functions. All these activities stimulate children to imbibe social ideas and a spirit of social service more and more with the result that they learn about the social customs, traditions and beliefs in a natural way and also learn the socially desirable values namely—sympathy, co-operation, tolerance, social service, sacrifice and adjustment. Not only this, through contacts with the other members of the community children also learn very deeply that duties and rights, freedom and discipline are greatly essential for the natural and wholesome development of their personality. In this way, we see that community exerts a great influence on the social development of children.

Influence on Cultural Development—Each community has its own culture. The children of that community come into active and lively contact in the community functions, festivals and conferences and learn to respect their culture through imitation. They act and react as their elders do. We see that rural and urban communities imprint their own special cultural traits and features upon the minds of their children. This difference can be clearly seen from the language, pronunciations, manners and behaviour of those children.

Influence of Political Ideas—Lectures by political leaders, political meetings and conferences organized by the community give political lessons to children of the community. They learn about various political parties, their political philosophies and manifestoes. These all go to form their own political conviction. In this way the community influences on the political ideas of children indirectly.

Influence on Vocational Development—The community influences the vocational development of children. They carefully observe the vocations followed by the members of their community, learn about the problems and techniques involved in various vocations, form their own opinions about them and ultimately choose any one of them for their future life.

Influence Through Other Devices—The community provides many informal devices and materials to children for their development in various aspects of personality. Radio and T.V. broadcasts, theatres, picture houses, museums, zoo, magazines, newspapers, reading rooms and libraries are the various and varied devices to influence the development of children of the community.

Educational Functions of the Community

(1) Establishment of Schools—The community establishes various types of schools so that the culture of the community may be preserved, developed and transmitted to its children. Many communities establish their own communal schools to train their children for the welfare and advancement of their community interests.

(2) Formulation of Aims and Control on Education—The community determines the aims of education. It also supervises and guides the educational process followed in the schools established by it.

(3) Provision of Universal Education—The community determines the various stages of education. At the same time it strives to provide universal education

(4) Provision of Vocational and Industrial Education—In modern age there is a great demand for vocational and industrial education. Hence the community establishes vocational, industrial and technical schools according to its needs.

(5) Adult Education—Community welfare and its development needs that adults should also be educated. Thus the community makes provision for adult education also.

(6) Finance of Schools—To shoulder the responsibility of running the schools smoothly and efficiently arrangement of required finance is essential. The community makes necessary provision of finance for school buildings, furniture and salary of teachers.

(7) Co-operation Between Citizens and School Leaders—Close Cooperation between citizens and leaders of schools is necessary. Hence the community tries to maintain as much close cooperation between parents, managers of institutions and teachers.

Merits of Community as an Agency of Education

Merits of education provided by community are given below:

(1) Community education is meaningful.
(2) Education provided by Community emphasises the principle of utility.

(3) Community education gives real life experiences to the children. They get practical experience of objects and their working. Thus children get real learning.
(4) Community education emphasises upon the principle of activity. Instead of simply hearing the lectures, children learn effectivity by doing and manipulating things and processes,
(5) The community imparts its cultural heritage to the children.
(6) The community creates consciousness in children about their rights and duties and thus develops in them those qualities and capacities which make them active and dynamic citizens.
(7) The community bestows upon children the capacity to think creatively and constructively. This makes them responsible and self reliant citizens.

De-merits of Community as an Agency of Education

Demerits of education provided by community are given below:

(1) The community, for its own narrow ends, manipulates the process of education as a play thing and uses it for its selfish ends.
(2) The community, to maintain its own superior status, creates blind faith in children.
(3) Community develops communal feelings which lead to chaos in national life. Our society is still suffering from this nasty and dangerous poison which vitiates national life.
(4) A community often takes recourse to repression and rigid discipline. It spoils the natural development of children.

QUESTIONS FOR ANSWER

1. Define Community and write a note on the educational functions of Community.
2. Write a note on Communit[illegible] an agency of education as well as on the merits and demer[illegible] of Community as an agency of Education.

9

The Religion (An Active and Informal Agency of Education)

Every society observes some rituals, religious ceremonies and ways of worship in accordance with their religion. Thus, religion is a family tradition, hence its impact upon the child is utmost. Therefore, role of religion on child's education is as strong as that of the family.

Meaning of Religion

Etymologically, the word religion is a combination of two Latin words namely—'Re.' and 'Legere' which mean to bind back or to establish connections. As such, religion signifies those moral bonds of love, sacrifice and social service which hold the human community together. Thus the essence of true religion is love, effection, sympathy, co-operation, tolerance, sacrifice, fellow feeling and such other qualities which shape human behaviour and his character. Gisbert has rightly remarked—"Religion establishes a double bond—one between man and God and the other between man and man as children of God."

Definition of Religion

The following definitions will clarify the concept of religion more clear:

(1) Whenever and wherever man has a sense of dependence on external powers which are conceived as mysterious and higher than man's own, there is religion."

—*Dawson*

(2) "Religion is the recognition of all our duties as divine commandments." —*Kant*

(3) "The essence of religion is faith in the conversation of values." —*Harald Hoffding*

(4) Religion is a vision of something which stands beyond, behind and within." —*A. N. White*

(5) "Religion is the dynamic belief in and submission to God or to gods on whom man feels dependent." —*Gisbert*

A Brief Review of History

The past history of the world clearly brings out that from ancient times the religious and moral principles have influenced the aims, curriculum and techniques of education. In those times, religion held sway in almost all the western countries. It was only through religious education that people were taught to live in unity, peace and co-operation. The 'Reformation Movement' in England had left the work of education entirely on churches and other religious institutes.

In the nineteenth century, gradually, the concept and practice of secular education began to hold the field and replaced religious education which used to be monopolised by a particular sector mission.

In the 20th century 'The Religious School Movement' in America replaced the old pattern of education by general and liberal education with the result that the policy of 'Religious Neutrality was incorporated in the American Democratic Principles and Policy.

In India and other Eastern countries, education has been religious since ancient times. According to McDonell, Indian education bears the imprint of religion since very early ages of human history. In those days, religious persons used to be teachers also. They inculcated moral and religious values in the minds of children.

During Muslim rule also, education maintained its religious character. But during the British rule religious naturality was practised by the rulers. This policy of religious naturality was opposed tooth and nails by Indians with the result that denominational schools began to be opened.

The Hindus insisted firmly that education devoid of religion will destroy their religion and culture. Hence from 'Hunter Commission' of 1882 to 'The Punjab University Commission' various commissions and committees recommended some sort of religious education to be associated with the general and common system of education in India.

Impact of Religious Values

The influence of religion in human life and society may be listed as follows:

(1) Religion inculcates in children the essential moral and human qualities of courtesy, tolerance, sympathy, fellow feeling, equality and faternity etc., which forms a noble character of man and develops his personality.

(2) Religion infuses hope and faith in man. He gets mental peace and develops in him sufficient courage and self confidence to face the problems of life successfully.

(3) Religion is that dynamic aspect of culture which infuses in human being moral qualities. These qualities are expressed in all fields of human life.

(4) Religion sublimates and redirects our sex instinct into desirable channel. It is so potent a factor that influences all aspects of human life and society of which he is an integral part. Prof H Kabir has rightly remarked—"Religion resolves many of the conflicts. It releases energies that recognise neither difficulties nor defeat."

The above discussion makes it crystal clear that religion is essential to man and society.

Relationship Between Religion and Education

There is a very intimate relation between religion and education. An effective educational system inculcates only those values in human beings which are valued and recognised by all the philosophies of the world. According to E.D. Burton—"Religion and education are close and real friends. Both are related to spiritualism in contrast to physical and material phenomenon. Both try to free the human being not from his physical surroundings but try to free him from the slavery to physical environment."

Education broadens human outlook. It tries to modify human behaviour according to those ideals and values which are recognised by religion as of worth and importance. Thus proper placing of religion in the system of education gives us those powers and capacities which develope human beings and the society to which they belong.

Religion inculcates those moral qualities which mould the educational system on democratic lines. The democratic and secular policy which aims at providing equal opportunities for all the citizens of our country is rightly based on true religion. It is why we inculcate in our children a spirit of self discipline, sense of duty and responsibility so that they are able to rise above their selfish motives and work for the welfare of others with a spirit of devotion and dedication.

Education is intimately related also to culture which is an inseparable part of religion. The curriculum which incorporates cultural values and ideals in the educational system naturally gives due place to religious values and ideals.

In the complicated and complex society of today, Naturalism and Pragmatism can not preserve the moral and spiritual values of life. Both these philosophies advocate material values and prosperity quite unrelated to the values of human life.

The need of the day is that education and philosophy should lead man to higher and higher towards achieving the noble and immortal ideals of Truth, Beauty and Goodness so that he leads a peaceful life and ultimately realizes God in himself.

The philosophy of idealism serves as a sound basis for noble ideals and values which an educational system should incorporate. Thus Idealism is an integral part of religion and as such idealistic values are the real religious values.

From the above discussion it becomes clear that both religion and education aim at the wholesome and fullest development of human personality which includes mental as well as spiritual development. To achieve this aim religion and education are closely related from ancient times.

We see that in ancient times religious persons were teachers also. They taught children to discharge their duties to self and society both and thus developed their personalities to the full so that they were able to lead their lives happily and peacefully. In short, the aim of religion and education being the same both are very intimately related to each other.

"Religion and education are natural allies. Both recognise and have to do with the spiritual as against an exclusively material attention to the physical. Both seek to emancipate man from contact with his environment, but from slavery to it, to enlarge his horizon and quicken his aspiration."

—*E.D. Burton*

(Education in Democratic World)

The Aims of Religious Education

The aims of religious education are as follows:

Development of Democratic Traditions in Schools—According to Ryburn religious education is undoubtedly important for the life of a human being. It helps to establish and incorporate democratic process and way in the working of the schools also.

Truly speaking religion is related to two facts namely—(1) relation of man to God, and (2) relation of man to the world and other human beings. Religious education should emphasise both the relations so that children may believe in the omnipresence and omnipotence of God. This will make them God fearing with the result that they will desist from evil doing which gives rise to conflicts and discords.

Preservation and Development of Culture—Religious education preserves culture which is its own integral part. The two develop hand in hand and reinforce each other. Hence education should conserve culture as well as reinforce it so that it is able to meet the ever growing needs of society.

Development of total Personality of the Child—Religious education embracing all the activities of human life should develop the personality of child to the full. Without such education total personality of child can not be developed. Hence religious education should ensure independent, self reliant and self confident personalities.

Redirection and Sublimation of Instincts—Religious education should mould, purify and sublimate the raw instincts of children into desirable channels of behaviour. It should reform habits, form desirable attitudes and ultimately develop in children the desired social awakening which is essential for the progress of individual as well as society.

Development of Moral and Spiritual Values—Religious education does not impart training in any particular way of worship or performance of specific rituals and ceremonies. It inculcates among children those moral and spiritual values which go to form developed personalities of individuals. With the inculcation of those values the individual tries to pursue higher and higher ideals and thus enjoys peace and happiness in his life.

Development of Wider Attitude—Religious education makes a man dynamic and enlightened. This develops in him a wider attitude towards life. He begins to take interest in social service by sacrificing his selfish motives. Not only this he becomes courageous enough to face the problems of life boldly and solve them to the best of his insight and efforts.

Development of Character—Religious education develops the character of the child through the inculcation of social, moral and spiritual values in him. According to Madden Ward—"Religious strength of character includes humility, which recognizes one's inevitable fallibility and submits to the correct process of group thinking and Co-operative action."

Due Care—A Must for Religious Education

We are living in nation-states having inhabitants of various religious faiths, therefore, due care is a must for introducing religious education in schools. We suggest following precautions should be taken while introducing religious education in schools:

Religious education should be imparted only to those children who wish to opt it after receiving the permission of their parents or guardians.

Life histories of great persons of the world, stories of moral greatness, examples of patriotism, fellow feeling, service and sacrifice should find place in the educational system as the same naturally and imperceptibly inculcate religious and moral values.

Critical outlook of adolescents should be developed so that they themselves avoid blind beliefs and rationalise their faith and action.

The ideals and values of true religion should be imbibed by children in a natural way. For this, the activities of the school should reflect all the higher moral ideals and values.

Unity of all religions should be emphasized in the education of the school. Since all religions have virtues, therefore they should be discussed in the right earnest. In the words of M.K. Gandhi—"The fundamental principles of ethics are common to all religions. These should be certainly taught to students."

Narrow religious education prepares the child for the other world. It neglects the needs of individual and demands of society. This should not be allowed to happen.

In the garb of religious education narrow communal or sectarian education is provided. This spoils the natural development of the child. Thus healthy principles and virtues of all religions should be incorporated in the education so that fanaticism, bigotry and blind beliefs are avoided.

To impart the education of all the virtues of all the religions of the world, the school environment should be so congenial and conducive that children receive virtuous education in a natural way. No compulsory indoctrination of dogmatic education should be allowed at all.

No child should be compelled to receive any kind of religious education directly or indirectly.

Life of teacher should be so ideal that children are inspired to imbibe the ideals of good conduct and character in a natural way.

Religious education should not receive so much emphasis that schools become temples, guruduaras, churches and mosques.

Religious Education and Secular India

On 15th August 1947 we achieved our freedom. As our country is a country of diverse religions, castes and creeds, our leadenrs adopted the ideal of secular education. They thought that any kind of narrow bigoted and communal education would create divisions and dissensions in the nation due to which our very independence would be in jeopardy.

Hence they separated religious education of any sort from the national pattern and propagated the ideal of secular liberal education. Viewing the defects of religious education, our Indian Constitution also emphasizes the secular ideal.

According to Article 19 all citizens are free to follow any creed or sect. No religious tax can be imposed on them. According to Article 22 no religious education can be imparted in any Government school.

Only those institutions can impart religious education which are founded by some 'Trusts' for this purpose. Even in such schools there is no compulsion on any child who does not like to opt for that education. In short, our country is committed to the ideal of secularism.

The Secondary Education Commission Report (1952-53) also opines—"In view of the provision in the constitution religious instruction can not be given in schools except on a voluntary basis and outside the regular school hours: such instructions should be given to children of a particular faith and with the consent of the parents and management concerned. In making this recommendation we wish to emphasise that all unhealthy trends or disunity, rancour, religious hatred and bigotry should be discouraged."

From the above, it is clear that the state has no religion. It is committed to democratic ideals and beliefs. As a matter of fact religion and democracy are same. Both strive to develop the innate tendencies and capacities of the child to the full. This is true of the religion and democracy all over the world. Both are committed to foster individual good and the good of the society.

QUESTIONS FOR ANSWER

1. Define religion and write a note on the aims of religious education.
2. Write a note on the precautions to be taken while introducing religious education in a state like India.

10

The State (An Active and Informal Agency of Education)

Education influences the social structure and associations of human beings very effectively, hence, the state being a well organised super association of human beings which came into existence to carry out the functions of all the social associations more effectively, has taken up the responsibility to educate its citizens as per its needs and means.

Meaning of State

It is clear from the above discussion that state came into existence by the close and integral union of various associations. As such, state is an enormous and powerful super structure of associations. It differs from other association in the sense that each individual belonging to any other association recognises the superiority of state and obeys the laws made by it.

Not only this, scientifically also, state has a definite territory, an association of human beings living on that territory, an organised structure of government and sovereignty. In this sense there are four important elements of state namely—(1) Territory, (2) Population, (3) Government, and (4) Sovereignty.

Definition of State

To make the meaning of state more clear, some definitions are given below:

(1) "State may be defined as an organised political community with government recognised by people."

—*I.L. Kandel*

(2) "State is a community of persons, more or less numerous, permanently occupying a definite position of a territory, independent and so of a foreign control and possessing an organised government to which the inhabitants render a habitual obedience."

—*Garner*

Historical Review of Relationship Between Education and State in India

Vedic period—During vedic period there was no relation between state and education at all. In those days education was imparted by learned Rishis and Munis called 'Acharyas' or Gurus. Children used to live in the 'Gurukuls' or 'Ashrams' of those Rishis and Munis and received free education in the laps of nature.

These Gurukuls needed no financial assistance from the state. Hence there was no state control over them. Society maintained them and the state only admired and appreciated their efforts. It simply guided and moulded their activities as and when needed.

Brahmanic Period—During this period also, education was maintained by voluntary and private agencies. In other words, there was no direct control of state education. Taxila, the famous university of our country came into existence during that period. Kings and rich persons of society used to give donations to this institution and also provided stipends and scholarships to those who received education in it.

But a significant change which occurred during this period was that education fell from the high pedestal of mission and service of the nation to a sort of profession in the hands of same pundits and purohits.

Budh Period—Private universities of the vedic and Brahmanic period changed into public institutions as we have today. Nalanda, Nadia, Vallabhi and Vikramshila were the famous universities of this period.

These universities came to be run by 'Association' and 'Samities' and maintained their high reputation and smooth management in all matters. In short, they enjoyed complete autonomy and state control was next to nothing.

Muslim period—During this period the 'Maktabs' and 'Madarsas' turned into agencies of procelytisation and religious conversion to Islam of the infidels by the Muslim monarchs and the mullas.

British Period—During this period the decree of 1835 set the seal on English Education for India. The Wood's Despatch of 1854 recommended the establishment of universities, Departments of Public Instruction under important officer to be called the Director of Public Instruction and the appointment of other officials to work out and supervise the plans.

The Hunter Commission of 1882 recommended the establishment of model schools by the government and withdraw from the direct management of secondary schools by encouraging voluntary and private bodies to run them on grant-in-aid basis. Thus Departments of Public Instruction began to be established with more and more officers to complete the task of education.

Modern Period—On 15th August 1947 India attained its political freedom and after a careful consideration, decided to transform itself into a secular democratic republic. Since then, education has been decentralized. Now education is a responsibility of the State Governments.

The Kothari Commission (1964-66) has distributed the responsibility of education among the central, the state and the Local bodies. All these authorities share the responsibility of educating the nation as per needs and resources of the states.

Relationship Between State and Education

There are two views about the relation of state and education as under:

(1) Individualism.
(2) Collectivism.

(1) Individualism—Locke, Mill and Bentham etc. individualist thinkers firmly believe that the function of the state is only to protect and guide its people. It should not interfere in the sphere of education in any way. This is known as the 'Doctrine of Laissez-faire.'

According to this doctrine, the individual has accepted the discipline of organised society for some definite objectives only. It does not mean that he has subordinated his freedom and liberty in toto.

There are many spheres of life where he is completely free to choose and act. Education is one such sphere. In this way according to individualist thinkers, state should not interfere in the sphere of education at all otherwise it will bring more harm than good.

(2) Collectivism—Mathu Arnold, Carlyle and Ruskin etc. are the supporters of collectivism. They hold the view that the function of the state is not only to protect its citizens from internal or external dangers alone but also to control the education as well.

Since the progress and development of state depends upon educated citizens possessing desirable habits, competence and sound character, in the opinion of Mathu Arnold, State must have full control even on higher education.

In short, the advocates of collectivism firmly believe that full control over education by the State will be advantageous and beneficial to all its citizens in all respects.

Each state has its distinct political set up, its culture and civilization, its, industry and commerce and various other needs. They are quite different from those of others. All the above mentioned factors influence and shape the system of education of that state.

Hence each state tries to influence and control its education in some way or the other. State may be classified as under:

(1) Totalitarian State.
(2) Democratic State.

(1) Totalitarian State—The supporters of totalitarian state believe that state is omnipotent and supremely sovereign in all fields of life. It has a superior and higher entity than that of

those who form and organise it. As such, it can have absolute control over all its citizens. As able and capable citizens form and run a state efficiently and only education develops such citizens, therefore the state must have complete control over education for its existence and advancement.

In short, the supporters of the totalitarian ideology emphasize that the whole educational system must be centralized. Hence in a totalitarian state education is completely centralised with the result that all aspects of education, namely—aims, curriculum, methods of teaching and discipline etc. are all closely guided and supervised by the Central government.

(2) Democratic State—The inherent powers of a democratic state are limited and well defined. The state distributes its absolute power amongst its citizens by decentralization. This means that people become responsible for their own welfare. They plan for their own good and execute the plans themselves.

The state provides more and more opportunities to its citizens to plan and execute such plans for their happier, richer and better development. In the following lines we are throwing light on the relation between state and education keeping into consideration the pattern of a democratic state.

The Synthesis

The individualists and the collectivists both insist on their extreme ideologies. Modern thinkers neither favour the doctrine of Laissez-faire alone nor accept the rigid control on education by the state. They regard both the ideologies as extremes and wish to strike a balance between the two.

According to them, the task of education is so important that the cooperation of all the agencies is essential to complete it. No doubt, State is an important agency of education but it is not all in itself. Hence the state should neither show complete neutrality towards the education of its citizens nor try to control it in toto but must work in active cooperation of all other agencies namely—the family, the community and the church.

Hence whereas on one hand the family, the community and the church should be allowed to help education in their own way, the state on the other hand should also guide and supervise the various stages of education through its policy of limited interference.

In this regard Rayment has rightly remarked, "The function of the state is to protect and promote, not to absorb or take the place of family and the individual. In the sphere of education it is the state's right, and even duty to protect the interior right of the family and the church.

Similarly, the state ought to make good the deficiency due to incapacity, unworthiness or other defects of parents and generally to protect, according to rules of reason and the faith, the moral and religious education of the young by moving any public impediment.

The national state can rightfully demand and ensure that the citizens have a proper knowledge of their civil and national duties and attain a certain standard of intellectual and moral culture."

Educational Functions of State

The following are the main functions of education in a democratic state:

1. *Construction of a National Scheme of Education*—In a democratic state education is just like the soul in a body. Thus each state constructs a national scheme of education, keeping into consideration the multifarious needs of its citizens after detailed discussion with its prominent educationists, educational philosophers and ministers.

After the construction of such a comprehensive scheme of education, it is cooked out and executed in such a way that no one is discriminated on the basis of colour, caste, sex as well as economic and social status. In other words, each individual gets equal opportunities to grow and develop

2. *Training in Citizenship*—The progress of state depends upon the ability, capacity and strength of character of its citizens. Hence the second function of a democratic state is to provide political, social, cultural and economic training to its citizens so that they are able to grow into dynamic, resourceful and national minded individuals to serve their nation with full sincerity, zeal and devotion.

Political training or training regarding the political ideology of the state is given by way of free film shows, military demonstrations, radio, magazines, newspapers and television shows. Social training is given through social service programmes, social functions and other variety programmes.

Cultural training is given by establishing various institutions like museums, picture galleries, exhibitions, zoos, clubs for entertainment and arranging, national tours, national fairs and free film shows. Much in the same way, economic training is given by imparting best possible vocational and technical training.

3. *Provision of Schools*— The function of state is to establish primary, secondary and various types of other schools. A democratic state establishes such schools and also the voluntary agencies run such schools to fulfil the needs of its citizens.

4. *Adult Education*—The function of state is to provide adult education for the uneducated and illiterate adults. It is really a matter of great pleasure that India has very recently launched such a scheme on a very huge scale.

5. *Finance of Schools*—Financing is greatly essential to establish schools of various types and stages. The state provides adequate financial assistance to all the schools established either by the state or run by other voluntary agencies.

6. *Universal, Compulsory and Free Education*—The success of a democratic state depends upon those citizens who make use of their rights and discharge duties correctly. Therefore democratic state provided universal, compulsory and free education upto a certain standard.

7. *Encouragement to Guardians*—Opening more and more schools does not bring in them all the children of the nation. To achieve this objective, the state motivates the parents in such a way that they begin to take interest to educate their children.

8. *Provision of Efficient Teachers*—Establishing various types of schools, provision of universal, compulsory and free education upto a certain level requires the services of a large number of competent and efficient teachers to run those schools and to work out those schemes successfully.

The state opens more and more training colleges and various types of training institutions to make available the vast army of capable teachers.

9. *Provision of Military Education*—In this modern age of conflict each citizen is expected to defend the state against a foreign invasion. Hence the state provides military education in all the schools and colleges so that in times of emergency the trained citizens are able to be vigilant and defend the state.

10. *Provision of Standard Books*—Good education depends upon the availability of good and standard books. The state persuades authors and publishers to prepare good and standard books of reasonable price.

11. *Provision of Scholarships*—Many talented, gifted and intelligent children of indigent means can not pursue their education properly and go ahead further. The state provides scholarships and stipends to the needy and deserving ones without any discrimination, of colour, cast, creed or sex.

12. *General Control and Direction of School System*—Each state determines the aims, curriculum and methods of teaching various subjects together with the evaluation system keeping into consideration its own demands and needs of its citizens.

Not only this, it extends proper guidance and keeps close supervision in such a way that the entire educational system runs on the right track. The defaulting institutions are brought to book, reformed and made to run on proper lines with motives of public good and national service.

13. *Organisation of Boards and Committees*—The state organizes committees and Boards for determining the aims, curriculum, methods, the examination system and other relevant activities concerning education.

14. *Appointment of Commission*—Sometimes the state appoints Commissions of enquiry to know about the working, deficiencies and drawbacks of schools and suggests measures for improvement and progress.

The Secondary Education Commission and the Kothari Commission were appointed in India for this purpose and the government is executing the recommendations of these Commissions gradually.

15. *Encouragement to Educational Research*—The modern age is an age of research. Hence each state encourages educational

research according to its needs and requirements to solve its own problems and explore new areas of improvement. We, in India, are beginning to realize its importance and schemes of research are coming up overhear also.

QUESTIONS FOR ANSWER

1. "In a welfare state education is the responsibility of state". Justify.
2. Write a note on the history of relationship between education and state in India.
3. Write a note on the educational functions of the state.

11

The School (An Active and Formal Agency of Education)

In wider meaning the term 'school' includes all those institutions, which impart instructions (education) on regular basis, such as schools, higher secondary and intermediate colleges, Degree and P.G. Colleges, Universities, Technical institutions and centres of spcialised studies in various fields of knowledge.

The term 'School' originated from the Greek word 'Skhole' which means 'leisure'. The reason of associating 'leisure' with school is that, in Ancient Greece, liberal education was not imparted to all. It was a privilege of the highest class in society which had enough leisure to cultivate the specialized aspects of culture through liberal education. Today, school stands for a specialised and formal agency set up by the society for imparting education to the rising generations.

Definition of School

Great educators define school as follows:

"A school is a vibrant community centre, radiating life and energy all-round, a school is a wonderful edifice, resting on the foundation of good will of the public, good will of the parents, good will of the pupils. In a word, a well-conducted school is a happy home, a sacred shrine, a social centre, a state in miniature and bewitching Brindavan, all beautifully blended into a aesthetic structure." —*S. Bala Krishna Joshi*

"School is a special environment, where a certain quality of life and certain types of activities and occupations are provided with the object of securing the child's development along desirable lines." —*John Dewey*

"Schools are institutions devised by civilized man for the purpose of aiding in the preparation of the young for well adjusted and efficient members of society" —*J.S. Ross*

Origin of School

In olden times, when the social life was very simple, the family provided the child with all the activities and experiences he needed. Then, so long as occupations were centred round home or village, the family, the church and the local community served as a school for life. The children learnt by imitating the work and life process of their parents and neighbours.

But, by and by as the society became more complex with the growth of civilization, and as human knowledge and experiences grew in written form, home or family and other informal agencies of education were found inadequate for the efficient transmission of cultural heritage to the future generation.

Thus arose the necessity of a formal agency of education called the school. By and by, the knowledge and skills secured by the children became so complex that it became rather impossible for the home to transmit the same to the children. Thus, education of children became a specialised occupation of those persons who were highly learned and qualified for discharging this function efficiently.

These persons began to be known as teachers, and the agency through which the teachers imparted education to the children came to be known as School. In recent times, the school has assumed a very comprehensive role. So much so that the functions of the family and the community have also fallen on school.

Now, the school has to discharge not only its own educational functions, but also to provide what home and community provided in the past. "The school has to provide total education, i.e. education for knowledge, for skills, for understanding, for culture, for making a contribution, for a sense of belonging, for attitudes and for a proper orientation to the modern world."

Moreover, with the coming in of democracy, universal education has not only become a necessity in the modern world, but also an accepted social ideal. So, the school is required to discharge very important functions in modern society.

Need of School

In ancient times human life was very simple. Knowledge had not grown so vast as it is today. Human needs were very simple and could be easily fulfilled by informal agencies like the family and the community. Gradually with the development of vast and varied knowledge and growth of over population needs of man increased and the form of culture and civilization also became so complex and complicated that it became almost impossible for parents to transmit it to their children.

Further, most of the parents and other members of the family became so busily engaged in their own vocations or other professions that they were not capable enough to educate their young oncs diverse subjects of the curriculum.

Hence the need was felt for some such institution which could preserve, transmit and develop the cultural heritage. In short, the formal agency of education namely the school came into existence on account of a rapid rise in the means of transport and communication, urbanization of growing population and the position of women as wage earners.

Mention may here be made that in the beginning, the school benefited the rich and well-to-do people only. It is the modern democratic society of today which has begun to cater to the educational needs of the poor and the neglected.

In almost all the countries of the world namely China, Egypt, Greece, Rome, Babylonia and India the schools came into existence by the same process and the same circumstances of society.

Complimentary Nature of Home and School

As far as the education of the children is concerned, the functions of school and home are complementary. The school alone cannot discharge all the above mentioned functions without the active co-operation of the home. Therefore, the family influence plays a very important part in the development of the habits, attitudes and behaviour of the child.

There is, therefore, a great need for building up mutual understanding and co-operation between home and school. Both home and school should co-operate actively in imparting education to the children.

Securing Co-operation between School and Home

School and home must co-operate to achieve the aims and objectives of education. This much needed co-operation can be secured by the school and by taking a number of important steps and by organising a number of activities. The following steps are important to achieve this objective:

1. *Parent-Teacher Association.* The chief instrument of bringing the school and the home closer to each other is the formation of parent-teacher association. This association should meet at least twice or thrice during a year to discuss the progress and problems of children at home and at school. Ways and means should be found to solve the problems of the children and to speed up their progress in studies.

2. *Parents' Day.* Once a year a day of the school programmes should be set apart for inviting the parents of the students to the school. On this occasion, they should be taken round the school and shown what is actually going on in the school. Problems of individual children may also be discussed with parents, and their co-operation sought in the solution of those problems. The problems of the school should be discussed with the parents for finding solutions for the same.

3. *Visits by the Teachers.* The teachers may sometimes visit the homes of the pupils in order to know the background of

the pupils and finding causes of their peculiar problems. Through such visits, the parents may be informed about the educational progress of their children and their general behaviour in the school. Such visits will help the school to know a lot about the physical and social conditions of the children and thereby handle them in a more psychological way.

Thus, the two great factors, the school and the home, influencing the life of the child, can be made to work for bringing about the maximum possible development of the children.

4. *Inviting parents to school functions.* Parents should be invited to the school at various functions organised by the school. These functions are the Parents' Day, the Prize Distribution, Celebration of the Independence Day, the Sports Day, the U.N.O. and the Human rights Day. Such occasions will encourage parents to associate themselves with the work and ideals of the school.

5. *Sending Progress Reports of Students.* Another important means of securing co-operation between school and home is that of sending regularly the progress reports of the students to their parents. The cumulative record of each pupil maintained in the school should also be sent to the parents for information as the child is promoted from one class to the next higher class.

This will enable the parents to know in detail about the physical, academic, social and moral development of their children in school. This co-operation between the school and the home, brought about by these and other measures can contribute much towards the progress and education of the children.

Importance of School

Some of the points which highlight the importance of school are as follows:

1. *A Special Environment*—Informal agencies do not impart education according to a pre-planned scheme. Hence the effect of such indefinite environment affects adversely upon the growth and development of the child.

On the other hand, school provides a simple, pure, interesting and well organised environment before the child according to a pre-planned scheme which ensures the physical, mental, emotional and social development of the child in a natural way. Hence school is an important agency of education.

2. *Harmonious Development of Personality*—The family, the community and the church together with other informal agencies do not have set aims and objectives of education. Their plans and schemes of education are also indefinite.

Sometimes the vagueness of activities affects the personality of the child adversely and develops in him undesirable habits and attitudes. On the contrary, the aims and activities of school are pre-planned. This ensures the harmonious development of the child. Hence the importance of school can not be underestimated.

3. *Extensive Cultural Heritage*—In modern times knowledge has become so vast and varied cultural heritage so extensive that informal agencies like the family and the community are quite incapable to shoulder to responsibility of transmitting this huge treasure of knowledge to the rising generation. School is the only formal agency to complete this task.

4. *Link between Home and the World*—The family develops in the child various qualities and values namely love, sympathy, sacrifice, cooperation, tolerance and service. But all these qualities remain connected with the members of the family and its four walls. This makes the child narrow minded.

School is a connecting link between the family and the external world. In school the child comes in contact with children belonging to different families This contact widens his outlook with the result that the child becomes capable enough to face the challenges and multifarious problems of life and the wider society outside.

Raymont has rightly remarked, "The school is a half way house between the entirely domestic life of early childhood and the larger life that awaits the youth when he quits his parental roof."

5. *Co-operation of Different Agencies*—School is the only agency through which cooperation of different agencies namely the family, the community and the state may be successfully achieved. It is why all these agencies try to extend their full co-operation in all the activities of school. Without the active

cooperation of these agencies school can not achieve its objectives.

6. *Development of Cultural Pluralism*—In school, children belonging to different religions, castes, creeds and social hierarchy come together and mix up freely with each other in friendly atmosphere with the result that they develop sympathy, co-operation, tolerance and respect for the views and cultures of others in a natural way. It is why school is an important agency to develop cultural pluralism amongst children.

7. *Propagation of Ideals and Ideologies of State*—School is an important agency for the propagation of ideals and ideologies of each state in the shortest possible time. It is why all the democratic, fascist and communist states have assigned due importance to school today.

8. *Perpetuation and Development of Society*—Society reviews and develops itself through the active cooperation of school. All social problems and needs of society are flashed in one way or the other in school which provides the desired solutions for all the problems of society. In this way social progress goes on and on with the help of school.

9. *Encouragement to Corporate Life*—Individual life needs socialization. The child should be encouraged to be more and more social in his outlook and behaviour. School provides these experiences for the child to understand social behaviour and develop in him a sense of social responsibility and corporate life.

10. *Creation of Educated Citizens*—In democracy, school has a special importance. Children learn their rights and duties and develop love, affection, sympathy, co-operation, tolerance and responsibility in school. With the development of these socially desirable values they prove useful citizens when they become adults.

11. *School a Better Place of Education than Home*—Under the influence of group life in school a child learns many social qualities and courtesies. Since the physical surroundings of school are healthy, there is ample provision for games, sports and various kinds of cultural activities. A family can not provide all these facilities. Hence school is a better place than home for the socialization and culturalization of the child.

Two Concepts of School

The details about two types of schools are as follows:

Traditional School

Traditional school imparts only formal education. Such schools came into existence when family failed to impart the needed education to its children. In early times, the church and the state were not separate institutions. In those days, the priests used to be teachers also and their places of imparting education were the premises of the churches.

Those priests or teachers had made the education so costly that children belonging to well-to-do families only could receive it. Later on, the state separated from the church and democratic trends began to appear in the working of the state.

Gradually, with the availability of paper in 13th century and invention of printing press in the 15th century more and more opportunities came to be available for more and more people to receive education. Today, these traditional schools have become the teaching shops where teachers are the sellers of knowledge and the children its purchasers.

In other words, the teachers, in such schools, try to thrust upon the minds of children the ready made titbits of knowledge by employing unpsychological methods and techniques without caring for their interests, inclinations, aptitudes, needs and capacities.

Discussing about such traditional school Pestalozzi has rightly remarked—"Our unpsychological schools are essentially only artificial strifling machines for destroying all the results of the power and experience, that nature herself brings the life in them (children). We tyrannically stop the delightful course of their unrestricted freedom, pen them up like sheep, pitiously chain them for hours, days, weeks, months, years to the contemplation of unnatural and unattractive letters".

Modern or Progressive School

Like Pestalozzi, other educationists namely Herbart, Froebel Montessori, Nunn, Tagore and others have emphasized child-centred education. All these educationists have opposed the traditional schools in which ready made knowledge is thrust upon the minds of children forcibly without caring for their individual differences.

They made numerous psychological experiments regarding the education of children. As a result of these experiments progressive schools came into existence. In short, progressive schools developed in contrast to the unpsychological tendency in traditional schools. Basic features of progressive school are as follows:

1. *Practical Knowledge*—In contrast to traditional schools which impart bookish and theoretical knowledge curbing the innate tendencies of a child, progressive schools impart useful, constructive and practical knowledge to the child. In these schools, the curriculum is based upon real life experiences.

The child recreates such learning experiences himself and learns out of such experiences the solution to his real needs and problems of life. Such school are playing their part very well in western countries. They are coming into existence gradually in our country also.

2. *Social Values*—Traditional schools are too much academic and monastic. They are cut way from real life and hence they are of little value to the child in actual day-to-day living. On the other hand, progressive schools work under the light of social ideal and develop the child with reference to such ideals and aims.

These schools encourage children to come in active contact with the libraries and youth welfare centres organized or run by the community or government. The miniature school life is brought into active and lively contact with the wider world outside. Children are made actively conscious of their obligations to the community, society and the nation. Not only this, they are led and guided in such ways that they develop their personalities to the full in active and vital correlation with the development of society to which they belong.

3. *Development of Personality*—Traditional schools emphasize only the mental development which is only one aspect of the whole process. On the other hand, progressive schools try to develop the whole personality of the child. This includes

physical, mental, emotional and social development. This is real development.

In the words of F. Tracey—"The true end of all education is the complete realization of the ideal personality. The ideal product of the educational process is balanced personality."

4. *Centre of Community Life*—A community opens schools for its own good and progress. As such, it is the chief function of school to impart such education which develops the child's personality in intimate relation with the development of the community.

Traditional schools carry out their teaching work keeping the children away from the real life of the community. On the other hand progressive schools are such centres of community life where children are developed according to the demands of community.

In the words of Prof. K. G. Saiyidain—"Since these demands are always changing and modifying themselves, it is necessary that the school should be in vital rapport the life outside the school."

5. *Importance of Child's Personality*—In traditional schools more importance is given to subject matter in comparison with the child. Hence dozes of content are forced down into the minds of children without paying any attention to their interests, inclinations and capacities.

In other words more importance is given to child rather than the curriculum. In progressive schools the personality of each child is honoured. Hence each child is provided such congenial and conducive environment in which he develops his personality according to his innate tendencies, capabilities and speed.

In the words of Prof K. G. Saiyidain—"Thus the modern school seeks to replace information by experience and chooses the most significant and abiding aspects of experiences for its subject matter and thereby makes school life active and meaningful."

6. *Importance of the Principle of Activity in Education*—In traditional schools a child receives education as a passive listener whereas progressive schools stimulate and motivate children to self-choosing and self-learning which is the best

way of learning. It infuses a sense of serious and sincere efforts together with heart felt responsibility.

In the words of Prof. John Dewey—"The environment of a progressive school is simplified, purified and balanced. Under such an atmosphere the child is afforded ample opportunities to experiment for himself and acquire many social ideas."

Functions of the School

Some educators divide functions of the school into formal and informal functions but in real consideration they are complimenting nature. Therefore, hereunder, some very important functions are listed:

1. *Conservation and Perpetuation of Society*—One oi the most important functions of school is to maintain the continuity of social life by handing down traditions, experiences, values and customs of the society from one generation to the other. The progress of the society depends upon the transmission of knowledge and skills from one generation to the next. This important function is faithfully and efficiently performed by the school.

2. *Development of Mental Powers*—The first formal function of school is to develop the mental powers of the child so that he is able to think freely, clearly and logically. To complete this function the school structures such experiences for the child that he is able to develop his inherent mental faculties according to his needs, interests and capabilities for his own good and good of the society.

3. *Cultivation of a Dynamic and Adaptable Mind*—The second formal function of school is to impart such knowledge to the child which is not an end in itself but a means to achieve some end. The end is cultivation of a dynamic and adaptable mind which is resourceful and able to create new value for future life.

4. *Preservation, Improvement and Transmission of Culture*—The third formal function of school is to preserve and improve the national culture and then, transmit it to the rising generation.

5. *Vocational and Industrial Education*—The fourth formal function of school is to impart vocational and industrial

education to children according to the demands of society. In a poor and developing country like India the school must be alert to impart vocational and industrial education to children according to their interests and capabilities so that they are able to support themselves and serve the country with sincerity.

6. *Re-organization and Reconstruction of Human Experiences*—The fifth formal function of school is to reorganize and reconstruct human experiences. As a matter of fact, the function of school is not to preserve the continuity of society only. It has to meet social problems, to reform the society and ultimately to purge it off its dead wood. Fur this, a continuous process of research in all the higher branches of knowledge is a must and the school should be equipped to do it.

7. *Development of Citizenship*—The sixth formal function of school is to develop in children the essential qualities of citizenship so that they may become active and responsible citizens imbued with qualities of leadership leading the nation on the path of progress in all spheres of national life.

8. *Development of Character*—The most important formal function of school is to develop children morally and socially so that they are able to acquire firm and noble character. In early times the family and the church developed the character of children jointly, but now it has become the function of school to develop the character of children by allowing them to participate in such moral, ethical and social activities which may inculcate in them the socially desirable values and lead to the formation of a strong good character.

9. *Promotion of Culture and Civilization*—The school not only transmits the cultural heritage to the rising generation, it also helps to promote culture and civilization. An Cannon has said, "If each generation had to learn for itself what has been learned by its predecessors, no sort of intellectual or social development would be possible and the present state of society would be little different from the society of the old stone-age." Thus the school performs the important function of constantly re-organising and re-structuring human experiences for the promotion of culture and civilization.

10. *All-round Development of the Individual*—The functions and responsibilities of school have increased manifold during the recent years. Its function is no longer the transmission of

the knowledge of 3 R's. As the concept of education has developed and become more comprehensive, the school has to assume a more comprehensive role. Now, the school aims at the development of the whole personality of the child.

Education is now defined as all round development of the personality of the child, physically, intellectually, morally, socially and spiritually. Through its curricular and co-curricular activities, the school caters to the child's social, constructive, artistic and other impulses.

Thus the child not only acquires knowledge but also develops the requisite habits, skills and attitude. In this way, the school helps to bring about all round development of the child's personality.

11. Promotion of Social Efficiency—To lead a successful life in the modern society the individuals must acquire social efficiency. In a democratic society, the children must be trained in the democratic ways of life through education and the school programmes must be planned accordingly. Training for effective participation in a democratic society and cultivation of a planned sense of rights and duties is an important function of the school. This is done by the school by having a clear concept of democratic ideals, and then directing the educational programmes accordingly.

12. Adjustability in Society. John Dewey says, "We send children to school to learn in a systematic way the occupations which constitute living." Brown says that, "The school has a direct responsibility of preparing the individual child for post-school adjustments."

A child spends a period of his life in school. After completing his school education, he is generally to adjust himself in the society outside the school to the best of his capability and capacity.

If this adjustment is proper, the school has succeeded in its aims and objectives. So, one of the main functions of the school is to turn out of its portals such young men and young women as may adjust themselves properly and usefully and lead successful lives on private, public and professional levels.

13. Physical Development—The first informal function of school is to develop the child physically. For this, the entire environment of school should be such which leads to the physical well being of children.

14. *Development of Social Feeling*—The second informal function of school is the development of social feeling in all the children of school. As a matter of fact; school is a miniature of society.

Hence the school should provide such a social environment before children by organizing students' unions, social service camps, social functions and parent-teacher associations etc. so that all the socially desirable values namely sympathy, cooperation, tolerance, social awakening and above all-discipline develop in them in a natural way.

15. *Emotional Development*—The third most important informal function of school is to develop the child emotionally. For this, the entire environment of school must be artistic. In other words, there should be garden, flower plants and other beautiful natural objects.

The school building and the campus should be neat and clean. The walls of the rooms should be whitewashed annually and the rooms be decorated tastefully. Trips, tours, exhibitions and debates also stimulate the emotional and aesthetic sense of children.

Drawbacks of Indian School

The system of education in schools has some drawbacks because of various reasons, which may be listed as follows:

1. *Lack of Constructive and Creative Activities*—Modern education lays emphasis upon creative and constructive activities. But alas! our schools neglect such activities. Most of them have no idea even of such desirable activities.

As a result our children on growing adults are incapable to participate in any sphere of national reconstruction and international development.

2. *Lack of Well Trained Teachers*—On account of the population explosion, our schools are over crowded and the teacher training institutions lag behind. The result is that adequate number of trained teachers are not available. Due to lack of well trained teachers education is suffering in quality, precision and proper direction.

3. *More Academic and Monastic*—School education is so academic and monastic that it has become, quite unrelated to real life situation. In other words, the education imparted in our schools is quite dull, lifeless and purely theoretical having less relation with real life.

4. *Unable to Develop Social Progress*—In fact, school is a replica of society. It should face the problems of society and foster such attitudes in the children which may lead to social advancement, progress and development. But education imparted in our traditional schools neither leads to individual progress nor progress of society.

5. *Nature of Schools*—Indian schools were organised to meet the needs of British rule. Though our country is now a Sovereign Democratic Republic, yet the pattern of these schools is still the same. As such, it is a hope against a hope to expect these schools to preserve, purify and transmit the cultural heritage of our country.

6. *No Co-operation of Other Agencies*—Whatever form, structure and scope of Indian school may be, still it can not replace the family. Thus to carry out its function it should seek the active co-operation of the family, the community and the church. We find that there is no such cooperation.

7. *Emphasis of Subject Matter*—In Indian schools too much emphasis is laid on the subject matter to the neglect of child. The natural interests, aptitudes and capacities of the child are not only neglected but more often they are curbed and doses of theoretical knowledge are forced down into the mind of child.

8. *One-Sided Development*—Our schools do not try to promote the complete development of the personality of child. Only one or the other aspect of personality is randomly emphasized and that too in a haphazard way.

9. *Unpsychological Environment*—The entire environment of Indian schools is lifeless, dull and often repulsive. Most of the schools in villages and towns run in improvised shanty structures containing either stools or carpets only. The rooms of such schools are dirty, dark and dingy without proper air circulation and light. Only a very few schools have any library, laboratory, and other essential materials. The campus of such

schools is like a courtyard where there is no garden, field and canteen.

In such schools only bookish theoretical ready made titbits of knowledge are imparted to children without employing proper strategies, tactics, techniques and methodology. Dictation by teachers, cramming by students and passing out in any way is the only objective of such teaching shops run on commercial lines with money motive.

10. *Stable and Rigid Curriculum*—The curriculum of our schools is framed by Government and the school carries that into practice. It is stable and rigid. The framers of such curriculum do not take any notice regarding the local conditions, need or requirements of the place and above all the nature of children who are to take that curriculum. Teachers can not modify it the least. Such rigid and lifeless curriculum is mechanically doled out to the children who profit very little from it.

11. *Defective Methods of Teaching*—In our schools methods of teaching are examination oriented and care very little to the inherent interests, aptitudes, needs and capacities of children. On the other hand they crush the initiative and originality of those for whom they are employed.

12. *Negligence of Individual Differences*—Psychological researches have emphatically proved that all children are born with distinct inherent capacities and powers. Education should draw and develop these native endowments. In our schools, factory like drilling, moulding and sharpening is done without any regard to individual differences, needs and aptitudes.

13. *Lack of Character Formation and Moral Development*—The whole atmosphere and working of Indian traditional schools is such that no inculcation of moral values and attitudes in children is possible.

As such character formation remains a distant dream. It is really a very sorry state of affairs that our schools do not aim at such essential goals and ends of life to be achieved.

14. *Lack of Vocational Education*—School education is simply bookish and theoretical without any practical experience. There is no provision for vocational education in our schools with the result that after getting certificates and degrees children either search table jobs or lead a life dependent upon others.

15. *Emphasis on Bookish Knowledge*—In our schools education is purely theoretical and academic. It starts with books and ends with books. In Western countries much emphasis is laid upon games and scientific training through experiments and inventions whereas our bookish education is mainly examination oriented.

How to Make Indian Schools Progressive

To achieve this we should attempt on the points:

1. *Centre of Community Life*—Indian schools should serve as community centres for children. They should engage all the children in various developmental and recreational activities in such a way so that, on one hand, all the desirable values namely morality, strong character, self reliance, sense of emotional and national unity together with national discipline develop in them in a natural way and, on the other hand, they actively participate in the development of the community to which they belong.

2. *Emphasis of Social Values*—Indian schools should develop children in social environment. For this, they should encourage children to come in contact with social centres, social institutions and also participate actively in various social functions. It will not only establish a bond between the smaller world of school and the wider world outside but also develop in children all the socially desirable values which are greatly essential for the success of democracy.

3. *Emphasis on Constructive and Creative Activities*—Indian schools should emphasize the principle of creativity in the education of children. According to this principle children should themselves plan and structure learning experiences. They should initiate and continue all varieties of constructive activities. Co-curricular activities, exhibitions, competitions, social and cultural programmes may also stimulate children in these directions.

4. *Provision for the Training of Teachers*—Trained teachers know their job well and do it efficiently in comparison with those who are not trained professionally. As the number of children increase, correspondingly provision of sufficient

teaching staff should be made by the management and the government.

The government should provide more and more facilities for the training of teachers. At the same time in service training schemes should also be widened in their scope and facilities. Not only this, training should be made inexpensive and working conditions, security of service, pay scales be increased to invite really intelligent and capable persons to the teaching profession.

5. *Democratic Nature of Schools*—India is now free from foreign alien rule. After careful consideration it has transformed itself into a secular democratic republic. Thus we should scrub the old bureaucratic and authoritarian pattern of our schools by changing their working in conformity with the democratic ideals and processes so that each child may learn to live democratically.

Thus the nature of Indian schools should, now, be democratic so that children are able to adjust with the environment and bring out a change in them according to the changing needs and situations of society.

6. *Co-operation of Other Agencies*—The family, the community and the state together with all other agencies of education should co-operate the working of the school. Then only the Indian schools will be worthy to be known as progressive schools.

7. *Emphasis on Child's Personality*—In addition to curriculum, full attention should be paid to the development of the child in accordance with his innate endowments. That is the real purpose of education. In other words, education should be child centred.

8. *All-Sided Development*—Personality has various aspects. None is to be neglected. Our schools should foster all-round development of personality namely—Physical, mental, emotional and social.

9. *Emphasis on Character Formation and Moral Development*—Emphasis on the development of moral values is essential for the proper development of character. In a democratic country like India only those citizens who are imbued with moral qualities and firm character can lead the nation to greatness.

Hence all the policies, programmes and other activities like scouting and guiding etc. of our schools should develop moral values and strong good character in our children.

10. *Provision of Vocational Education*—Our schools should make children self-reliant by training them in some craft or vocation according to their needs, interests and capacities. Vocational education shall enable them to live independently on their own labour and efforts in the capacity of socially efficient citizens.

11. *Emphasis on Practical Knowledge*—Our schools should minimize imparting bookish and theorctical knowledge. They should try to give more and more creative, constructive and practical knowledge to children. For this, our curriculum should be based on life experiences as experiences gained through self learning prove useful in practical life. As a matter of fact the moto of work experience is current these days. It should be sincerely worked out.

12. *Phychological Environment*—Our schools should provide congenial and conducive environment to the children. Then only, it will be possible for our young ones to develop their inherent tendencies and capacities to the best of their efforts by their own initiative and creativity.

13. *Flexible Curriculum*—Curriculum followed by our schools should be flexible, suited to local needs and situations. At the same time teachers should also have the freedom to modify it according to the requirements of children and social conditions.

14. *Dynamic Methods of Teaching*—No doubt curriculum is important but equally important are the strategies, tactics, techniques and methodology of teaching which work out the curriculum. Dalton Plan, Assignments, projects etc. are some of the important useful methods.

15. *Emphasis on Individual Differences*—Keeping into consideration the principle of individual differences, our schools should try to meet individual needs and problems as far as possible. Only then, education will be effective and profitable in developing values that equip children for their future life full of stress and strain.

QUESTIONS FOR ANSWER

1. What do you mean by a school? Discuss its need importance and functions.
2. What are the differences between a traditional school and a progressive school? Enumerate the distinctive features of progressive school.
3. What are the drawbacks of Indian schools? Give suggestions to make Indian schools an effective agency of education.
4. Write a note on the origin of school as an agency of education.
5. "Educational functions of the school and family are of complimentary nature". Justify.
6. Write a note on educational functions of the school.

12

Non-Formal Education

In chapter two of this book, captioned as 'Forms of education' a reference has been made of non-formal education, therefore, hereunder only some of the basic details about this form of education are given.

Non-formal education has emerged as one of the alternatives of the formal system of education. It envisages need-based education in a free atmosphere. The word 'non-formal' has been derived from the word 'forma' by using the prefix 'non' to formal which itself means concerned with the form or 'structured'. So, 'formal education' means structured education which is more concerned with the form and less with the matter.' The concept of non-formal education being of recent origin is yet in the developing stage. It widely differs from person to person and from place to place.

Non-Formal Education (NFE) differentiated from Formal and Informal Education

Non-Formal Education may be differentiated from the conceptual framework of formal education and informal education. The NFE is life long and with flexible points of entry, while formal education is finite and limited to a period meant for teaching and learning, with fixed point of entry and exit. In formal education acquisition of knowledge is the goal; in non-formal education, the goals are understanding one's needs, environment and social relationship.

Non-formal education develops an open-end critical and self reliant awareness. It is a process of sharing, exploring, analysing and judging together. There is maximum participation of the learner. It is need based and future oriented. NFE is "any organised, systematic, educational activity, carried outside the framework of the established formal system, whether operating separately or is an important feature of some broader activity, that is intended to serve identifiable learning clientele and learning objective.

Informal education is "the process by which a person imbibes attitudes, develops skills, cultivates values and acquires knowledge without there being any organisation or system about it. This would include the deliberate attempts of parents and elders in the family and community to help the young ones grow and adapt themselves to the environment. Informal education would also include all incidental learning that takes place while at work or at play and during travels as well as spontaneous learning though films, radio and television."

Objectives of Non-Formal Education

The broad-based objectives of Non-formal education may be enumerated as under:

1. To enable the maximum number of non-school going children of 9-14 age group to join the non-formal stream so that we may help in achieving constitutional directive.
2. To enable the learners to learn basic skills of reading writing and arithmetic so as to make them self-reliant in day-to-day life.
3. To develop general awareness about the socio-politico-economic problems of local, slate and national importance so as to seek their solutions.
4. To enrich knowledge/experiences the vocations/professions in which the clientele is involved by utilizing local and outside resources.
5. To develop basic skill to handle/repair modern ordinary gadgets with which the learners are familiar and have access to.

6. To develop in them desirable personal and social habits as well as healthy attitudes towards our charished national ideals and values.

Features of Non-Formal Education

The salient features of Non-formal Education may be stated as under:

1. Relevance. The content of Non-formal education programme must be need-based and relevant to the age-group concerned. There will not be a uniform content for all but it will differ as per time, climate, culture and ecological conditions etc.

2. Flexibility. Opposed to formal system which is too rigid, the NFE programme will be flexible as regards time, place, duration, attendance, syllabi, methods and evaluation etc.

3. Practicability. The programme of Non-formal Education will not be theoretical alone but will be translated into practice. It will be a functional programme.

4. Own time Education for Shortened Duration. Unlike formal system, Non-formal Education will be provided for nearly two hours and the timings are to be adjusted according to the convenience of the clientele.

5. Delinking with Degrees, Diplomas and Certificates. Those joining Non-formal Education would not care for degrees, diplomas and certificates. Moreover, no stigma of pass and fail would be attached.

Dimensions of Non-Formal Education

In view of the objectives and characteristics mentioned above the dimensions of Non-formal Education may be prescribed as under:

1. Healthy living.
2. Acquaintance with ecological conditions.
3. Socialization and confrontation with socio-politico economic problems.
4. Vocational skills.
5. Manipulative skills (3 R's)

Essentials of Non-Formal Education (NFE)

Non-formal activities should be:

— outside the formal system of education.

— consciously and deliberately organised and systematically implemented.

— organised for a homogeneous group—such group has to be identified in terms of their learning needs.

— programmed to serve the needs of the group. This will necessitate flexibility in design of the curriculum and the schemes of evaluation.

Approaches to Non-Formal Education

While formal education is a system with its own distinct structure, interlocking parts and internal coherence, non-formal education is a non system or an open system; it is simply a collective label covering a wide assortment of organised educational activities outside the formal system which serve the identified learning needs of a variety of groups—children, youth, adults, men, women, farmers, artisans, merchants, rich, poor, etc. and which change as he needs change.

There are as may as four schools of thought on this subject and they need some examinations.

1. *De-schooling Society*. Iwal Illich is deeply committed to equality and to the dignity and autonomy of the individual. He is greatly concerned with improvement in the quality of life. It is his view that these basic values have been adversely affected in the modern industrial society. He would, therefore, prefer to replace the modern industrial society, by a convivial society—where, every individual has full autonomy and facilities for growth:

where consumerism ceases to be a goal;

where an individual's access to essential goods and services is based on equality and justice;

where an appropriate technology is adopted so that a new system of production by the masses replaces the present system of mass production;

Some persons are strongly in favour of non-formal and incidental channels of education, which, in his opinion, are adequate to meet all our needs. On the other hand, he finds that the formal school with all its rigidities and direct compulsions, and with its vast army of professionalized full-time teachers, is an instrument of mis-education rather than of education and hinders rather than helps the spread of proper education among the people. They are also of the view that the weaknesses of the formal school are so great that it is beyond repair. They, therefore, recommends that the formal school should be totally abolished or that the society should be de-schooled.

2. *Radical Transformation of the Formal-school.* Whether one does or does not agree with the proposal of Illich for de-schooling, one thing is certain: everyone is convinced that it is absolutely essential to carry out a radical reform of the formal school so that it emphasizes learning rather than teaching; becomes elastic, flexible, and diversified; develops programmes of part-time education and self-study; and uses all community resources, including non-teachers. Side by side with the reform of the formal school steps are also needed to reform non-formal and incidental education and to integrate them with the formal stream.

3. *The Additive Approach.* The official reaction to the strong criticism of the formal school and the equally strong case made out in support of non-formal education programmes is generally to take action on the following lines:

(*a*) To carry out some reforms in the formal school, mostly of a patch work character, which do not make any significant impact on its weakness, and

(*b*) To initiate a few programmes of non-formal education in addition.

4. *The Integrative Approach.* This proposal attempts simultaneous action on three fronts:

(*a*) A sustained and large-scale programme of radical reform in the formal school is developed. Speaking of the conditions in India, for instance, it may be said that the single point entry must go.

The school system should be elastic, flexible and diversified. It should not be exclusively full-time, and the alternative channels of part-time and full-time education should be fully developed. The almost exclusive dependence on full-time teachers must be given up and all teaching resources of the community must be utilized.

(*b*) The existing forms of non-formal education are studied and improved. New forms of non-formal education are also introduced where needed. In fact, the whole emphasis is shifted to a large scale development of non-formal education.

(*c*) There is a simultaneous effort to improve the quality of incidental education also.

Need for a New System of Education: All things considered, our best alternative obviously is to evolve a new system of education which will incorporate within it all programmes of formal, non-formal and incidental education, which will operate all the three channels of full-time, part-time and own-time education and give them equality of status, which will make full use of all institutions for purposes of learning, which will replace the present exclusive emphasis on full-time professional teachers by the use of all human resources, and will be sufficiently elastic, diversified, and flexible to provide all the necessary opportunities for learning to all individuals throughout their lives. This is probably best expressed in the following principles, considerations and recommendations of the Report of International Commission on Education:

(1) Life-long education should be the master concept of educational policies in the years ahead, for the developing countries.

(2) Every individual must be in a position to keep learning throughout his life.

(3) Education must be carried on at all ages of man, according to each individual's needs and convenience. He must, therefore, be oriented from the out-set and from phase to phase, keeping the real purpose of all education in mind: personal learning, self-teaching, and self-training. Education must cease being confined to school walls. All kinds of existing institutions, whether designed for teaching or not, and many forms

of social and economic activities, must be used for educational purposes.

(4) Education should be dispensed with and acquired in a multiplicity of means. The important thing is; not the path an individual has followed, but what he has learned or acquired.

(5) Artificial and outmoded barriers between different essential disciplines, courses and levels and between formal and non-formal education should be abolished. Recurrent education should be gradually introduced.

(6) An over-all open system helps learners to move within it both horizontally and vertically and widens the range of choice available to them.

(7) Each person should be able to choose his path more freely, in a more flexible framework, without being compelled to give up using educational facilities for life, if he leaves the system.

Non-Formal Education in India (NFE)

NFE is one of the recent concepts being adopted in Indian Education. In the context of the Indian situation, non-formal education has assumed a lightly different connotation. It has been accepted as complementary and supplementary to the formal education. It has been widely accepted by our government and people because the formal system has failed or is inadequate to fulfil our commitment to the constitutional directive (Art. 45) that is, to achieve universalization of elementary education for all the children of 6-14 age group within the fixed time limit. Further, non-formal education is aimed at providing educational facilities to those children of 9-14 age group who, on account of one reason or another, could not complete elementary education or dropped out before they could do so.

The programme of NFE basically differs from that of Adult Education Programme (AEP) on age. In the former case it is 9-14, while in the latter case it is 15-35 years. Moreover, in NFE the emphasis is more on socio-academic component besides the learning of 3 R's. In AEP, the emphasis is more on socio-economic (including vocational) aspects.

Programmes: There are certain categories of people who stand in special need of non-formal education.

(1) *Out of School Youth*: Out of school youth in the age group of 15-25. The size of the group is about 20 per cent of the total population. Its members are generally alert, inquisitive, impressionable, and capable of being inspired by emotional commitments to the service of people and the country. As Educands therefore, they offer rich and potential material that is much easier to handle than either children of younger age or adults.

The content of non-formal education to be developed for this age group will include:

- Improvement of vocational skills to enable them increase their income;
- Citizenship or an understanding of the problems facing the society and the country;
- General Education;
- Sports and games;
- Hobbies and Recreation;
- Health and family planning; and
- Participation in programmes of social or national service.

By and large, these programmes will have to be part-time. But in many cases short full-time courses can also be arranged with great advantage.

(2) *Adults*: To begin with, we divide programmes of adult education into two parts: *(1)* Continuing education for those who have already completed elementary, secondary and higher education and *(2)* education of the poor and deprived groups which will include further education of those who are illiterates, literacy programmes, and even the further education of those who are illiterate and may not desire to literacy.

(3) *Women:* We should develop programmes for women similar to those which have been described earlier for men. Programmes for better care and upbringing of children, family planning, preservation of food, nutrition, and improved culinary practices have special interest and significance for women. The training of women workers for delivery of health care services and for provision of non-formal education emphasised.

Condensed courses which help women who have missed regular school to complete their formal studies in a short period and seek employment have been found to be useful; and there is urgent need to develop worker's education programmes for women workers in the organised industry.

(4) Emerging Leadership: A new leadership from masses, and especially from rural areas is now emerging in many walks of life. It is particularly growing in the political sphere where it is getting elected to membership of local bodies, state legislatures, and Parliament. Very often it is found that this new leadership is not fully equipped to discharge the responsibilities which it has assumed. The development of non-formal education programme for this social group, with a view to enabling it to discharge its responsibilities satisfactorily is obviously a programme of high significance and priority. A similar group is that of 'Opinion-leaders' in rural areas who play a significant role in moulding community thinking and action in their localities. Their training through non-formal channels will have far reaching consequences for development and social transformation.

QUESTIONS FOR ANSWER

1. Define Non-Formal Education and differentiate it from formal and informal education.
2. Write a note on the objectives, features and essentials of Non-Formal Education.
3. Give an account of the Approaches to Non-Formal Education.
4. Write a note on the Indian concept of Non-Formal Education.

13

Distinction Between Training, Instruction, Teaching and Education

The basic fact is that unless the people understand true meaning of education, they will not be able to understand its utility and importance in personal, social and national life. Generally the terms training, instruction, teaching and education are not distinguished from each other but for educators they have different meaning and society must accept it. Therefore, hereunder, an attempt is being made to make the same clear.

Training

This word which we often meet in educational discussion has a certain clear connotation and carries with it also often a number of derogatory implications. First of all it can refer to the actual drill or practice which a person may undertake to prepare himself for an improved performance, the training which an athlete or an apprentice may undergo, the reference being to the preparation itself whether it be running or gymnastics or the repetition of supervised practice with tools or some other such instruments.

This word has often been mischievous in educational discussion. It is associated with the tricks of the trade, with dependent attitudes and with a limited understanding of the purpose of any activity.

It is significant, for example, that we speak of 'teacher training' and 'training colleges'. At the universities in England, for some years the official title for the department of education was 'The University Training Department.' The official title now is 'The University Department of Education.'

The training colleges, however, still have this word associated with them. In intellectual activity it is a mark of esteem that you have something more or less independent and individual to say.

Training places emphasis upon a man's dependence, upon being taught by others, upon learning within the framework of a known programme.

In the early part of the 19th century in Scotland, David Stow elaborated a programme of preparation for teaching and founded what he specifically termed 'the training system', and in this practical work in classroom played a large part. The Normal School was the result of this training system—the school from which the norms or standards of practical teaching could be obtained.

We are told in proverbs that if we train a child in the way he should go, when he is old he will not depart from it. This emphasis upon laying down and establishing ways of acting, a routine, a procedure, a solution to all eventualities on the basis of practice, represents on the one hand a necessary part of anyone's mastery of a subject, of a trade, but on the other, in the case of relationships to ideas or to people, it may be too rigid to be creditable.

Here, then, we have a word 'training' which is legitimate in that it defines the skills and practices which have to be understood and mastered but which does not include the equally important principle of independence, the necessity to improvise with all the overtones of judgement, intelligence and freedom which this suggests.

It is interesting to notice that training is probably linked with vocational preparation, and education is linked with liberal preparation. Technical education is often thought of as representing the training tradition but technology may give more room for liberal traditions.

Instruction

This word represents the passing on of information. The emphasis here is upon what is communicated and its importance. This is another word which represents part of the educational process but which very often produces confusion in discussion. We can see this sort of difficulty arising in such a sentence as 'children should profit from the instruction of their elders.' The emphasis in instruction is upon the factual material which is being presented by an instructor.

The implication is that the material is clearly understood by the instructor, has been ordered for presentation by him and is presented to the pupil. Perhaps it could be summed up by saying that this term represents a state of affairs something like the following 'here is material which has been sorted out to be presented to you. You should absorb it—take it or leave it.'

Teaching

There is a two-fold difference between instruction and teaching which is not easy to disentangle. First, the emphasis in teaching is upon a relationship between people, the teacher and his pupils. Secondly, there is an implication of the necessity for follow-up so that the teacher may be assured that what he has presented has, in fact, been understood and learned.

It is quite true that teaching, like training and like instruction rests to some extent upon certain methods, techniques, tricks of the trade. However, in addition teaching presupposes an interest in the learning process of the pupils and the interaction of the minds of teacher and taught.

It is to be expected that the emphasis in this interchange will be now upon the teacher, what he has to say and how he says it, now upon the learners, his growth in understanding and his mental initiative in grasping and transforming what is being presented to him.

The word 'teaching' has also other references arising from historical associations. For example, in England, the term 'teacher' has to be differentiated from 'schoolmaster.' The word schoolmistress, for various reasons of association, is very often thought to be slightly less advantageous in relation to schoolteacher than the word schoolmaster.

It is sufficient at this stage to have indicated that while the words 'teaching' and 'teacher' have certain associations with the relationship between people and the learning process involved, the shadings of repute can be very subtle and fluctuating.

Education

It is now commonly held that this word derives from educare which refers to the bringing-up of children physically and mentally. It is a word of such wide reference that at times, it is of necessity. For example, we read that it is concerned with all the qualities which are acquired through individual instruction and social training, which further the happiness, efficiency and capacity for social service of the person educated.

Adams points out that education has for its aim not merely to supply a certain amount of knowledge but also to modify the nature of the pupil. It is noticeable that in the history of the development of the institution of school we have been moving steadily away from the narrower concept of school instruction, of training in specific knowledge or techniques, towards the notion of the school and other agencies as part of an educative society. This is to be detected in the shift and enrichment of the meaning of the word 'education' itself.

It would be wise at this stage to distinguish between the narrower and wider senses in which this term is used.

Wirelmm Dilthey speaks of education as the planful activity of grown-ups to shape the mind of the younger generation, and Adams takes this farther in his examination of the bi-polar process mentioned above. Here one personality acts upon another in order to modify the development of the other. That is to say, that the process is not only conscious but deliberate, for the educator has the clearly realized intention of shaping and modifying the development of the pupil.

Dilthey and Adams have this in common, that they see in education the influence of person upon person in which the older generation wishes to prepare the younger generation in terms of idea, knowledge and attitudes. In the foreground of this activity stands the school as an institution in which there is concentrated the purpose of presenting knowledge deliberately and on the basis of a consciously planned programme.

Only relatively recently, with the entry of psychological considerations, has the importance of emotional factors in learning and indeed the educational significance of the emotions at large been thought to be important.

This may lead us now to consider the broader concept of education. One of the classical statements of this wider and necessarily vaguer view of education is contained in J.S. Mill's address as Rector of St. Andrews University, Mill said, "Whatever we do for ourselves and whatever is done for us by others for the express purpose of bringing us somewhat nearer to the perfection of nature (education) does more: in its largest acceptation it comprehends even the indirect effects produced on character and on human faculties by things of which the direct purposes are different, by forms of government, by the industrial arts, by modes of social life: nay, even by physical facts not dependent on human will, by climate, soil and local position."

This is the assumption that education represents the organization of forces and influences which are to lead to a higher standard of behaviour and values—Mill speaks of the effects produced on character.

Education can only arise out of a social situation. Robinson Crusoe could teach himself to adapt to the needs of survival but the heritage of his training and experience as a member of society before he was wrecked on his island gave him resources which he developed with admirable ingenuity and good sense.

If the need for education arises out of people living together, one of its aims has to be to enable them to live together more successfully in the widest sense of these terms. Where societies or communities develop, normal ways of organizing their life develop, too, and these the sociologist calls the institutions of a society. Institutions come about from the clash and interplay of individual interests and when they have come into existence they in their turn help to define the area of acceptable conflict and harmony, that is to say they make their contribution to the development of the social and individual aspects of character, where character represents how a man behaves and what his motivation is to behave in that way.

Education, then is dynamic on both sides in that it deals with adaptable development of individuals and equally with a changing and developing society.

QUESTIONS FOR ANSWER

1. Draw a distinction between training and teaching.
2. Draw a distinction between teaching and education.
3. Draw a distinction between instruction and teaching as well as between instruction and education.

14

Educational Values

Personal and social values are attempted to be gained through education and these values are termed as educational values which are considered vital in opting for an educational aim as a matter of principles of education for formulating the curriculum. Hereunder, we discuss educational values very briefly.

Meaning of Values

According to Cunningham educational values become aims of education. According to these qualities, abilities and capacities are promoted in the individuals, which are inherently values of life. Brubacher speaks out this as—"To state one's aim of education is at once to state his educational values."

Educational values are related to those activities which are good, useful and valuable from the point of view of education. It has already been pointed out that according to Adams education is a bipolar process which has two parts—(1) The teacher and (2) The Child. The teacher, in order to mould and modify the behaviour of the child employs various strategies and tactics to achieve the desired behavioural change in the child. He performs all these activities, because he thinks them as valuable for the purpose in view.

As the teacher provides an environment of utility and value to the child, in the same manner the child participates only in those activities which he considers useful and valuable to him. Thus the teacher and the child participate only in those activities which they consider as educationally useful and valuable.

Etymological Meaning of Value—According to its verbal meaning value signifies that quality of an individual or thing which makes that individual or thing important, respectable and useful. This quality may be internal or external or both.

Philosophical Meaning of Value—In its philosophical or educational interpretation value signifies neither a thing nor an individual, but a thought or a point of view. As such, any thing which is useful to an individual becomes valuable to him. The very same thing may be quite useless to another individual and as such it is of no value to that individual. Thus from the philosophical standpoint, a value is directly related to a view point or thought.

THE TWO VIEW POINTS

Views About Educational Values

There are two views about educational values. They are—(1) Have these values an independent existence and (2) Are these values dependent upon the individual who does evaluation. The nature of these are of two kinds as under:

(1) Internal and Subjective.
(2) External and Objective.

(1) Internal and Subjective—Some educationists are of opinion that values depend upon personal ideas and experiences. In other words, a value is born out of a mind's power of imagination. They hold that those things are of any use to human beings which have values inherent in them. Things are of no use which have no value.

Hence educational values are internal and subjective. According to these educationists, curriculum construction, selection of educational aids, strategies and tactics all depend upon the teacher and the child. They determine their values according to their utility.

(1) External and Objective—Some educationists firmly hold that values are inherent in objects and activities in accordance

with their qualities and altitudes. According to their views the social environment influences the quality or the value of an object. In other words, it is the social environment which assigns any value to an object.

Hence each social value according to environment enters an object and becomes a part of it. These educationists do not regard a value as something internal and subjective, but assert that it is external and objective.

According to them, curriculum construction, selection of strategies, tactics and teaching aids are all used with relevance to the social environment in which the teacher as well as the child live.

The above discussion makes it clear that some educationists hold values as internal and subjective whereas others believe that they are external and objective. It should be borne in mind that either of them are one-sided and reveal only one side of truth.

The first group of educationists neglects the external social environment and the other remains indifferent to the interests inclinations, aptitudes and capacities of the child. In fact, the internal and external values are essential for an effective and wholesome process of education.

Thus educational values should be created keeping into consideration the nature of the child together with the nature of the objects and activities. In short, an educational value is created out of a synthesis of both—the subjectivity and the objectivity.

Kinds of Educational Values

About educational values Urban, Me Dougall, Brubacher and other educationists have expressed different views of which those of Brubacher need mention. In his book—'Modern Philosophies of Education' he has divided educational values into two categories as under:

(1) Related to Likes or Immediate.
(2) Related to Intelligent Likes or Remote.

(1) Related to Likes or Immediate Values—These values are those which fulfil the biological and psychological needs of

children. Only immediate objects satisfy these values. The remote ones have no relevance. For example—a child, having an interest and liking for fine arts, shall be able to satisfy his artistic taste by practising artistic activities only. In short these values are related to immediate needs and their fulfilment to achieve immediate self satisfaction.

(2) Related to Intelligent Likes or Remote Values—These values are closely related to intelligent and rational needs. It is a matter of common experience that each programme of school satisfies the diverse needs of teachers and children, but of these needs, only same are important. It is also a fact that all these needs are not likely to be satisfied.

Thus each individual has to make an intelligent selection out of all these needs and try to achieve maximum advantage from all the activities of the school. Hence these values are related to intelligently selected likes and needs. These values can be divided further into two categories as under:

(i) Instrumental Values.
(ii) Intrinsic Values.

(i) Instrumental Values—In the words of Brubacher—"Instrumental values are values that are judged good, because they are good for something." These values are useful in themselves and they are also instrumental in realizing some other values. For example, if a child wants to become a noted musician, knowledge of 'Tal and 'Swar' will be useful to him to realize his chief objective. This knowledge of 'Swar' and 'Tal' is an instrumental value for some higher values. These instrumental values are subjective and change according to change in circumstances. Thus instrumental values are of no use in other vocations and professions.

(ii) Intrinsic Values—Again in the words of Brubacher—"Intrinsic values are values, which are judged good, not for something else, but in and of themselves." These values are complete in themselves and are not dependent upon anything external. For example, furniture of a class is useful to the teaching process. Hence furniture has a value in itself. It may be borne in mind that intrinsic values are not subjective but objective in nature.

In the above lines, we have discussed the instrumental and intrinsic values with examples. Still there are many objects which are valuable from the point of view of both the categories.

Aesthetic Values—Values which give us pleasure and happiness are known as aesthetic values. Some educationists delimit these values upto the domain of fine arts only. Other educationists of the day hold that pleasure and happiness may be derived from other subjects of the curriculum also besides fine arts

It should be borne in mind that aesthetic experiences are vitally composed of feelings of heart as well as mind. Hence teacher should strive to familiarize children with various curricular as well as co-curricular activities to develop the aesthetic values more and more.

Hierarchy of Educational Values

As discussed above, J. S. Brubacher has divided values into two categories viz. (1) Related to likes or immediate and (2) Related to intelligent likes or remote. Most of the educationists regard the intelligent likes or remote values as of higher nature than the immediate ones.

Even in the latter category, they hold intrinsic value as of greater importance than the instrumental values. Instrumental values are subjective conditioned by time and place while intrinsic values are universal, relatively permanent and objective.

Be it noted that there are some educationists, mostly materialists, who rate instrumental values higher than the intrinsic values.

This controversy poses a problem in curriculum construction as whether subjects related to instrumental values should be assigned any place above or below or near the subjects connected with intrinsic values. As a matter of fact both kinds of values are interrelated, mutually complimentary, supplementary and are essential for the progressive growth and development of children.

Hence hierarchy of educational values is not of great significance. For a wholesome and proper development of children all values are essential in spite of the undoubted greater significance of intrinsic values.

Educational Values are the Determinants of Educational Aims

Educational aims are determined by educational values. As are the values, so shall be the aims of education. In other words, educational values take the form of educational aims. In this process of transformation, we have to depend upon some bases which according to J. S. Brubacher are as under:

(1) Historical Analysis.
(2) Scientific Analysis of Current Life.
(3) Activity Analysis of Child and Adults.
(4) Psychological Analysis of Human Nature.
(5) Job Analysis.
(6) Personal Opinion.
(7) General Opinion.
(8) Philosopher's Opinion.

Out of all the above bases, philosopher's opinion is regarded as the most important base for the determination of educational aims. This is because all the other bases are conditioned by time, place, circumstances and situations while the views of philosophers are relatively permanent for all times and places and in addition can point out towards directions of reform and modification of the prevalent aims.

But there is a controversy overhere also as different philosophers emphasize different values. Some think intrinsic values higher to instrumental values and others vice versa. But in spite of these differences in approach and view points, one thing is of utmost importance, that educational aims depend on and are based upon educational values. Educationists have divided these aims into two categories as under:

(1) General and Ultimate Aims.
(2) Specific and Related Aims.

(1) General and Ultimate Aims—The formation of general and ultimate aims of education is done on the basis of natural

and intrinsic values of life. For example, if the aim of education is self-realization, then the first step towards its attainment will be to understand the nature of the child and, after correct scrutiny try to know well his basic tendencies, capacities and abilities.

After this educational activities and programmes should be so organized that the basic capacities and abilities are developed to the fullest extent and the child is able to realise his self completely. In short, ultimate aims are determined on the natural and essential bases of intrinsic values.

(2) Specific and Related Aims—Specific or immediate aims of education are determined on the bases of instrumental values. Though the general and ultimate aims of education possess an all pervading importance, yet the teacher should try to break up a general aim into subsidiary aims which are quite specific, clear and definite.

This will make the educational process very effective and purposeful. For example, according to Herbert Spencer, the ultimate aim of education is—"Complete-Living." He has divided this broad aim into five specific categories and has assigned appropriate activities to each category. In the same way, to realize this aim of 'Complete Living'.

The National Education Association of America has divided this aim into seven specific aims of education in the following manner:

(i) Health.
(ii) Command of Fundamental Processes notably the three R's.
(iii) Worthy Home Membership.
(iv) Vocation.
(v) Civic Functions.
(vi) Worthy use of Leisure Time.
(vii) Ethical Character.

The above discussion clearly points out that the ultimate aim of education is 'Self-realization'. All the subsidiary specific aims contribute towards its realization to the fullest possible extent. In the words of J.S. Brubacher—"Aims, there must be tailor made for the occasion. We can not publish a list of them in advance.... Hence there are no educational aims which are unalterably or eternally."

QUESTIONS FOR ANSWER

1. Define the phrase 'Educational Values' and write a note on the kinds of educational values.
2. 'Educational aims are determined by educational values.' Justify.
3. Write short notes on:
   (a) Hierarchy of educational values.
   (b) Specific and related aims of education.

15

Principles of Curriculum Construction

Educational values effect the formulation of educational aims which determine the curriculum of education and the curriculum thus becomes practical aspect of educational system of the society.

Curriculum and Education

Education has to integrate the two processes—the individual process and the social process. In the former sense, it is identical with individual growth and the development of latent power in the child. From the latter point of view, it is identical with socialization, adjustment of environment and imbibing of culture. Both the processes are integrated.

While education is a process, curriculum is a means to the process. While education is learning, curriculum signifies situations for learning. While education deals with 'how' and 'when', curriculum deals with 'what.' While education is the product curriculum is the plan.

Objectives of the Curriculum

(1) To draw out, cultivate, excite and inspire the full development of each student.

(2) To create an atmosphere in which students will learn

to think critically and constructively and seek truth and solve problems.

(3) To help students in establishing values through intimate acquaintance with the humanities, the arts, the natural sciences, the social sciences and religion.

(4) To develop the character of students—integrity, honesty, judgement, co-operation, friendliness and goodwill.

(5) To prepare men and women for citizenship in a democratic society where freedom and liberty go hand in hand with law and justice and where responsibility, national and international, is a characteristic of the individual.

(6) To meet the needs not only of more students, but of students with wide range of ability aptitudes and interests.

Principles of Curriculum Construction

1. Child Centred Education

Curriculum should be child centred. The interests, needs, capacities, abilities, age and the level of intelligence of children should be kept in full view and close attention while constructing a suitable curriculum.

2. Relation with Life

Only those subjects should be included in the curriculum which are directly relevant to actual living because of its irrelevance to the actual living conditions of children. The old and prevalent curriculum is under heavy fire.

3. Utilizing Creative and Constructive Powers

Those subjects should be assigned prominent place in the curriculum which develop the creative and constructive capacities and abilities of children.

Raymont rightly says, "In a curriculum that is suited to the needs of today and of the future, there must be a definite bias towards definite creative subjects."

4. *Interrelation of Play and Work Activities*

The learning activities and experiences should be made so much interesting while constructing a curriculum that a child gains knowledge and learning from them in the play way spirit, finding them very interesting and captivating.

According to Crow and Crow, "The aim of those who guide the learning process should be so as to plan learning activities that the play attitude is introduced."

5. *Knowledge of Culture and Civilization*

Those subjects, activities and experiences should be included in the curriculum which convey to the children the knowledge and understanding of their cultural values and civilization. The curriculum should preserve and develop culture and civilization.

6. *Totality of Experience*

The integrated whole of human experiences should be included in the curriculum as one unit. The curriculum should include both the literary and academic subjects as well as the sum total of varied human experiences which a child receives in the school campus, in the class rooms, on the playing fields, in the libraries and laboratories and through the various informal contacts with the teachers and other educationists.

The Secondary Education Commission Report lays down, "Curriculum does not mean only the academic subjects, but it includes the totality of experiences."

7. *Achievement of Wholesome Behaviour Pattern*

Curriculum subjects, activities and experiences should inculcate in the children social and moral qualities which shape courteous behaviour towards others.

Crow and Crow remarks, "The curriculum should be so framed that it may help the children in the achievement of wholesome behaviour patterns."

8. Utility

Curriculum should include those subjects, activities and experiences which are useful to the present as well as the future life of children. Irrelevant and useless material should find no place in the curriculum. The dead wood in the present curriculum should be removed and replaced by needful and relevant materials.

9. Forward Look

Curriculum subjects and materials should be forward looking so that the child is able to solve the various problems coming before him in the immediate as well as remote future, and also to find out suitable solutions and achieve harmonious adjustment with the changing conditions and situations of life in a progressive ways. This capacity for adjustment should also enable the child to modify the environment according to his needs.

10. Variety and Flexibility

Different children have different inherent interests, aptitudes, urges, tendencies, capacities and abilities. Due to these variations and differences, there should be enough flexibility and elasticity in the curriculum to suit the varieties.

The Secondary Education Commission Report (1952-53) says, "There should be enough variety and elasticity in the curriculum to allow for individual differences and adaptation to individual needs and interests."

11. Education for Leisure

The problem of utilizing leisure time gainfully is of considerable magnitude in modern times. It is generally noticed that people have no plan to spend this time effectively. They often waste it or rather kill it. A good curriculum should develop capacities in the children to spend their leisure time in a useful manner.

12. Inclusion of All Life Activities

According to Herbert Spencer, the prime aim of education is

to achieve complete development of individuality. Hence all those activities and subjects should be included in the curriculum which promote physical, mental, moral, social and political development of a child in a harmonious manner.

13. Relationship with Community Life

Full consideration of local needs and situations should be kept in mind while constructing curriculum. All those social beliefs, attitudes, traditions and problems of community life should be given due place to make children understand them well and realize their responsibility towards them.

The Secondary Education Commission Report lays down, "The curriculum should be vitally and organically related to community life."

14. Developing Democratic Spirit

As India has accepted the ideal of a democratic republic curriculum should contain and emphasize those activities and experiences which promote democratic spirit, feelings and attitudes in the children together with democratic behaviour patterns based on democratic ideals and values.

15. Correlation

The impact and importance of a curriculum is destroyed if it is broken into unrelated fragments and unconnected units. On the other hand, if the integrated approach is employed in teaching various subjects, then this correlation leads to wider and deeper understanding and wholesome knowledge. Hence the curriculum should keep various units interrelated and lay stress upon correlation.

Basis of Curriculum Construction

1. Psychological Basis of Curriculum Construction

Psychological basis of education emphasizes that child is the centre of educational process. Education is for the child and child is not for education. Psychology has established the fact that a child develops through various stages.

There are individual differences in the interests, impulses, urges, needs, capacities and abilities among children. Therefore curriculum should be so flexible to meet the individual differences effectively and allow each child to develop along his natural path and progress at his own speed according to his natural directions of development. For this, the curriculum should contain various games, sports, creative activities and useful developing experiences.

2. *Scientific Basis of Curriculum Construction*

Scientific tendency in education or scientific basis of education emphasizes that the main and important place in the curriculum should be given to scientific subjects and secondary place should be given to the academic disciplines.

The credit of introducing and developing the scientific tendency in education goes to Herbert Spencer, according to whom the development of a human being should not be one-sided but complete in all aspects. Education should so achieve this complete development that an individual is able to solve all the problems and thus lead a happy life.

Thus, the main aim of education should be to prepare the individual for complete living. Herbert Spencer divided human activities into five categories and in order of their priority and prescribed definite subjects for each category.

In the first category are those activities which promote self-preservation directly. In the second category are those activities which promote self-protection indirectly. In the third category are those activities which promote human progeny and its protection. In the fourth category are activities which secure social and political protection. Fifth category includes activities concerned with the proper utilization of leisure time.

According to Spencer for the first category—Physiology, Hygiene, Physics and Chemistry, for the second category—Maths, Biology, Sociology and Physics, for the third category—Physiology Domestic Science and Psychology, for the fourth category—History, Politics, Economics and for the fifth category—Art, Music and Poetry should find proper place in the curriculum.

3. *Sociological Basis of Curriculum Construction*

According to sociological basis of education, the individual needs, propensities, interests, capacities and tendencies should be moulded through education to achieve social welfare and social development. Only those subjects and activities should be included in the curriculum which are useful from the point of view of society.

The curriculum should be constructed in accordance with the needs, requirements, conditions and aspirations of society so that qualities of sociability and citizenship are inculcated in each child. The curriculum should contain Language, Arithmetic, Health education. Physical education. Social studies, General science, subjects to enable children to earn livelihood, Experimental arts, Music and such other socially useful subjects which develop the individual side by side with the society.

Curriculum Reconstruction in India

In free India number of attempts were made to renovate and revamp the curriculum to make it suitable to the growing needs, aspirations and demands of a modernising egalitarian society.

Basic Education (1937)

The first major attempt in curriculum reconstruction in India was made in 1937 when Gandhiji propounded the idea of Basic Education. Dr. Zakir Hussain Committee elaborated it in the scheme of studies of Basic Education. After independence the Basic System of education was accepted as the national system of education at the primary stage.

The entire instructional programme was to centre round a craft. Besides craft, physical and social environment were also considered to be important factors in the curriculum. Correlation of various subjects was to be achieved through craft and social and physical environment.

University Education Commission (1949)

In 1948, a year after the attainment of independence, a

University Education Commission was set up under the Chairmanship of Dr. S. Radhakrishnan which recommended the adoption of Three-Year degree course and suggested suitable curriculum for this stage in 1949. Presently the U.G.C. has given guideline for curriculum for almost all the subjects in the Universities.

Secondary Education Commission (1952-53)

With Dr. A. Lakshmanaswamy Mudaliar as the Chairman the Secondary Education Commission made faithful analysis of the curriculum, revealed its defects, formulated principles and suggested the need reforms, which were not properly implemented and the Education Commission (1964-66) was appointed.

The Education Commission (1964-66)

For the first time in the educational history of the country, the Government of India decided to review the entire educational structure of the country by setting up the Education Commission 1964-66 under the Chairmanship of Dr. D. S. Kothari.

The Kothari Commission made a detailed survey of the curriculum followed in the country. It came to the conclusion that the curriculum was inadequate, out-moded and not properly designed to the needs of the modern times. There was widespread dissatisfaction with the curriculum due to tremendous expansion of knowledge in recent years. There was a good deal of 'Useless Education Lumber' in the school courses. There was an urgent need to raise, upgrade and improve the school curriculum.

Recommendations

(i) School curriculum should be upgraded through research in curriculum development by University Departments of Education, Colleges of Education and other such agencies. Research is also needed in the preparation of textbooks and learning materials.

(*ii*) The teacher should be oriented to the revised curriculum through 'in-service education.'

(*iii*) The schools should be free to devise the experiment with new curricula suited to their needs.

(*iv*) The State Boards of School Education should prepare advanced curricula in all subjects and introduce them in a phased manner in schools.

(*v*) In general or non-vocational school common curricula of general education should be provided for the first 10 years, and diversification of studies and specialisation should begin only at the Higher Secondary Stage. An unified approach should be made to the curriculum synthesising general education with specialised course.

(*vi*) The standard of attainment should be clearly defined at the end of each substage.

(*vii*) Science education should be given special importance. "Science and Mathematics", says the Commission, "should be compulsory in the first 10 years of schooling." Science teaching should be linked with agriculture in the rural areas and with technology in the urban areas.

(*viii*) The study of Mathematics should be emphasised in view of the importance of qualification on the advent of automation in the scientific and industrial revolution.

(*ix*) Teaching of Social Studies must be made effective for the development of good citizenship and emotional integration. The syllabus in Social Studies must stress the idea of national unity and the unity of man.

(*x*) The three language formula should be modified, and a new plan presented. It suggested that three languages (Mother tongue, Hindi and English) should be studied from class VIII, but, do not on compulsory basis. A classical language also should be introduced on optional basis from class VIII.

(*xi*) Emphasis should be laid on 'Work Experience'. Manual work should be emphasised at all the stages. It may take the form of hand work in lower primary, craft in upper primary, workshop training in lower secondary and experience in school workshop, farm or commercial or industrial establishment at the higher secondary stage.

Suggestions

In addition to the above recommendations, the following are also suggested:

(i) Programme of social service and participation in community development should be organised at all levels as suited to the different age groups.
(ii) Labour and social service camps should be run throughout the year and for this purpose, a special organisation to be set up in each district.
(iii) Physical education should be provided for the physical fitness and efficiency, mental alertness and the development of certain qualities of character. Hence, physical education programme should be re-examined and re-designed.
(iv) Organised attempt should be made for imparting moral education and inculcating spiritual values in schools through direct and indirect methods with the help of the ethical teachings of great religions.
(v) The Government of India should appoint committee of experts to survey the present situation of art education, and explore all possibilities for its extension and systematic development. Art departments should be set up in selected university centres to carry research in art education. A variety of co-curricular activities should be organised to provide pupils an opportunity for creative self-expression.
(vi) The recommendations of the Hansa Mehta Committee should be endorsed that there should be no differentiation of curricula on the basis of sex. Home science should be provided as an optional subject but not made compulsory for girls. Larger provision should be made for music and fine arts, and the study of mathematics and science should be encouraged.

(*vii*) The essential principle of basic education, namely: productive activity, correlation of curriculum with productive activity and environment and contact with local community should guide and shape the educational system at all levels. No single stage of education should be designated as basic education.

National Policy on Education (1968)

The Government of India considered the recommendations of Education Commission and adopted a National Policy on Education in 1968 which identified national goals of education. The policy resolution stated that the educational system must produce young men and women of character and ability committed to national service and development. The following five goals were clearly mentioned:

1. Relating education to the needs of the society.
2. Promotion of national integration.
3. Equalisation of educational opportunity.
4. Linking education with productivity and national development.
5. Acceleration of social transformation.

10+2+3 Pattern

National Policy. A new programme of curriculum development should be undertaken by the adoption of a broadly uniform pattern popularly known as 10+2+3 pattern throughout the country. This pattern meant 10 years of general education followed by diversified 2 years Higher Secondary Education and then 3 years of University Education.

QUESTIONS FOR ANSWER

1. Discuss the meaning and objectives of curriculum.
2. What are the important basis of curriculum? Explain.
3. Write a note on the principles of curriculum construction.

16

Principles of Organising Curricular and Co-Curricular Activities

After formulation of curriculum by the appropriate authority the schools are asked to teach the students accordingly. Since the school functions as a small society, it attempts for mental and physical development of the child. Therefore, there are some basic principles which should guide the schools to organise various curricular and co-curricular activities in the school. These guiding principles, in brief, are given hereunder.

Introduction

In the total programme of education, curricular and co-curricular activities occupy the central place. Curricular and co-curricular activities are complementary to each other. These activities help developing integral human personality. There was a time when the whole purpose of the school was conceived to be confined to the teaching of prescribed syllabi. Activities were regarded as extra or superfluous.

Participation in social and sports activities or outside the class-room activities was looked upon as a mere 'sideshow' or waste of time. It was thought that these activities had no link with the actual teaching programme.

Ever since the advent of modern education the position has changed. Out-of-class activities are no longer 'extra'. They are an integral part of school programme. They are now given the name 'co-curricular' activities and are believed to supplement the class-room work.

Children learn not only in the class-room but also on the playground, in the laboratory, in the library and also through so many informal and formal contacts. It has been rightly recognised that these activities have tremendous educational importance.

Curricular Activities

Activities that are carried out inside the class-room, in the laboratory or in the workshop and have reference to the prescribed courses of study are called 'curricular activities'. These activities are a part of the over-all instructional programme. There is full involvement of the teaching staff in these activities.

Curricular Activities Include

(a) Class-room activities. Such as those related to instruction work in different subjects such as instructional games, class-room experiments, scientific observations, guidance programme, examination and evaluation work, audio-visual education such as making different charts and models, etc.

(b) Activities in the Library. Such as reading books and journals, taking additional notes from library books pertaining to current lessons, making scrap books, making files of newspaper cuttings, etc.

(c) Activities in the Workshop and on the Farm. These activities have reference to various types of 'work-experience' or socially useful productive work.

(d) Activities in the laboratory. Such as those carried out in science laboratories, history room, geography room, language laboratory etc.

The importance of above activities lies in the fact that instructional work in any subject is incomplete without one or all of the above activities.

Co-Curricular Activities

Co-curricular activities are those activities which have indirect reference to actual instructional work that goes on in the class-room. In fact, today, there is only a sharp difference between curricular and co-curricular activities as the latter activities also supplement class-room teaching.

Educational Value of Co-curricular Activities

Co-curricular activities have great educational value. They are important from the following points of view.

1. *Useful in Physical Development*: Co-curricuiar activities, especially the physical activities, help the normal growth and development of the body. The activities like sports, athletics and games lead to the muscular development of students. These develop healthful habits and keep the students physically fit.

2. *Essential for Emotional Development*: These activities meet the psychological needs of pupils and lead to their emotional development. Their instincts are sublimated. Instincts like gregariousness and self-assertion which are so dominant in adolescents, find expression in one activity or the other. The activities also lead to emotional training. The pent-up emotions find effective outlet through the activities.

3. *Help in Social Development:* The co-curricular activities are carried out in social environment. The pupils work together, act together and live together. This helps in socialising the child. They develop social qualities like team .spirit, fellow feeling, cooperation, toleration etc. Activities like scouting first-aid, red cross, community living, shramdan etc. provide complete social training to children.

4. *Useful in Moral Development*: The co-curricular activities have a great moral value. These activities provide opportunities for moral experience and moral conduct. Through sports, the pupils develop sportsmanship. He believes in fair play. While discharging some responsibility, he has to be honest, just and impartial when he has to organise an activity, he develops quality of leadership.

5. *Academic Value*: Co-curricular activities supplement class work. These enrich and widen the bookish knowledge of

students. They get opportunities of observation and experience. For example, a trip or excursion to some important places can add to the knowledge of geography and history. Literary activities can enrich the knowledge of language.

6. *Cultural Value*: There are co-curricular activities which have great cultural value. The activities like dramatics, folkdance, folk music, pageants, variety shows, celebration of social and religious functions etc. provide glimpses of our culture. These activities help in the preservation, transmission and development of our cultural heritage.

7. *Aesthetic and Recreational Value*: The co-curricular activities bring a healthy change in the otherwise dull class-room routtine. The pupils feel relaxed and free when they perform activities like sports, cultural programmes, dances, dramas etc. The activities like drawing, painting, fancy dress, music, fine arts, preparation of models, flower shows etc., develop aesthetic sensibility.

8. *Proper use of leisure time*: Some co-curricular activities help in the proper use of leisure time. For example, crafts, hobbies and other creative activities can be pursued by the students. In the absence of such constructive work, they may pick up some bad habits. An idle brain is a devil's workshop, so goes the maxim.

9. *Training for leadership*: In these activities, the pupils are actively involved. They discharge various responsibilities and therefore, get opportunities to come forward and lead. They get training for leadership. Their talents are recognised and developed.

10. *Disciplinary Value*: The students get a number of opportunities to frame certain rules and regulations concerning activities. They also act according to the rules. They themselves impose restrictions on their freedom. Thus they learn mode of discipline which is self-imposed. They learn to behave with a sense of responsibility. Thus activities make them disciplined.

The Activities that can be Undertaken in the School

1. *Physical Activities*: Games, athletics, mass drill, N.C.C., N.S.S. swimming and boating, yogic exercises, gardening etc.

2. *Social Service Activities*: Scouting, girl guiding, red-cross work, shramdan, rendering social service during social and religious functions etc.

3. *Civic Training Activities*: Visits to civic institutions like the Parliament, municipalities etc. Student councils, student co-operative stores, school, banks, mock parliament, mock courts etc. provide useful civic training.

4. *Literary and Academic Activities:* Debates, group discussions, declamations, symposium, extension lectures, school magazine, wall magazine, recitations etc.

5. *Aesthetic and Cultural Activities:* Music, drama, pageants, folk dance, folk songs, variety shows, fancy dress, flower shows etc.

6. *Leisure-time Activities or Hobbies*: Photography, science, soap-making, clay-modelling, album making, collections of coins, pictures etc.

7. *Miscellaneous Activities:* Projects like running a cooperative store or a cooperative bank, village survey, cleanliness and beautification of school, celebration of social and religious functions, excursions etc.

There cannot be a comprehensive list of all the activities that can be carried out in the school. Every school has to select activities which can be conveniently undertaken with its available material and human resources.

Principles of Organising Activities

A number of principles should be kept in mind while organising these activities:

1. *Proper selection:* The activities should be properly selected keeping in view the level and interests of pupils and available facilities in the school. Educational value of the activity should be the main consideration.

2. *Adjustment in the time-table*: Activities should form an integral part of school programme. There should be activity periods in the time-table. Activities done after the school hours, do not evoke interest in pupils and teachers.

3. *Providing necessary equipment*: No activities can be organised properly without necessary equipment and provisions. The arrangement must be made well in time. Certain materials or equipment may be purchased by the school.

4. *Encouraging pupil participation:* Every effort should be made to encourage pupils to take active part in the school activities. There should be due credit or participation in activities. It may be in the form of prizes, merit certificates or assessment. Pupils should be asked to choose activities of their interest.

5. *Specifying time, date and place:* There should be proper specifications of time and place of an activity. Information regarding these specifications should be given well in advance so that there is sufficient time for preparation.

6. *Providing guidance:* For effective organisation and conduct of activity, the pupils should be properly guided, teachers who are conversant in the activity, should guide the students for successful participation. In the absence of such guidance, the activity may not serve its purpose.

7. *Balancing teacher's work load:* The teachers who are to organise these activities, should not be overburdened with academic work. A teacher who takes active interest in organising the activities, must be given due appreciation and credit.

Co-curricular activities serve their useful purpose, when these are properly organised. This is possible if the headmaster and the teachers are interested in organising these activities. These activities should not be considered extra, but an integral part of curriculum for the complete education of children.

Some Important Activities and Their Organisation

I. School Assembly

In the words of W.R. Smith. "School assembly can, serve as a focussing centre of all forms of extra-curricular life." Every school begins the day's work with a morning assembly wherein the entire school population assembles together for a common prayer or talks from the teacher. School assembly is an important unit and can foster the spirit of co-operation. It is to cultivate group consciousness and espirit de-corps. It promotes school loyalty and a sense of social unity.

In brief, school assembly serves the following purposes:

1. It unifies and integrate the school life. It makes for a common knowledge of rules, customs and traditions which means unification of the school spirit.
2. It facilitates the process of school administration. The headmaster or teachers can address the whole school at one time. Certain rules and regulations can be explained. Besides an announcement about certain programmes can also be made.
3. It offers an opportunity for self expression. The students learn confidence as well. They get training to face the audience, lead the prayer, make announcements, read newspapers etc. They also give brief talks.
4. It serves as a means of propagation of commendable work or established ideals of life.
5. It helps in the development of correct audience habits.

The programme of school assembly should be planned thoughtfully. It should be educational-cum-recreational.

Maximum number of students should be encouraged to participate in the programme. Proper discipline should be maintained. Co-operation of the students should be secured in these activities.

Nothing should be said against the sentiments of any persons or community. Students' goodwill must be won.

2. *Debates and Discussions*

Debates and declamations, discussions and literary activities, are useful in developing expression, oral as well as written. Public speaking and formal debating are the two main forms of oral expression in which systematic training should be given in the schools. Debates are helpful in developing clear, logical and vigorous thinking, in selecting material and organisation of ideas.

Debates and discussions increase the linguistic ability of the participants, enrich their vocabulary, improve their pronunciation and intonation. The speaker learns the art of education and gets training in oratory discussion and argumentation.

The debator has not only to investigate a problem or issue, but he has also to convince the audience about the correctness of his views. Formal debating is a very skilful and difficult art, and those who are successful in mastering it acquire a powerful instrument for influencing and guiding the action of their fellows.

1. Debates should be organised properly. This organisation needs a proper planning.
2. Different aspect concerning debates must be told to the participants well in time.
3. Topics for debates should be selected carefully. They must be interesting.
4. Speakers should be properly guided regarding references and source material. They need help and guidance for organisation and laying stress on a particular point.
5. Cramming up of the written drafts of speeches be discouraged. Students may, however, be instructed to jot down a few points for elaboration.
6. A successful debate depends upon proper style. It is, therefore essential that requisite training in this respect must be provided by the teachers.

It is suggested that the teachers should draw up a list of subjects and guide the speakers in various aspects of debates and discussions. It is desirable to inculcate among the pupils the true spirit of debating so as to produce good speakers, orators and thinkers.

3. Dramatic Activity

Dramatic activity is of great educational value. Dramatic tendency is general among children. It is business of the teachers to utilise it for the development of the individual and for the benefit and pleasure of others.

Dramatic activities provide a catharsis of pent-up emotions and a release from the inhibitions. They also prove a cure for the self-consciousness from which adolescents suffer. They make the participants "natural, spontaneous, and creative human beings."

As a technique of teaching: As a technique of teaching, drama serves a point of correlation for a number of subjects. Dramatic work is significant as it trains the imagination and develops initiative, originality and ingenuity. Experience in dramatisation gives the student greater appreciation of the dramas and discriminating recognition of the artistic and literary value of the best dramas.

It develops habits of poise and self control and thus aids in the development of personality. Dramatic activities also develop an attitude of cooperation. They afford the students opportunities for training in team-work.

Organisation of Dramatic activities: Dramatic activities should be organised properly and with care. The planning and arranging of the stage, and preparation of costumes, will require the cooperation of the pupils, members of the staff and even of parents.

The organisation of these activities requires the services of specialist teachers who are well versed in this art. The play should be selected carefully and must be suitable one possessing educative as well as recreational values. It should be prepared with utmost efforts.

4. Sports, Games and Athletics

Importance and value: In the total programme of co-curricular activities, enjoy the largest measure of popularity. This is mainly due to the strong appeal they make to the instinctive nature of boys as well as of girls.

These activities have a wholesome effect on the physical, mental, social and moral development of the individuals. This means that the activities on the playground go a long way in the development of the personality of the individual.

The playground is said to be the cradle of democracy. It is here that the students learn to work for the good of the whole, and respect the rules of the games. In fact, games provide opportunities for securing mental and moral discipline—the alertness, precision, determination, self control, courage, teamwork, leadership and sportsmanship.

This is also indirectly a step towards character development. In short, games, sports and athletics have great physical, social, moral, recreational and educational values.

Organisation: In view of their immense educational value, these activities should be organised and managed carefully. They should be an integral part of school programme. The possible dangers in the organisation and conduct of these activities resulting from ill-directed or excessive enthusiasm must be checked and avoided. Certain students get undue privileges. There is a vicious exploitation of few talented students and neglect of the many.

The opportunities for athletics should be provided to all pupils desirable to provide each pupil with the opportunity of playing the game in which he is interested and of playing it to the level of his capacity.

The most important thing in the organisation of these activities is proper guidance or control of athletics. The playground is known to be an uncovered school. There must be proper supervision and control of these activities.

For this reason, a D.P.E. or a responsible member of the staff should be present on the playground. A staff advisor for each principal branch of the activities may be appointed. Students must be given facilities with regard to coaching and other needed guidance.

Apart from these factors, due consideration should be given to the following points:

(i) Formation of small groups and teams.
(ii) Preparation of time—schedule of athletics and games, for a particular term.
(iii) Providing necessary equipment in sufficient quality.
(iv) Providing necessary facilities and light refreshment to the pupils.
(v) Arranging necessary guidance and coaching etc.
(vi) Arranging competitions, matches and athletic meets.
(vii) Proper maintenance of playgrounds etc.

The whole programme would be well co-ordinated and should be based on the spirit of amateurism. India needs almost a revolution in this sphere.

5. The Students Council (Bal Sabha)

The students council is an organisation of students, elected by students to serve as their official representative in all matters of concern to the entire school. It provides a medium through which student opinion may be heard and a forum for the consideration of common school problems.

The effective school in a democracy must give its pupils an intelligent understanding of the issues of democracy, make them well disposed toward democracy as a way of life and make them skilful in the cooperative activities through which democracy must function. The need for student council can further be emphasised in the light of the following purposes it serves:

(i) It furnishes citizenship training.
(ii) It gives a knowledge of the theory of democracy by furnishing a working model of government.
(iii) It provides a form for expression of students opinion and also promotes general welfare of the students.
(iv) It allows and prepares students for intelligent participation in managing co-curricular activities and other school affairs, and helps in solving the problems that arise in the school.
(v) It trains students for intelligent respect for law, order and authority.
(vi) It coordinates and regulates school activities.

In every school, student council must be started by extending it full support. Students should elect their class or section representative. Various office bearers to the council are elected by the student representatives in the presence of the school staff. They are assigned different duties. Meetings are arranged from time to time.

Apart from the activities explained above, the following activities also need special care and planning :

1. School Clubs
2. Scouting and Girl Guiding
3. Hobbies—creative and collective
4. Excursions
5. School Magazine and Publications

Conclusion

All the co-curricular activities should be organised in a spirit of devotion. However, these activities should in no way dominate the academic activities. A proper balance has to be maintained. "In the actual working out of these activities—academic, social, practical and sporting, the teacher will find that there are really no right boundary walls between them. Thus by planning a coherent programme on different activities rich in stimuli the school will not be frittering away either the time or the energy of the pupils but will be heightening their intellectual power also side by side by training them in other fine qualities."

QUESTIONS FOR ANSWER

1. "Extra curricular activities no extras but constitute an integral part of school curriculum." Discuss.
2. Discuss the exact role of co-curricular activities. What steps would you take to strengthen the organisation of such activities?

17

Principle of Responsibility—Role of Headmaster/Principal

Effective and efficient conduct of curricular and co-curricular activities in the school primarily depends on two basic pillars of school administration. Therefore, unless the Headmaster and teachers follow the principles concerning their duties and responsibilities the making of the child as per his capabilities will not be possible. In this chapter we are discussing only the duties and responsibilities of the Headmaster/Principal.

Introduction

Principal/Headmaster and teachers constitute the human equipment of a school. A magnificent building, the most ambitious curriculum and most sophisticated material equipment will remain meaningless unless they are given the human touch of an able administrator and his subordinate staff.

Both Principal/headmaster and teachers, by working hand in hand, infuse the real spirit in the otherwise lifeless walls of a school, made of brick and stone. It is the role of headmaster and teachers that will determine the worth—good or otherwise—of a school.

Importance of the Headmaster/Principal

The headmaster occupies an important position in the school.

The total life of the school flows out of his personality. He is the pivot of the school administration. In the words of P.C. Wren, 'What the mainspring is to the watch, the fly-wheel to the machine or the engine to the steamship, the headmaster is to the school." The headmaster is indispensable for the functioning of the school. The administrative machinery of the school runs efficiently only if the headmaster is competent.

W.M. Ryburn has said, "The headmaster holds the key position in a school just as the captain of a ship holds the key position on a ship." The success or failure of a school depends on the headmaster.

Dr. Jaswant Singh has aptly remarked, "The headmaster or the principal of a school is the hub of the educational process. On his ability and skill, as a sound and effective educational leader, depends the success of a school system."

The school is the lengthened shadow of the headmaster. He is the seal and the school is the wax. Everything in the school, the teacher, the pupils, the curricular activities, school plant etc. bear the impress of the personality of the headmaster. Suppose there is a school in which the teachers and the pupils pay attention to their work properly. Co-curricular activities are well organised.

The parents of children are satisfied with the type of education provided in the school. Naturally the image of the school will be raised because it is headed by a good principal or headmaster. On the other hand, if there is indiscipline in a school and the pupils and the teachers do not attend to their work properly, parents come to school with certain complaints, this means something is wrong with the administrator.

The headmaster of the school is not competent. Thus we see that the working of a school depends upon the quality and competence of the headmaster. He can make or mar the fair name of the institution.

The Secondary Education Commission has expressed the opinion: "On him the proper working of the school ultimately depends. The reputation of the school and the position that it holds in the society depends in a large measure on the influence that he exercises over his colleagues, his pupils and the general public."

Thus we see that a good school must have a good headmaster or a good headmaster makes a good school. The headmaster must possess certain qualities of head and heart which may be mentioned as under:

Qualities of Headmaster/Principal

1. *Sound philosophy of life:* The headmaster must have a sound philosophy of life. He should have some desirable principle of life. He should be a practical moralist. He must not be led away by temptations, prejudices etc. His personality will radiate the whole school atmosphere.

2. *Sound philosophy of education:* The headmaster must keep himself abreast of the latest educational thought and practice. He must know the objectives of education well and conform his educational practices accordingly. Only such a headmaster can raise the educational standard of the school.

3. *Leadership quality:* The headmaster must possess initiative and leadership quality. He is required to lead the teachers, the pupils, the parents and the high authorities.

4. *Administrative and organising ability:* The headmaster must have good administrative and organising ability. He must know how to organise each and every item in the school. He should know the problems of teachers and students, faced by them in the class-room, laboratory, library, playground etc. So to say, he must have professional insight and experience. He should develop a healthy administrative policy of the school.

5. *General Scholarship:* The headmaster must be head and shoulders above the members of the faculty, so far as general scholarship is concerned. The teachers and the pupils look to him for guidance and he must be in a position to provide the needed guidance. For that, he should himself be well informed.

6. *A Good teacher*: A headmaster must be good at teaching. He should have proficiency in the teaching skills. His teaching should be exemplary and source of inspiration for the teachers. A headmaster who is a poor teacher himself, cannot urge other teachers to teach well.

7. *Good health*: The headmaster's job is quite strenuous. He has to deal with all sorts of problems of the school daily. His energy is constantly consumed. Dr. Jaswant Singh has aptly said, "The job of the Headmaster is fairly arduous and

taxing. A person with indifferent health and poor stamina will not be able to hold his own or successfully discharge the multifarious and heavy responsibilities of this office. He must, therefore, take immediate steps to make up the deficiency in his health and evolve a daily routine which would ensure required physical efficiency."

8. Broad vision: The headmaster must rise above the narrow barriers of castes, creeds, religions, regions, languages etc. He should not have prejudices against individuals having different faiths. He must treat all the teachers alike.

9. Sense of dedication: The headmaster has to deal with various types of persons daily—the teachers, the pupils and their parents, the general public, the inspectors and supervisors etc. He must be able to maintain good relations with everybody. He must have sociable nature.

10. Judgement and decision: The headmaster must have good judgement and decisive nature. He should be able to take wise decisions. He should be quick in judgment and must not remain in a state of indecision.

11. Punctual and regular: The headmaster must be regular and punctual in his school duties if he wants the teachers and the pupils to be so. He should regularly attend to various aspects of administrative and organisational work.

12. Progressive nature: The headmaster must be progressive-minded. He should be receptive to new ideas. He should attend educational conferences, workshops, refresher courses etc. He should also visit good schools. Prominent educationists may also be invited to the institution.

13. Democratic Nature: The Headmaster must have democratic nature. He should not be an autocratic leader. He should take decisions after consulting the staff, the pupils and all concerned with school. A democratic leader is also a good follower. He will allow the other experienced person to lead in certain situations.

Role of Headmaster/Principal

The head of a school has to perform multifarious duties and responsibilities. He is responsible for anything and everything going on in the school. He has to deal with teachers, students and their parents, general public. He has to plan, organise and supervise the smooth running of the most important functions of the headmaster.

1. Role in Planning

Planning is the first and foremost duty of the head of a school. He has to plan a number of things in the school, with the cooperation of the teachers, the pupils, the parents and general public. Planning goes on throughout the year. It consists of the following phases.

(i) Planning before the opening of the school: The headmaster has to plan a number of things before the opening of the school. He should chalk out the policies and rules of admission. Dates of admission are to be publicized. He should convene the meetings of the staff and discuss with the teachers the activities and programmes for the whole year. Thus the school calendar may be prepared in advance. In case of need, fresh staff will be recruited before the actual functioning of the school. The headmaster must also check that the whole school plant is in fine shape, and the equipment is adequate. He must also see that various registers needed for different purposes are there in the school.

(ii) Planning during the first week: In the beginning the headmaster has to set the school machinery into motion. Work allotment to the teachers is an important function of the headmaster. He should urge the teachers to balance class-sizes and classify the students into suitable groups or sections.

Preparation of time table—general, teacherswise and classwise is another important thing to be done. Unless the time-table is prepared, school work cannot be started. General assembly of the students may be convened and instructions be given to the students. The prescribed text-books are to be announced.

(iii) Planning during the year: As the classes start, the headmaster starts attending to the activities and programmes mentioned in the school calendar. Detailed planning of each activity is to be done. The headmaster has to prepare the budget of the year, keeping in view the estimated expenditure in the session.

(iv) Planning at the end of the year: The headmaster will ask the teacher to prepare reports of the activities done during the year. Various records have to be completed. Holding of valedictory and annual functions has to be planned.

(v) Planning of the next year: The headmaster should convene staff meetings and appraise year's work. In the light of this appraisal, next year's work has to be planned.

2. *Role in School Organisation*

The headmaster is not to plan things theoretically; he is to give them a practical shape. In this regard, the must organise the following items:

1. *Organising instructional work*: The head of a school must organise the instructional work. He will ask the teacher to divide the year's work into smaller units. This will also involve the formulation of objectives, selection of methods of teaching, classification of pupils, framing of time-table.

2. *Organising school office*: The office work must also be properly organised. Routine work, registration, correspondence, maintenance of accounts etc. have to be organised so that office work is done regularly and efficiently.

3. *Organising co-curricular activities*: The headmaster must organise the activities of the school, with the cooperation of staff and students. There can be so many school activities like sports, scouting, girl-guiding, red-cross, parent-teacher association, celebrations of religious and social functions and festivals etc.

4. *Organising school upkeep*: The headmaster is to organise the school plant so that it is properly maintained, equipped and put to maximum use. Classroom, library, laboratory etc. are to be well furnished. Repairs may be done wherever needed.

3. *Role in Supervision*

The head of a school should not simply remain sitting in his office. He should supervise the working of the school, here, there and everywhere. He should supervise instructional work. He may have a round of the class-rooms. However, it is not to be a fault-finding business. The headmaster should supervise the activities going on in the playground, hall, art-room, library, workshop etc. He must supervise the proper use and upkeep of school materials. In general, he should supervise the behaviour of students, provide facilities for them, maintain cleanliness of the campus etc.

4. *Teaching Role*

The headmaster must share instructional work with the teachers. He should consider himself teacher first and teacher last. His teaching should be exemplary. This way he will also keep in touch with the work of the teachers and the achievements of students. The headmaster will understand the problems of the teachers and the pupils better—when he himself teaches.

5. *Role in Guidance*

The headmaster is not simply a fault-finder. Wherever he finds defects, errors and inefficiency, he should show the correct path. He must guide the teachers in the methods of teaching and organisation of activities. Students are to be guided in matters of study, activities and personal difficulties. A guidance cell may be organised in the school. Besides, the headmaster is to guide parents, higher authorities etc.

6. *Role in General Administration*

As the head of the school, the headmaster is responsible for all that is being done in or by the school. He is to issue necessary orders and get their compliance. He must see that the teachers and the pupils attend to their duties punctually and regularly. He must ensure that human and material resources of the school are adequate. Purchases should be made wherever needed, in accordance with the prescribed rules. He is responsible for the maintenance of accounts and submitting official information and correspondence.

7. *Role in Maintaining Relations*

The reputation of the headmaster and of the school mostly

depends upon the relations that he maintains with the staff, students and their parents and the community.

(i) Relation with the staff: The head of a school must work in a team spirit and he should regard the teachers as his co-workers He should not have bossing tendency. He must give due regard to the teachers, their views and their problems.

(ii) Relations with the pupils: "Great headmasters have been great friends of pupils." The headmaster should think that the teachers, the school and he himself, all are meant for the pupils. He must listen to their genuine difficulties and try to remove the same. He must provide proper facilities for their learning.

(iii) Relations with the parents: The headmaster must maintain link of the parents with the school. They may be invited to the school on important occasions. He should organise parent-teacher organization in the school. When the parents come to school they should be treated with courtesy and be given due respect.

(iv) Relation with the Community: The school is meant for the community and must be made a community centre. A number of community activities may be launched by the school. Community members may also be invited to the school on certain occasions.

QUESTIONS FOR ANSWER

1. "Principal/Headmaster is the leader of the school on whose guidance depends the effectiveness of the school teaching." Justify.
2. What are the functions of the Head of school? Select any one function and describe how it can be performed effectively?
3. "A good headmaster is not merely a good administrator." Discuss and explain what additional qualifications the head of school should possess?
4. "On him the proper working of the school ultimately depends. The reputation of the school and the position that he holds in the society depends in a large measure on the influence that he exercises over his colleagues, his pupils and the general public." Comment upon the above view of Secondary Education Commission.
5. Draw a pen-picture of your favourite headmaster, how he ran the school successfully.

18

Principle of Responsibility—Role of the Teacher

The teacher constitutes the human equipment of a school and he is rightly termed as the architect of educational system and master of child's testing. He is mirror of the society and nation builder. Therefore, there is a paramount need of good teachers for the good of the society and the nation. Hereunder we are discussing the importance, qualifications, qualities and role of the teacher and in the next chapter we will discuss the training and authority etc. aspect of a good teacher.

Importance

The teacher is of a paramount importance in the teaching-learning process. The teacher is the pivot in any system of education. The whole system of education revolves around the teacher. He is the person upon whom depend all the activities of the school. The importance of school building, school furniture and equipment, curriculum, the text books etc., cannot be denied. But, without the teacher, they are all meaningless. It is not the school-building and the equipment, but teachers which make a school.

Teaching is a tri-polar process. It has three indispensable constituents—the teacher, the taught, and the curriculum. Of these three, teacher is undoubtedly the most important, because, it is the teacher who is set in motion in process of teaching.

But, it is not simply the teacher, but rather good teachers that are required. Thus, there is a need of really good teachers. In this connection, Dr. E.A. Pire says, "If a nation's teachers are C3, the nation itself cannot but be C3, and let there be no doubt about this— if we wish to be an A-1 nation, our teachers will have to be A-1."

The importance of good teachers is emphasised by Prof. Humayun Kabir by saying: "Without good teachers, even the best of system is bound to fail. With good teachers, even the defects of the system can be largely overcome.

The importance of the teacher is also highlighted by the Secondary Education Commission in the following words : "We are, however, convinced that the most important factor in the contemplated educational reconstruction is the teacher—his personal qualities, his educational qualifications, his professional training and the place he occupies in the school as well as in the community."

The reputation of a school and its influence on the life of the community invariably depends on the kind of teachers working in it. Thus, the need of really good and competent teachers cannot be over-emphasised.

In the words of Kothari Education Commission 1964-66, 'Of all the different factors which influence the quality of education, and in contribution to material development, the quality, competence and character of teacher are undoubtedly the most significant.'

Qualifications/Qualities

The teacher plays an important role in the school. He is not simply to impart knowledge but also mould the habits, tastes and character of pupils. He is to achieve educational objectives through the curriculum of the school. In order to discharge his duties effectively, he must possess certain qualities and qualifications which may be described as under:

1. General Academic Background.
2. Professional efficiency.
3. Personality traits.

1. *General Academic Background:* The teacher must have academic qualifications as per government order for the post

on which he is appointed. The teacher is required to answer questions which require a fair command of the subject. He should have sufficient knowledge so far as the pupils are concerned. That is why minimum qualifications are laid down for the recruitment of teachers in schools.

For primary school, the teacher should be at least matriculate. For high schools, the teacher should be at least graduate. For secondary classes, he should be an M.A. In addition to the knowledge of his subject, he should have sufficient addition to the knowledge of his subject, he should have sufficient general knowledge. For that, he should have literary tastes. He must be a well read person. He should be trained in teaching.

2. *Professional Efficiency:* Knowledge of the subject matter is not sufficient to be a good teacher. A first rate scholar may be a poor teacher. He must have some pre-service training, so that he is conversant with the ins and outs of teaching. While in service, he should attend short-term refresher courses, workshops, seminars and educational conferences so that he goes on adding to his professional efficiency.

The teacher should have a sense of dedication to the teaching profession. He should relish teaching and teach enthusiastically. Teacher's enthusiasm, professional insight and sense of dedication are his valuable assets.

3. *Personality Trails*: Teacher's personality traits have deep impact on the pupils. The following traits in the teacher are worth mentioning here:

(i) *Love for children:* The teacher must love his pupils. He must understand them individually and try to help them overcome their difficulties. His attitude should be sympathetic and friendly.

(ii) *A man of character:* The teacher should have high moral character. He should have sound principles of life. His ideas and conduct will affect the children profoundly.

(iii) *Emotionally stable*: The teacher must be emotionally stable. He must be free from complexes, worries and frustration. An emotionally unstable teacher cannot do justice to his work.

(iv) *Good expression:* The teacher must be able to express his thoughts clearly. His oral and written expression must be good. He has to write reports and so many other things. His speech, pronunciation and voice must also be impressive.

(v) *Sense of Humour:* While in the school, the teacher should have a smiling face. He should have a cheerful look while teaching. His sense of humour will help him overcome very serious situations, which can be sometimes laughed away.

(vi) *Social Traits:* The teacher should have a sociable nature. He must maintain good relations with his colleagues, pupils and their parents and general public. He must be able to mix well with people. Only then he will be able to develop social virtues in the students.

(vii) *Leadership quality*: The teacher should be able to provide effective leadership to the children who are immature and need guidance in matters of study, activities, courses etc.

Role/Functions of Teacher

Teaching is a complicated job. It is not mere communication of knowledge to the students. Even knowledge cannot be handed over to students like currency. The teacher has to attend to a number of factors while working in the school. Some of his functions may be discussed as under :

1. *Role in Teaching:* Teaching is the first and foremost duty of the teacher. The teacher should prepare his lessons regularly. He must motivate the pupils and use methods and techniques of teaching suitable for a particular group of students. He must always try to improve his teaching skill. He should give regular home work and correct it regularly. Activities on the part of pupils should be properly stimulated and directed.

2. *Role in Planning:* In order to be a successful teacher, the teacher must plan his work well. At the first place, he should plan his teaching work. He should decide how much work is to be done in a particular month and in a particular week. Daily teaching work must also be planned. He should

plan the use of teaching aids in advance. Activities of the pupils are also to be planned by him.

3. *Role in Organising:* The teacher has to organise a number of things in the school. He has to organise the school plant. He should see that the class-rooms are well-equipped. He is to make seating arrangements, distribute equipment and attend to its proper up-keep. He has to organise instructional work, dividing the syllabus into units, classification of students, construction of time-table and co-curricular activities are also to be organised. Library work, laboratory work, sports etc. need proper organisation.

4. *Role in Supervising:* The teacher has to supervise a number of tasks and activities. He is required to supervise attendance of pupils, their daily work, home work, their work habits and behaviour. He has to maintain order and discipline in the school. He may have to supervise pupils in the hostel.

5. *Role in Guiding:* The teacher is not to simply supervise pupils and their work but also he is to give suggestions and guide them. Pupils need his guidance in matters of study, activities, selection of courses etc. Pupils' study habits and work habits have to be guided properly. He must pay attention to all children, particularly to the delinquent, abnormal and mal-adjusted children. Guidance in health matters is also to be given.

6. *Role in Evaluating*: Work of the pupils and their participation should be evaluated by the teacher from time to time. It is evaluation which will throw light on teacher's work and pupils achievement. Evaluation will point out weaknesses in the teaching and learning process and the teacher can adopt suitable remedial measures. The teacher has to conduct house tests and report the progress of pupils to parents and the headmaster, policies of promotion have to be chalked out in the light of evaluation.

7. *Role in Recording*: The teacher has to maintain record of pupils' achievement in different subjects and activities. Also he has to record their admission, attendance, their score in different tests, realisation of fee etc. The teacher may also be required to maintain school records such as property register, supply of equipment, issue of books etc. He is also to write annual reports of various activities and functions done during the year.

8. Role in Maintaining Relations: It is the duty of the teacher to maintain good relations with the pupils, their parents and general public. For this purpose, parents-teacher association may be organised by the teacher. The relationship with parents will solve many problems. The teacher must have healthy and cordial relations with the headmaster and his colleagues. For all this, the teacher should have a sociable nature.

QUESTIONS FOR ANSWER

1. Discuss the various functions of a teacher. What should he do and bear in mind in order to become a successful teacher?
2. Being the headmaster of a secondary school what general principles will you follow in staffing your school?
3. What is the importance of a staff council in the school? How can it be organised effectively ?
4. "All the recommendations for the improvement of education are meaning-less unless right type of teachers are recruited."
5. If you are responsible for the selection of teachers for a Higher Secondary School, what qualifications and qualities would you look for in the candidates for positions in your school?
6. A teacher requires much more than merely the mastery in the technique of teaching. Discuss.

19

Principles Governing the Authority of the Teacher

Introduction

During schools hours the child is handed over to the care of the teacher, who is not only responsible for giving instruction, but also stands in *loco parentis* in the regulation of the child's conduct. Precisely how far the school-master's authority shall in certain respects extend, is partly a matter of law and custom, and so varies from country to country and from age to age.

The educator himself must inevitably, according to a principle which prevails not less in the moral than in the intellectual sphere, represent concretely what will later take on a more abstract form. The educator, whether parent or teacher, stands provisionally as the source of moral law and of moral sanctions.

The authority thus vested in the teacher has to be exercised by him with a view to moderating the spirit of disorder. The elements of that spirit exist, as we have seen, in certain of the child's native impulses; impulses which, though they do not point to a vicious disposition, since they do not issue from a bad will, would still, if allowed to run riot, place an effective check upon the educative influence of instruction and guidance.

When, however, we speak of introducing the spirit of order into the child's life, we must not be understood to mean that he should be reduced to a state of dumb, abject submission. The sort of order aimed at should be just that which is necessary to make the work of instruction proceed smoothly, and to render operative the silent influence of the teacher's personality, for, beyond this point, order becomes stagnation, if not something worse. It now remains for us to examine those measures to which the teacher may resort in curbing the wider and more impetuous of the child's propensities.

What we have to aim at, then, in our direct efforts towards the formation of character is, in the first place, to train the child to good habits, among which the habit of obedience must take high rank, for, as Miss Martineau says, this is a necessary preliminary to the formation of all other habits; and, in the second place, to give the child as many opportunities as he can bear of choosing for himself between alternative courses of action in order that he may be trained to act rightly in the more complex situations of life.

Now, as we have seen, the raw material of voluntary action lies in certain native and instinctive tendencies which do not at the outset possess any moral quality at all. To the inexperienced and untrained child, there is no reason why asking should be preferable to seizing or snatching, eating plain food to eating sweetmeats, taking his own to taking another's, neatness to untidiness, order to disorder, knowledge to ignorance. His impulsive tendencies are at least as likely to lead him wrong as right.

Hence the necessity, in the early years, of imposing our will upon him, of keeping him on the straight path by the exercise of arbitrary authority and by insistence upon obedience. The native impulses must be transformed into desirable habits, though the process may, at times, be somewhat meaningless and unpleasing to the child himself.

The above discussion makes it very clear that the teacher owns the responsibility to help the child to form desirable habits and good character and for this purpose he should be trained while he does his teacher's training course. This aspect of his knowledge is of moral nature, rather being a part of his theory curriculum for the degree of B. Ed. or M. Ed. This practical aspect of his moral knowledge will make him real teacher to exercise his authority as a teacher. Hereunder, we discuss some of the aspects concerning the authority of the teacher while guiding the child.

Rule of Control

1. First among these we may place the expedient of keeping the child well and suitably occupied. There is much wisdom in the saying, "Satan finds some mischief still for idle hands to do." Incessant activity is a law of the child's being; and the first requisite of a wise system of control is that this activity should be directed into desirable channels. Prevention is here certainly better than cure.

2. Another requisite of a good system of government is that he who governs should be a vigilant observer of his charges. "Begin betimes," says the sagacious Locke, "nicely to observe your son's temper, and that when he is least under restraint, in his play, and, as he thinks, out of your sight.

See what are his predominant passions and prevailing inclinations; whether he be fierce or mild, bold or bashful, compassionate or cruel, open or reserved, etc. For as these are different in him so are your methods to be different and your authority must hence take measures to apply itself in different ways to him." And as with the parent so with the teacher. No teacher can study too carefully or can know too well the individual characters of his pupils.

How far he should by his interference make the children aware of his watchfulness is another question. Under some circumstances when, for example, a child is exceptionally turbulent, or snows signs of developing a grave moral fault—it is no doubt well that he should know that a vigilant eye is upon him.

3. But when all is done that can be done to keep the child well occupied, and to keep a watchful eye upon him, occasions will inevitably arise when the educator must issue definite and specific commands. These occasions will be numerous in the early stages, but should gradually become fewer as the years advance.

First, let commands be limited to the smallest possible number. The teacher or parent who is continually giving minute directions about the smallest details of the child's conduct is simply reducing the latter to a condition of moral helplessness.

Secondly, it follows from the above that it is a bad plan to repeat one's commands unnecessarily. To give an order once should be enough: frequently to give it a second time is to lead the child to expect the repetition, and to beget a habit of hesitating obedience.

Thirdly, having reduced our commands to the smallest possible number, we must next see to it that when we do command, we do so with firmness and decision.

The educator who would gain obedience must show that he expects it, and that the possibility of its contrary is in his view so remote as not to have entered into his calculations.

Fourthly, firmness and decision in giving an order must be held to imply that the order has been properly considered before being given. In most cases, the teacher will be so sure of his ground that hardly a moment's thought, if any at all, will be necessary; but when the circumstances are unusual they should be carefully weighed before the decisive step is taken. It is demoralising to have to revise or cancel one's command.

Fifthly, let a command assume the positive rather than the negative form. "Do" is a far better word of command than "don't" especially when the latter anticipates an act that may never have been performed at all.

Sixthly, as corollary to our first maxim, that commands should not descend to unnecessary detail, we may add that they should be general rather than particular. Some children who were visiting a relative were informed by the latter that there were certain faults which she could not tolerate, among which were, untruthfulness, disobedience, untidiness, and so on.

When the children on their return home repeated this to their in mother, she quietly replied: "That is all very right and proper, but if you make sure of one thing it will save you from all these faults; in all you do, be sensible."

There is a world and wisdom in this simple saying. As far as possible and as soon as possible, our multitudinous special requirements—speak the truth, don't take what is not your own, be clean and tidy, don't speak rudely, don't plant your elbows on the table or put your knife in your mouth—should all be merged in one demand: act with good sense.

4. A rule of conduct is a sort of permanent command; it is a standing order of the home or school authority. The same remarks that have been made concerning commands apply therefore to rules. They should be as few as possible, indicating, not all that is expected of the child, but only what is required in certain cases where misunderstanding is likely to arise.

They should, moreover, be well thought out beforehand, and then expressed with perfect clearness. Under these conditions, the rules of a school may well promote the ends of good government. It should always be remembered, however, that the purpose of rules is the ultimate abolition of rules.

Punishment

The measures of control we have so far considered are all of the preventive sort. We now pass to those repressive measures summed up in the word punishment. A punishment we take to mean the intentional infliction of pain of some sort, as a consequence of some special offence against the laws, written or unwritten, of a school or other community. In a school it may take the negative form of withholding some expected pleasure; or one of various positive forms, such as the imposition of tasks and bodily chastisement.

Punishment is a bad thing; since it tends to weaken the bond of sympathy between teacher and pupil, parent and child. It is the last resort of flouted authority.

Frequent punishment is therefore a sign of weak government. When all other means often fail, the reason must be that those other means are feebly or fitfully exercised.

Three views are commonly put forward as to the proper aim of punishment: (1) the preventive, deterrent, or exemplary; (2) the corrective or reformative; and (3) the retributive. According to the first the purpose of punishment is to deter others from committing a like offence; according to the second, it is to reform the offender; and according to the third, it is to cause the offence to recoil upon the offender's own head.

From the educator's standpoint, too, there are elements of truth in every one of the three views above enunciated, though he will place the stress differently. His prime object is doubtless the reformation of the offender. But if the offender is a member of a school society, where order has to be maintained and work carried on, the educator will look also to the deterrent function of the punishment.

This idea must not, however, be pressed too far; since "making an example" of a pupil may easily lead the teacher to the infliction of punishments quite out of proportion to the offence. The reformative and preventive views must, in short, be supplemented by the retributive.

The law of the school society has been broken, and must be vindicated; and this vindication, if it be effected by a punishment suitable in kind and degree, will tend at the same time to reformation and prevention.

But what is the test of the suitability of punishment? Rousseau declared "that punishment must never be inflicted on children as punishment, but that it ought always to come to them as the natural consequences of their bad acts." and Spencer in his well-known essay on "Moral Education," works out this thesis with all his accustomed vigour of expression and felicity of illustration.

Spencer points out that the child who thrusts his finger into a candle-flame, or runs his head against the table, has been taught by Nature a lesson that he is not likely to forget. It is characteristic, he proceeds, of Nature's lessons that they directly connect right-doing with pleasure, and wrong doing with pain.

He infers that parents and teachers should take a leaf out of Nature's book, instead of constituting themselves Nature's proxies; in other words, that punishments should be the "natural" outcome of offences.

If the child persists in making a litter, he must be refused his toys; it he is habitually late for his walk, he must be left at home; if he breaks or loses his toy or his knife, he must suffer the inconvenience of doing without it. When we come to more serious offences, Spencer seems to admit that the difficulties are greater, but he argues that they are not insuperable. The natural consequences of a theft, for example, are of two kinds, direct and indirect; the direct consequence is that of making restitution, and the indirect and more serious consequence is the grave displeasure of parents.

In estimating the value of this theory, we observe, in the first place, that the advantages it attributes to Nature's punishments are by no means so evident as we are led to suppose.

After all, however, this is only one of several conditions which a well-devised system of punishments ought to fulfil. These conditions, so far as they affect public legislation, have been stated once for all by Bentham, and as some of his canons are equally applicable to school and family government, a summary of them will not be amiss.

First, punishments should be proportionate to the offence, and to this end they should be susceptible of degrees of intensity and duration; moreover, a fixed punishment for a given offence is not altogether wise, since the circumstances of the act and the sensitiveness of the culprit are varying factors.

Our discussion of the canons of effective punishment naturally leads us to consider the various forms of punishment which have become customary in schools. Some of these involve a greater or less degree of shame of disgrace, whilst others carry with them, in addition, some amount of bodily pain or discomfort.

Simple reproof should be sufficient in the vast majority of cases, where healthy relations exist between teacher and taught; and it is a great part of good government to know exactly when and how to use this weapon. That fine tact and discrimination are needed is clear, since a rebuke may assume any form, a mild word or even a slightly altered manner, to the severest public "wigging".

Being compelled to assume a position or posture of disgrace is an effective punishment for refractory members of junior classes. Provided the frequent use of coarser measures has not dulled his sensibility to the lighter penalties, a young pupil will sufficiently feel the disgrace of being made to stand on a bench etc.

The system of marks for conduct, taking the form either of deducting good marks or giving bad ones, is employed by some teachers. Satisfactory results are said to have been obtained by crediting each pupil with a certain number of marks at the beginning of the term, from which deductions are made for misbehaviour.

Detention after school hours, or during recess, is applicable to a large number of the common faults of schoolboys, and seems to satisfy most of the conditions of effective and suitable punishment, except that, since it necessarily involves careful supervision, it is apt to be inconvenient to the teacher himself.

Compulsory stillness and silence during the period of detention is the "characteristical" penalty for unlawful whispering and talking; whereas unpunctuality and laziness (which, however, usually means being busily engaged upon the wrong thing) will be most suitably met by requiring the defaulter to make up the lost ground.

The subject of fines as a mode of school punishment need not detain us. The authenticated story of the girls who occasionally resolved to "have three penny worth" of conversation at prohibited times will serve in place of a serious discussion.

We come now to the vexed question of corporal punishment. In discussing this it will be well to clear the ground by pointing out that the savage and vindictive castigations, so common in the not remote past, are now by universal consent abandoned.

The Rewards

The subject of punishment naturally suggests that of rewards. As punishment is the deliberate infliction of pain for special demerit, so is a reward the giving of pleasure for special merit. Of course, the chief reward of all, a still and quiet conscience, comes without our intervention.

The rewards commonly bestowed fall roughly into two classes—those which do and those which do not take a material shape. Of the former gifts of books and of money are the usual types; whilst the latter may take the form of praise, or of marks for good conduct or meritorious work, or of more or less important positions of honour and trust.

It is sometimes objected to all rewards that, appealing as they do to the ambitious impulses, they lead to jealous rivalry; that they substitute a lower for a higher motive; that they "make a merit of superior natural gifts"; arid that in any case they can influence only the few who have the greatest chance of obtaining them.

To the first objection it may be replied that the ambitious impulses have their good as well as their bad side; and that the instinctive desire to excel, provided it be kept within moderate limits, may surely be as harmless a spur to success during school life as it undoubtedly may become in after years.

The second objection, that an inferior is substituted for the best motive, must be allowed. But the whole theory and practice of the exercise of authority rests upon the patent fact that the highest motive is not always available.

The wheels of school life would certainly run smoothly, if every child were prompted by an inner sense of duty to habits of neatness and punctuality and industry.

The cardinal principle of any good system of rewards is that it should not serve the merely temporary purpose of securing good conduct on a particular occasion, but that it should take account of permanent effects on character: in other words, a reward should be an instrument not only of government and control, but also of training.

It follows that a reward should generally be given for a prolonged series of efforts rather than for any particular performance; and, as a consequence of this, that rewards should not be common, but should be reserved for instances of signal merit.

In conclusion, let us apply these canons to the different forms of reward most commonly adopted. Praise is the readiest and the most delicate instrument at the teacher's disposal, and upon its wise employment his success greatly depends. If he never bestows praise, he sacrifices a valuable asset.

It is a patent fact that supervision, commands and rules, rewards and punishments, are instruments whose value varies greatly according to the person who employs them.

QUESTIONS FOR ANSWER

1. Write a note on the factors which are expedient for keeping the child well and suitably occupied.
2. Write a note on the theories of punishment which may be followed in the school.
3. "Reward means giving the pleasure for special merit." Write a note on the importance of reward in the schools.

20

Principle of Assessing Student's Progress—The Cumulative Record Card

Assessment of student's progress as important as effective and efficient teaching and conduct of all curricular and co-curricular activities by the school administration—the principal/ headmaster and teachers in particular with judicious exercise of authority. The most modern method of assessing student's progress is ensure proper care to keep record of his educational achievements as well as his personality traits.

Hereunder, we will discuss various aspects concerning cumulative recordcard, which with due care would give clear picture of students's progress.

Cumulative Record Card

Cumulative Record Card is one of the modern evaluative devices. It is that card which contains the results of different assessments and judgements held from time to time during the course of study of a student. It is an evaluation tool which presents a comprehensive record of the achievements or otherwise of each student. A school which keeps adequate record of the educational progress of each student, his personality traits and his academic achievement, will find that evaluation of a student's status at any particular time is made easier and richer than it could otherwise be.

Importance of CRC

The CRC of a student is needed for the following important points:

1. To give a complete picture of a pupil's all-round progress.
2. To know the child, his potentialities, talents, interests, growth of personality through successive stages, his achievements in different fields etc.
3. To give proper guidance to the teachers, headmasters, administrators, parents as regards the important aspects of the students curricular and co-curricular life.
4. To facilitate the process of internal assessment of pupils.
5. To help parents and teachers in deciding the course of studies for their wards at the crucial secondary school stage.
6. To help parents and teachers in the after-school placement of pupils.

How to Gather Material for CRC?

There are numerous ways of gathering information and material about pupils for onward incorporation in the CRC. A list of means might well include the following:

1. Autobiographical information
2. Health records
3. Standardised Test Results
4. School Grades
5. Anecdotal Records
6. Teacher's Notes
7. Notation of Parent Conferences.

All this vital information tells a story and provides data for understanding a pupil's potential and his progress as well as strong and weak points of his physical, mental, social and emotional behaviour and capabilities. Thus the CRC becomes the centre of information for teacher's study.

Contents of a CRC

A Cumulative Record Card actually contains the following information:

1. Personal data
2. Information about home circumstances
3. Health information
4. Psychological report
5. Scholastic achievement
6. Performance in co-curricular Activities
7. Educational and Vocational Plan
8. Personality characteristics
9. General over-all Remarks

Specimen Form of Cumulative Record

Below we reproduce the specimen form of Cumulative Record as suggested by the Secondary Education Commission (1953):

Name of Pupil
Date of Birth
Name of Parent
Occupation
Address of Parent or Guardian
School History
Names of schools studied...year...Reason for Transfer
Family History: Position of the child in family
Family Discipline
Home circumstances
Pupil's Ambitions
Parent's desire regarding career

A. Scholastic Attainments

Subjects	*Grade/Marks*
1. First Language	
2. Second Language	
3. English	
4. Mathematics	
5. Science	
6. Social Studies	
7. Bifurcated course	

B. Activities, Practical

1. Craft
   - (*a*) Turnover
   - (*b*) Craftsmanship
   - (*c*) Application

   Total Grading
2. Social and Citizen Activities
   - (*a*) Collections
   - (*b*) Expression
   - (*c*) Service
   - (*d*) Proficiency batches
   - (*e*) Team spirit — Total Grading
3. Physical Education
   - (*a*) Physical efficiency
   - (*b*) Participation in Games etc. — Total Grading
4. Drawing and Painting
   - (*a*) Technique
   - (*b*) Expression
   - (*c*) Originality — Total Grading
5. Music
6. Dancing

C. Health Report

Height
Weight
Chest Expanded......... Normal ......Contracted
Medical Officer's Report

D. Personality Traits

Initiative
Integrity
Persistence
Leadership
Self-confidence
Emotional control
Social Attitude

E. General Remarks

1. Position of responsibility held
2. Special remarks, if any
3. Signature of class teacher
4. Signature of headmaster.

It is important to note that a CRC must contain items of factual information about the pupils. This device should be used by all schools with a view to eliminating progressively the annual promotion examination. It is suggested that 25 per cent of the total number of marks in each subject should be allotted to the assessment of the candidate's performance as given in his school record.

Maintenance of Cumulative Records

The following points should be noted in this regard:

(*a*) The teachers incharge of various activities or teaching various subjects should maintain the records after periodical assessment of pupils.

(*b*) The class teacher will maintain the file containing the record cards of all the students. He will be responsible for getting necessary entries made.

(*c*) CRC of each pupil will remain with the class teacher. However, it should be easily accessible to the other teachers whenever they want to make entries.

(*d*) The teachers should make regular entries in the columns of the forms at the time of a particular event or test. Record of written work may be kept by the teacher and entries made for fortnightly and monthly.

QUESTIONS FOR ANSWER

1. Discuss various sections of a Cumulative Record Card.
2. "A Cumulative Record Card is a mirror of student's academic as well as co-curricular progress." Discuss.
3. What is Cumulative Record Card? Why it should be maintained?
4. Write a note on the need of Cumulative Record Card.
5. Discuss the contents of Cumulative Record Card.

21

Principle of Social Control

Control of the society over the individual is a must to control his undesirable and harmful tendencies. Therefore, as a matter of principle education must infuse in the individual a sense of respect for social control so that the individual becomes useful to the society. Hereunder, we will discuss relationship between social control and education.

Definitions

"Social control is a collective term for those processes and agencies, planned and unplanned, by which individual are taught, persuaded or compelled to conform to the usages and values of the group to which they belong."

"It is clear from the above definition that social control includes those laws by which an individual behaves in concurrence with the mores of group." —*Brearly*

"Social control is that system of measures, suggestion, persuasion, restraint and coercion by whatever means, including physical force, by which a society brings into conformity to the approved pattern of behaviour a subgroup or by which a group moulds into conformity its members."

—*Gillin and Gillin*

"By social control is meant the way in which the entire social order coheres and maintains itself, how it operates, as a changing equilibrium." —*MacIver and Page*

"Social control can be defined as the sum total or rather the whole of cultural patterns, social symbols, collective spiritual meanings, values, ideas and ideals, as well as acts or processes, directly connected with them, whereby, inclusive of society, every particular group and every participating individual member overcome tensions and conflicts within themselves through temporary equilibria and takes steps for new creative efforts." —*Gurvitch and Moore*

Types of Social Control

Karl Mannheim's View

Different sociologists held differing views upon the types of social control. Karl Mannheim has accepted the following two types of social control:

(i) Direct social control. This is the control exercised upon the individual by the reactions of the people living in proximity. Such control is found existing in the family, neighbourhood, play group, and other primary groups. An individual is deeply influenced by the opinion and views of his parents, colleagues, neighbours and those who work with him. His behaviour is determined or controlled by their criticism, derogation, praise, suggestion or persuasion, etc. This is direct control.

(ii) Indirect social control. This is the control exercised upon the individual by factors which are separated from him. Control of the individual by secondary groups is of this type. Its prominent means are traditions, institutions, customs, rationalised behaviour, changes in situations and social mechanism, etc. The means of social control are invisible and subtle. In the existing complex society, the influence of the opinion, law, custom, etc., is controlled in this way. It is not that there are no individuals behind this control but these individuals are not seen by the persons affected.

Kimball Young's View

Kimball Young has divided social control into the following two types:

(i) Positive. Reward has an immense values upon the activities of an individual. A large part of the population of

society desires to be rewarded by the society. And, consequently, they constantly endeavour to conform to the traditions, mores, values and ideals accepted by the society. For this, they are retarded in the form of social recognition, fame, respect, etc.

(ii) Negative. Under this, those types of social controls are comprehended in which a person is prevented from doing something by threat of punishment, while it encourages the people to indulge in certain types of activity by promising regard. Fear of punishment helps to prevent people from violating the socially approved customs, traditions, values and ideals, etc.

In addition to the above-mentioned form of social controls, two other forms: formal and informal have also been recognized. The formal types are those which are specifically designed for control, and include government, law, police, army, jail, penal code, etc.

Informal social control includes those methods which develop by themselves according to the needs of society such as, mores, traditions, customs, social ideals, etc. Hayes has accepted two forms of social control:

(a) Control by sanction. In this, social control is effected by awarding the obedient and punishing the miscreant.

(b) Control by socialization and education.

Agencies of Social Control

It would have become evident from the foregoing description of the various types of social control, that there are many direct and indirect, formal and informal means of social control. Among the important means of social control, Ross has enumerated family, educational system, belief and religion, social suggestion, social ideal, ritual and festival, art, leadership, law and administration besides physical force.

Giddings has accepted the importance of belief, social direction or guidance, religion, social ideals, social festivals, art, leadership, intellectual factors, education and propaganda, law and administration and force, as means of social control.

Social Control and Education

According to Ruskin, "Education consists in making people polite what they ought to be." The ideals and patterns in these are promoted through education. Here, the word "education" is used in a comprehensive sense. It is only in this meaning of the word that the sociologist studies or contemplates it.

Education teaches man to live according to Nature. Education gives him ability to succeed in his struggle for existence. Education is an art of adaptation. For man adaptation is more social than natural. Hence, education adapts man to society. In this way, education is an important means of social control.

Education is in the family, playground, club, office, in fact, everywhere. At every place the individual is taught something and socialized. In the family, in school, on playground, he learns to follow the opinion and advice of others and learns to comply with the traditions and mores.

Theoretical education, viz., reading and writing, serves to form the intellectual base for all this and with practical education he learns to put this into practice.

The organisation or system of society is disrupted and thrown into confusion when the educational system contradicts or when the activity of education does not function correctly and social control fails to function. Hence, education is a necessary condition for the proper exercise of social control.

Without proper education the harmony of the individual and society is not merely difficult but well nigh impossible. Education makes social control normal. It makes social control self-control and the individual does not experience its burden.

QUESTIONS FOR ANSWER

1. What is social control? How is it achieved through education?
2. Explain social control in the context of educational institution.

22

Principle of Social Values

The principle of social control is exercised to ensure the application of the principle of social values in education because individuals constitute society which has certain ideals, models and norms about behaviour, conduct duties and responsibilities towards one another. Therefore, hereunder, we will discuss implementation of social values in educational system.

Definitions

Values relate to the aims of human life. For the achievement of the aims men frame certain notions and these notions are called values. In the words of W.H. Kilpatrick, "That out of man's capacity for goal seeking behaviour arise his wants and efforts and out of these come in consciously chosen ends (goal). Because ends conflict, man is led to weigh his goals against each other. When this is done critically enough values emerge."

According to Mr. Henderson, "It has been pointed out that man acts to satisfy his wants, anything which satisfies, a human want becomes thereby a value. To say, that our conduct is motivated by our value is another way of saying that we act to satisfy our wants."

Social Values and Education

Individuals constitute society which has certain ideals, models and norms about behaviour, conduct, duties and responsibilities towards one another. Love, universal brotherhood, sincerity, honesty and integrity of character, firm attitude of rendering help and performing actions and works of general benefit etc. are some of the constituents of healthy social life. True education aims at developing individuals into social beings having these virtues.

Schooling is a preparatory stage for cultivating the sense of social values. In the laboratories, students work in a co-operative way and develop a scientific attitude towards social life. In libraries, while sitting together for study they practise patience. In the hostels, while leading a corporate life they imbibe the spirit of living together like brothers, behave harmoniously sinking their differences and experiences.

Activities correlated with academic aspects afford opportunities for bringing about their physical and intellectual development and strengthening common bonds of spirit. Activities like N.C.C ., N.S.S., Boys Scout and Girls Guide help the students to develop themselves physically. These inculcate patriotic virtues in them and enthuse in them preparedness for safety and security of the country at the time of need.

Thus, teachers impart social values to the students in school systems. Education aims at developing individuals into social beings having these virtues.

Social values have been emphasised at every stage of social development. Ancient Indian educational institutions attached importance to social values. The students in the 'Gurukulas' rendered service not only to their students, community, but to the institution as a whole. They would go to the habitations for collecting meals from worthy householders who took it as their duty to set apart of portion of the cooked meal for the students.

In medieval times, the system continued. But with the occupation of India by the foreigners, new system of education was ushered. Emphasis was laid on Muslim education with Western education. Western education aimed at producing white collar clerks to help Britishers to run the administrative machinery of the state. From this period onwards, Indian social virtues disappeared from Indian mind.

With the dawn of independence education has been accepted as a nation building activity. India developed a national system of education, to help in the all-round development of the educands. The achievements so far are not satisfactory, social values should be developed both inside and outside educational institutions. Students should learn that love for country means love for nation, and love for the mankind leads to international sympathy.

This paves the way for education for international understanding, which is the cry of the day for world peace.

Strategies for Inculcating Social Values

Social values can be inculcated by introducing a programme for educational values of social service. Social service implies service to society or groups of individuals bound together by rules or conventions or other considerations for achievement of objectives and aims.

The individual has to render service to himself and bring about his growth in such a way as to enable him to prove of use for the society. He should prove himself useful to the members of the family, to the neighbours, to the state, to the country and to the world.

The educative process has to see it that the development of the individual is consistent with this aim of usefulness and fitness in the objectives and aims in general.

Education is a stage of preparation for cultivating the sense of social services in its theoretical aspect through teaching of lessons, dwelling on social virtues and through practical in laboratories where students work developing scientific attitude under the supervision of experts.

The following activities should be undertaken by the schools to impart educational values of social service to the students:

1. *Pre-school stage:* Education at the pre-school stage consists in the upbringing of infants in home atmosphere. Attempts should be made to cultivate virtues of affection, love, truthfulness and obedience at this stage of education.

2. *Primary stage:* At the primary stage, affection for all love for the country, truthfulness in behaviour, obedience to

elders, curiosity for knowledge, and appreciation of nature should be cultivated.

3. *Junior high school:* At the junior high school stage, straight-forwardness, frankness, uprightness, affection and kindness for all sense of rendering help to others in times of need should be cultivated. Foundation should be laid for the formation of character and cultivation of qualities of leadership.

4. *Secondary stage:* At the secondary stage, love for all mankind, preliminary knowledge of different aspects of nature, kindness and help to all living beings, dignity of manual labour, respect for the constitution of the country, sense of maintaining country's independence, freedom of thought, speech and action in the just and right context and interest for the defence of the country should be cultivated.

5. *College and university stage*: At the college and university stages, all these virtues should be developed and their practical aspect strengthened.

6. *Extra-curricular activities:* Programmes of manual labour as cleanliness of neglected localities picnics, excursion etc. should be arranged to provide opportunities to the students for moving among different people and seeing monumental achievements in the country for broadening outlook and understanding humanitarian values.

7. *Campaigns against disease:* These may be arranged by the students of higher education.

8. *Education of disabled people*: Provisions should be made to educate the deaf, the dumb and the blind etc.

9. *Anti-illiteracy drives*: Schemes for removing illiteracy should be undertaken out of love for the benefit of mankind.

10. *Development of aesthetic sense*: Training in drawing and painting should be arranged in order to develop aesthetic sense.

11. *Music and dance*: Music and dancing are parts of the cultural aspect of social service. Hence, necessary training in this respect should be imparted.

12. *Social service by girls*: Girl students should be encouraged to organize mass-cooking, mass-knitting of woollen equipment, visit orphanages, voluntary service to orphan children such as pairing off their nails, washing and bathing them.

13. Construction work: Students should be engaged in minor construction works like repairing and constructing roads, houses, digging well and tanks etc.

14. Service during calamities: Students should render voluntary service during natural calamities.

Training in Citizenship

A citizen feels that he is a part of the community and that he is there to share its burdens. Attempts should be made to give education for citizenship to promote the cause of liberty and democracy. Citizens are not born, they are to be trained. Therefore, the following strategies may be undertaken in order to develop the sense of citizenship among the students.

1. Education for citizenship: It should become a dynamic element in our pattern of education.

2. Development: Attempts should be made to inspire the students to develop a sense of cooperation for worthy causes, capacity for critical thought and freedom to place his point of view reasonably.

3. Debates and discussions: School should provide activities like debates and discussions on the issues and problems of our country. Mock parliament, mock panchayats, mock assemblies etc. should be arranged in order to inculcate proper civic values and attitudes.

4. Excursions: The schools should organise excursions to places of historic, religious and cultural importance.

5. Socialization: Students should learn to work in the social context and to come into contact with their fellow-men and women in a variety of ways in order to achieve their personal desires.

6. Productive work: Every boy and girl should willingly undertake useful productive work which may be mental or manual as a result of which he does not remain a burden or a parasite on others and can render some service to society.

7. Special camps: Special camps like N.C.C. or A.C.C., NS.S., I.V.S.P. (international voluntary services for peace) should be organised to provide a natural environment for the students to develop a sense of comradeship resulting from free group activities in work and play.

8. *Self-government*: Students should be encouraged to organise self-government in order to learn the art of dividing different activities amongst themselves to carry their duties in a disciplined manner and to obey their freely chosen leaders, so much essential for good citizenship.

9. *Relations among students*: Teachers should have a good understanding of adolescent psychology and be able to establish sincere and friendly relations among the students.

10. *Co-operative society*: In order to encourage co-operative group work, schools should organise co-operative societies, where they should actively participate.

11. *Pen-friends clubs*: Students should be encouraged to organise pen-friends clubs, on national and international level.

12. *Celebrate birthdays of great men*: The school should celebrate birthdays of great men and women of our country like; Lord Krishna, Gautam the Buddha, Shankaracharya, M.K. Gandhi, Gopabandhu, Tagore, etc., besides the celebration of important days like the Independence Day and the Republic Day etc.

Education and Values

According to Reid, "Education is part of life, and clearly our questions about values and education are inseparable from larger question of values in life. Values are embodied in educational practice." Thus education develops a sense of discrimination between good and bad. This discrimination is based on values and these values are tested in schools.

To quote W.H. Kilpatrick, "The teacher must have an essential part of his professional equipment, which is here called 'map of value.' Such a map consists of his hopes, aims, ideals, all the criticised values which he will use as aims in guiding those things. Teaching should aim continually on keeping this aggregate of values, life and growing but especially it should include all that the teacher hopes for students to learn so as life for them becomes as rich and fine as possible."

In other words, "Aims are an end in themselves and values are the product." Values of education are the same as of life. These educational values are individual as well as social.

Contribution of Educational Values

Educational values contribute the following advantages for individual and social life:

1. Development of healthy and balanced personality.
2. Capacity to earn livelihood and acquire material prosperity.
3. Development of vocational efficiency.
4. Creation of good citizenship.
5. Reorganisation and reconstruction of experience.
6. Adjustment with the environment and its modifications.
7. Fulfilment of the needs of man.
8. Development of character.
9. National integration and national development.
10. Leaders and skilled workers.
11. Promotion of social efficiency.
12. Cultural values.
13. Utilisation of leisure.

Therefore, educational values play a significant role in the life of man. Through them, one is able to lead his personal and social life successfully. To sum up in the words of J.S Brubacher, "Hence, the ultimate aim of education is self-realization, the fulfilment of man's instinctive potentialities for many in addition to the realization of eternal life. All proximate aims of education take their direction from the aim which itself stands imperishable eternal."

According to Adams, education is a bipolar process having two parts:

(1) the teacher, and
(2) the child.

In order to mould and modify the behaviour of the child the teacher employs various strategies and tactics to achieve the desired behavioural changes in him. He performs all these activities as he thinks them valuable for the purpose in view. As the teacher provides an environment of utility and value to the child, in the same manner the child participates only in those activities which he considers useful and valuable to him.

Both the teacher and the child participate only in those activities which they consider as educationally useful and valuable. According to Cunningham, educational values are aims of education. Through education qualities, abilities and capacities are promoted in the individuals, which are inherent values of life.

QUESTIONS FOR ANSWER

1. Explain various kinds of educational values and point out their hierarchy.
2. Describe social values in education. What are educational strategies to inculcate them?
3. Write short note on Training in Citizenship.

23

Principle of Social Change

Social change is a natural process in human society and education promotes social change in all fields of life. In modern world society is changing very rapidly, therefore, the principle of social change assumes very important place in the present day educational system. Hereunder, we will discuss, very briefly, various aspects concerning impact of social change in education and relationship between social change and education.

Definitions

To make the concept of social change more clear, we are giving some definitions as under:

(1) "Social change is a term used to describe variation in or modification of any aspects of social processes, social interactions or social organisation." —*Sir Jones*

(2) "Social changes are variations from the accepted modes of life whether due to alterations in geographic conditions, in cultural equipment, composition of the population or ideologies and whether brought about by diffusion or invention within the group." —*Gillin and Gillin*

Factors of Social Change

Social change is a continuous process. There are some important factors which help this process. These factors are—(1) The physical environment, (2) Scientific inventions and researches, and (3) Interdynamics. In the above lines, we have mentioned that according to Ogburn, social change first occurs in the material culture and then in the non-material culture. But Ottaways holds that these cultural changes do not take place one after the other, but it is a product of the interdynamics of the two. Ottaway has clearly stated that social or cultural change occurs because of the interaction of technological researches or scientific inventions and the ideals, values and aims of society.

As these factors namely; technology, techniques and values play an essential role in any social change, it is necessary to understand the meaning and significance of these words. Technology is that branch of science which develops various techniques. Techniques are those means which fulfil various basic needs of human beings in a society. In the end values are those objectives, beliefs, thoughts and abstract concepts which make human life dynamic, successful and purposive.

From the above discussion, it becomes quite clear that neither technological techniques alone nor the values in themselves bring about any real social change. It cannot also be determined definitely that which one of the above two has a greater share in achieving social change.

In fact, when technology changes, it affects change in values and when values change, they bring out the corresponding change in technology. In this way, technological techniques as well as values are both the essential basis of social change. Both are equally important and essential. Both actively interact and bring about social changes.

Factors Resisting Social Change

We have discussed above the factors which promote social changes, but there are still some factors which resist this change. The factors which resist social change are as under:

1. *Cultural inertia*: Cultural inertia is the first important factor which resists social change. Cultural inertia refers to those blind beliefs, customs and traditions which come down to us from our forefathers and which we stick to rigidly and blindly thinking them as sacred and indelible. This rigid, conservative

and narrow outlook makes us static and averse to any change. The outcome of this inertia is that our society remains backward in many respects and an aversion to modernization is evident. Education should break this inertia and rigidity.

2. *Fear of new things*: Fear of new things is second factor which stands in the way of any social change. In fact, some minds are always very apprehensive and doubtful about any change. According to Ogburn and Nim-Koff, most of the people show a tendency to stick to traditional routine life and are therefore averse to gain anything new for fear that these new elements may not turn to be harmful and injurious to them. They are contented with the status quo, the present state of affairs and are always praising the old traditional patterns of thinking and behaviour. This tendency needs to be changed through education. Only then, any social change will be welcomed and adopted by general people.

3. *Vested interests*: Vested interests is third factor which resists social change. Generally, it has been observed that there are some old traditions and beliefs which satisfy the vested interests of a few privileged section of society. Such people with vested interests, resist any change because of the danger to their self-interests. In other words, people having vested interests vehemetly resist social change. Education is the only means to sublimate self-interests and make them welcome any social change.

4. *Degree of isolation*: Degree of isolation is the fourth factor which resists social change. In fact, there are some people in society who refuse to come into contact with persons of other cultures. They try their best to remain in isolation and insulated from other influences. These people resist any kind of social change. For example, the backward communities and tribal groups resist any outside contacts apprehending danger to their self-centred narrow spheres of life full of special privileges and aids of many kinds.

Education and Social Change

Education fulfils the needs of society and propagates such ideas which promote social change in all fields of life. Education becomes, in this way, a social process by means of which society moulds children according to its needs and approved patterns of behaviour. It is for this end in view that a society organises its educational activities according to its needs and aspirations. In the light of social change, we are discussing below the functions of education:

1. *Perpetualizing eternal values*: A society has some eternal values which stabilize and consolidate it. Ralph Litton, while discussing this principle, has stated that whenever these eternal values lose their hold due to social changes, the society begins to decay and degenerate. In such times of crisis, education protects these eternal values, saves them from pernicious effects of social changes and promotes their knowledge and acceptance in such a manner that in spite of social changes, people in general keep faith in these values. In our society, such eternal values are of moral and spiritual nature. Education should protect, preserve and promote these values.

2. *Promoting capacity to welcome and accept social change*: Education propagates in the society both the materialistic and non-materialistic techniques. It prepares the mentality of people to welcome and adopt desirable social changes easily and gladly. It may be noted that people will welcome and adopt any technique or pattern only when they become convinced of its utility and desirability. Education, thus, structures a wholesome and conducive environment for these social changes to become acceptable to all.

3. *Evaluation of social changes*: A society is constantly under a process of transformation of various forms and nature in all fields of human activity. Teachers, by critical evaluation, determine the desirability or otherwise of these social changes. In other words, education lays down the required standards and criteria of values with reference to which this process of evaluation takes place effectively, and only after that, desirable social changes are propagated whereas the undesirable ones discarded and decried.

4. *Aids the coming of new social changes*: Education strives to banish social evils, blind customs and traditions through various social reformation projects, political movements, social service schemes and also tries to bring in needed social changes and reforms.

For example, in India, public movements, agitations against child marriage, forced widowhood, caste insulation, untouchability and social injustice resulted in desirable social changes.

5. *Transmission of culture*: Through its function of transmission of national culture from generation to generation as a continuous process, education lends stability and continuity to the society. Not only this, education prepares society to adopt needed and desirable social reforms.

In this sense, education is the creator, generator and director of all social changes. In short, education is a conservative, consolidating and stabilizing force and in addition, it is a creative force as well.

6. *Promotes unity and total integration*: When conflicts arise between various groups and sections of a society, education tries to solve those conflicts by advocating thoughts and feelings which bring about unity in diversity and achieve integration of all. Education, in India, has this sacred mission to perform by educating people to rise above petty caste rivalries, communal feuds, linguistic conflicts and regional discords and try to achieve the cherished ideal of national integration and national glory.

7. *Maintaining human and social relations*: In an industrial society, development of new techniques and devices, very often, lead to social laxity, disunity and discord among sections of people. Education strives to maintain and consolidate human relations in spite of these social changes in attitudes and patterns of behaviour of people.

8. *Education of social changes*: Education employs various methods to promote knowledge and understanding among people about social changes occurring in society. When the understanding of social changes develops, people gladly welcome and actively co-operate in all the plans to bring about social change.

9. *Removal of obstacle*: Various obstacles impede the march of social changes and reformations. Education informs people about their importance and desirability. Not only this, it tries to remove the mental reservations and complexes in the minds of people, which obstruct the progress of change.

10. *Increasing the areas of knowledge*: Education promotes in the individuals the capacity to increase their areas and scope of knowledge more and more for their benefit. It opens new

vistas for deeper and deeper investigations and researches, which bring about desirable changes in material as well as non-material aspects of culture. Thus, education prepares ground for the advent of social change.

11. Leadership role of social-changes: By promoting democratic feelings and progressive attitudes in the people, education makes them capable to initiate and guide for needed social changes by fighting successfully against social evils, customs and blind traditions. Thus, people become capable for realizing their own true personality to the full and promote social welfare to greater and greater extent. Education, in this way, prepares people for leadership roles as social reformers and nation builders.

Education Follows Social Change

Education and social change are very intimately related. Hence, education should prepare the background for social change. Not only this, education should also spell out the kinds of desirable changes needed by society and how these changes are to be brought about. For this, education should try to study and understand the various problems of society in specific areas from time to time and should become the integral part of social development. When education will assume this responsibility, society will grow more and more by adopting needed social changes.

But picture seems to be just the reverse. We see that instead of initiating and leading social changes, education today follows social changes. In other words, when changes occur in needs, technology and values, education also adopts itself to these changes. More clearly, education, follows social changes. Below, we are discussing some of the chief factors which compel education to follow social change:

1. Educational changes because of social forces: Social aspirations, social values and social dynamism are some of the social powers. When these forces change, change occurs in the educational process also.

2. Educational changes because of social needs: Society has various needs which affect the process of education for the purpose of their own satisfaction. It means that educational changes occur because of social needs and aspirations. Compulsory, free and universal education, diversification of secondary and higher education, adult education, agricultural, individual, vocational, professional and scientific education are the various forms and varieties of education which have been brought about by the needs of modern Indian society.

3. *Educational changes because of cultural changes*: Many changes in education occur because of cultural changes. It may be noted that first the material aspect of culture changes and then the non-material aspect of culture gradually changes. Thus, when cultural changes occur, changes also occur in education.

Teacher and Social Change

Teacher and social change are related as body and soul. As the very thought of body without soul is futile, in the same way, any social change without teacher is a mere figment of imagination. But it should be borne in mind that a teacher can initiate and promote social change only when he knows fully well the needs of society as well as the nature and direction of social change. In fact, social changes are of various kinds. They are (1) Evolutionary, (2) Wave like, and (3) Cyclic order. In the same way, directions of social changes are various. The prominent among them are (1) Even, and (2) Uneven. Teacher should become well-versed in all kinds and directions of social change and then try to mould the process of social change in such a way that it is acceptable to all people. The teacher should also keep in mind the fact that social changes are not even at all times.

He must know the fact that social changes brought about by such cultural factors which are not acceptable to the people of another culture, will not be welcomed by all people. Such plans and programmes of the teacher and the undesirable social change brought about by him shall be designated as uneven. In other words, when social changes are uneven, the educational changes are also correspondingly uneven. Hence, the teacher should protect society from such unhealthy and harmful changes.

History bears eloquent testimony to the fact that since very early times, teacher has co-operated society wholeheartedly in bringing about desirable social change. That is why, he is known as nation-builder even today.

But it is a sorry state of affairs that teacher of today is mute, inactive and indifferent towards the needful social change. That is why, he has lost his respect in society today. If the teacher wants to achieve the same honour as before, he should try to understand the needs of modern society and bring about the needed change according to the call of the time.

Importance of School in Social Change

School as such is a social institution of great importance. The role of school in bringing about social change is as follows:

1. *Relation with social order.* The size, form, nature and organizational set up of a school depend upon the prevalent social order. But social order has some aims, ideals, values and traditions. The school tries its best to realize these ideals and values. In other words, the organization of education conforms to the needs and values of society. This means that school works according to the social order. If social changes occur in society, school is bound to reflect the same changes in its working and operation.

2. *Influence of national policy.* The current national policy has a powerful influence on the school. In other words, school co-operates wholeheartedly in satisfying the needs and aspirations of the nation. For example, our national need is to increase the production of goods. We see that our schools are extending their hearty co-operation to meet the demand of scientific and technological education.

3. *Simplification of socio-cultural patterns.* In Indian society, socio-cultural patterns are varied and often complex. Their preservation without the help of school is next to impossible. A school tries to simplify and categorize these bewildering variety of socio-cultural patterns and preserves them for use and understanding by children.

4. *Development of capacities and efficiencies.* A school is not only concerned with the preservation of cultural heritage, but it looks to the future also. In other words, school tries to foresee the future needs of society and for the purpose of meeting

them tries to develop more and more capacities and efficiencies of the individuals.

5. *Meeting the economic needs of society.* Education promotes the economic efficiency of individuals who achieve their own economic prosperity as well as the prosperity of the society of which they happen to be integral parts. As the school meets the economic needs of individuals, therefore, it plays an important role to add to the prosperity of society.

6. *Promoting continuity.* A school preserves the cultural heritage of society. Not only this, it transmits this heritage from one generation to another and this promotes continuity of society in a very effective manner.

7. *Contact with wide environment.* The environment of a school is very wide and varied. In comparison with the narrow and limited environments of a family or neighbourhood, school tries to provide for children a very wide and varied environment by its diverse activities, programmes and experiences.

8. *Glorious future.* In modern times, a school strives to plan for a very bright and glorious future of society. Thus, it not only preserves the glories of the past but also tries to make society achieve greater and greater heights of glory and fame in future times.

QUESTIONS FOR ANSWER

1. What is social change? Enumerate the factors which promote and resist social change.
2. How does education bring about social change? Discuss the role of teacher in this connection.
3. Discuss the role of school in social change.

24

Principles Concerning Cultural, Religious and Moral Values (Education and Religion)

The real aim of education is the fullest and proper development of human being, which includes his cultural, religious and moral development along with his mental, physical and social development. There are some basic principal methods for the cultural, religious and moral development of the individuals, which we will discuss hereunder, very briefly.

Education and Culture

In the words of Sorokin and MacIver, "Culture implies man's moral, spiritual and intellectual achievements." Bogardus holds: "Culture is composed of integrated customs, traditions and current behaviour patterns of human group. Culture is the stock in trade of group. It is antecedent complex of value into which every individual is born. It is a medium within which individuals develop and mature."

Kinds of Culture

According to the subject there are different kinds of culture:

(1) Individual culture,
(2) Communal culture,

(3) National culture, and
(4) World culture.

Every individual has some personal traits and qualities which guide his habits of thinking and behaving in all fields of human activities. These personal likes and dislikes, interests, modes of thinking and patterns of social behaviour constitute his personal culture. In the same way, different communities have their distinct traits of life styles comprising specific modes of community beliefs and styles of living.

All the members of different communities exhibit different traits known as community culture. Likewise, every nation has some distinct national traits and attributes of character which condition its national patterns of ideals, values, modes of thought and behaviour. Such national traits are known as national culture.

Further, a rapid rise in the means of transport and communication has shrunk the whole world into one small unit with the result that different nations of the world live together as members of a world community having common values of life. Such values namely—co-operation, sympathy, social service, social awakening and social sensitiveness etc., constitute world culture.

According to contents there are two types of culture in each society:

(1) Material culture,
(2) Non-material culture.

1. *Material culture.* Material culture includes all those man-made things and objects which human society has created for its physical welfare in times of peace and war. Items such as clothes, utensils, home, roads, ornaments, TV, radio, various machines, gadgets and various means of transport and communication are some examples of material culture.

2. *Non-material culture.* Non-material culture includes all those ideals, attitudes and values which modify the behaviour of an individual. Language, literature, art, music, religion, customs and traditions etc., are some examples of non-material culture.

Education and Cultural Lag

Due to rapid progress of scientific inventions and technological advancement, material aspect of culture has gone ahead and its area has been greatly widened. The modern society is gradually adopting more and more of these techniques and scientific achievements in their day-to-day styles of living, while the non-material aspect of culture has been left far behind.

This vast difference between the material culture and the non-material culture is known as social and cultural lag. As the pace of material culture cannot be slackened, the need is to speed up the changes in the non-material cultural patterns of thinking and living. Both should proceed together in a corresponding pace as the two wheels of a chariot. Education is the only means to bridge this cultural lag.

We see that through scientific inventions, investigations and discoveries many of our own Indian people are enjoying the fruits of the material culture, yet there are still vast masses of people who are steeped in ignorance, inertia and utter backwardness. Education can do this job of eliminating this cultural lag and inspire the general people to march on the road of progress and modernisation as best they can.

Education and Culture

Education and culture are intimately and integrally connected. Hence, the cultural pattern of a society conditions its educational pattern. For example, if a society has a spiritual pattern of culture, then its educational procedures will emphasize the achievement of moral and eternal values of life. On the other hand, if the cultural pattern of a society is materialistic, then naturally its educational pattern will be shaped for the attainment of material values which promote pleasures of senses and material comforts. It may be borne in mind that a society devoid of any culture will have no definite educational organisation.

Hence, it may be safely asserted that the culture of a country has a very powerful impact on its educational pattern. This mutual influence is being discussed in the following lines.

Influence of Culture on Education

Culture influences the following aspects of education:

1. *Influence of culture on aims of education.* The meaning and aims of education are determined by the cultural ideals, values and patterns of a society. In other words, as is the culture of a society so shall be its aims of education.

2. *Influence of culture on curriculum.* The aims of education are achieved through curriculum. As the aims of education are determined according to the culture of society, so the curriculum is conditioned according to the culture of society. In other words, as are the ideas, ideals and values of a society, the educational curriculum of that society is conditioned according to the ideals and needs of that society to realize its cultural values. In short, the system of education tries to realize the cultural needs of society through curriculum which conditions activities and programmes.

3. *Influence of culture on methods of teaching.* Culture and methods of teaching are intimately connected. It is why, the changing cultural patterns of a society exert powerful influence upon the methods of teaching also. In ancient times education was teacher-centred and tried to force into the minds of children specific doses of knowledge in quite disregard of their natural interests and needs.

The result of this artificial progress of education was mechanical cramming and rote memorization. In modern times education has become child-centred. Thus, the interests, inclinations, aptitudes, needs and capacities of children are taken into full consideration before exposing them to specific educational experiences, activities and programmes.

In this way, education is now a method of preparing children for successful and effective living during the present times and for the times to come. In short, cultural and social needs condition the methods and techniques of teaching in a very powerful way.

4. *Influence of culture on discipline.* Cultural values also influence the concept of discipline. The present cultural patterns of thinking and living are directly linked to our concept of discipline. In ancient and middle ages societies where authoritarianism ruled, the concept of discipline was repressionistic. But in modern times when democratic values

of life are being accepted all over the world, the concept of discipline has come to mean impressionistic or emancipatory or self-discipline.

5. *Influence of culture on text-books.* Curriculum is contained in text-books. We have discussed above the powerful impact of cultural values upon the curriculum. These text-books are written according to the formulated or determined curriculum. It may be borne in mind that only those text-books are welcomed if they foster and promote cultural ideals and values. On the contrary, they are discarded and often banned if they militate against the cultural ideals and values of a particular society.

6. *Influence of culture on teacher.* Each individual teacher is imbued with the cultural ideals and values of the society of which he happens to be an integral member. Only such a teacher achieves his mission successfully. It is only such a teacher who is able to infuse higher ideals and moral values in children. The idealism and higher ideals of teacher are imbibed by children imperceptibly but definitely. It may be noted here that the idealism and higher ideals of teacher are comprised of the cultural ideals and values of his society of nation.

7. *Influence of culture on school.* According to the ideology of pragmatism, a school is a miniature of society. The total activities and programmes of the school are organised according to the cultural ideals and values of the society which establishes and organises the school. Hence, school is the centre of promoting, moulding, reforming and developing the cultural patterns of the society which establishes that school for its own good and welfare.

Influence of Education on Culture

Just as culture influences education, much in the same way education also exerts its powerful influence upon the culture of a country. In the following lines, we are explaining the various ways by which education influences the culture of a country:

1. *Preservation of culture.* Each country believes and flaunts the superiority of its own culture over the rest. Hence, it tries to preserve its culture in its original form. Education is the

only means to complete this task. In other words, education preserves the culture of society.

2. *Transmission of culture.* The process of preservation includes the process of transmission as well because through transmission of culture from one generation to another is the best guarantee of its preservation. The famous sociologist Ottaway has rightly remarked, "The function of education is to transmit the social values and ideals to the young and capable members of society."

3. *Development of culture.* The function of education is not only to preserve and transmit the culture of society, but it also brings about the needed and desirable changes in the cultural ideals and values for the progress and continued development of society, without which social progress will stratify and come to naught. In other words, education culturises individual, modifies cultural processes by research and deeper investigations into all areas of human requirements.

4. *Maintaining the continuity of culture.* Culture is the life blood of a society. Without culture a society is bound to decay and die sooneror later. Education upholds the continuity of culture through its diverse activities and programmes. It may be noted that a society establishes schools to preserve and transmit its culture from generation to generation. But some schools try to develop cultural chauvinism and superiority complexes among its children. This is very undesirable. Children should be motivated to learn more and more from cultural interaction among various cultures and develop the qualities of tolerance, adjustment together with mutual give and take, that they are able to benefit themselves from the contribution of all cultures. This cultural integration and cultural synthesis is the dire need of the world society in modern time.

5. *Helping the development of personality.* Education aims to develop the personality of the child. For this, it employs diverse cultural patterns of thinking, behaviour and items of cultural values so that children are physically, mentally, socially and emotionally developed to the maximum extent.

6. *Removing cultural lag.* When material culture develops at a fast pace due to scientific researches and inventions, non-material culture consisting of ideals, values and norms lag behind creating a gulf between the two. Education is the only

means to bridge this cultural lag by its activities and programmes of development.

It is clear from the above discussion that whereas on one hand, education culturises an individual, on the other hand, it preserves, transmits and develops the culture of a society. In short, education and culture are mutually interdependent, complementary and supplementary in all their aspects and activities.

Role of Culture in Man's Life

Culture plays vital role in man's life. Education of various elements of culture can help man in the following aspects:

1. Adaptation to the natural environment.
2. Adaptation to the social environment.
3. Development in individual's personality.
4. Socialization of the individual.
5. Proper use of leisure.
6. In understanding other cultures and proper meaning of liberality.

Education in culture is imparted by the family, society and school.

Religious Education

The aim of contemporary education is not only the mental, physical and social development of the individual, but also his religious and moral development, that is why modern educationists have stressed the importance of moral education for the country.

Vivekananda said that religion is the basis of education, although here he does not imply his own or someone else's religion. This comment also implies that the aim of religious education is not to propound the theories of any one particular religion but to create faith towards universally accepted religious values.

The presence of religious faith helps the individual to face all kinds of adverse conditions with the belief that he can progress at least a little, irrespective of the darkness of the outlook. Hence, religious faith helps man in his progress, raises him to a high level, and also assists him in developing democratic qualities.

Religion is the foundation of all moral character, because without religion man cannot have faith in truth, beauty and goodness. The freedom that we want to grant the child through education is not possible without religion. Besides, even culture has no meaning in the absence of religion which also acquaints us with the final goal of life. Without knowing this goal, education cannot progress. Religion is the basis of true humanitarianism.

It is evident from the foregoing comments that religion should be given its appropriate place in the curriculum for education. Vivekananda has recommended that modern science should be used to awaken the educand's knowledge. History, geography and literature should be taught to the educand along with the teaching of religion which must be used to teach them the greatest truths.

Dr. S. Radhakrishnan also supported the teaching of religion at the various levels of education. He said that we will have to plan for a rational religion for our conflict ridden emerging humanity, a religion that does not ridicule man's soul filled with unrestrained individualism and hesitation born out of conflict.

Mahatma Gandhi has also attached the greatest significance to religious education and he has advocated the educands should be acquainted with the basic elements of all religions. Sri Aurobindo has considered religious education to be the most important aspect of education.

Aims of Religious Education

Religious education must not include importance and methods of retuals but aim at the following:

1. Mental development.
2. Refinement of human values.
3. Socialization of the individual.
4. Development of democratic values.
5. Cultural development.

6. Sense of respect for man.
7. Complete development of the child.

V.T. Thayer rightly says, "The school must therefore concern itself with the whole child and no child can become whole without instruction in religion."

Place of Religious Education in a Secular State

Some people opine that religious education should not be encouraged by the state in a secular country like India, and they argue that religious education should be given by religious institutions and society, not by the school.

This attitude has no justification because education must aim at the complete development of the individual, an aim that cannot be fulfilled in the absence of religious education.

A secular state does not imply a state which is hostile to or indifferent towards religion, because all that the term secular implies is that the state shall not insist upon the adoption of any particular religion, because there is no state religion.

It is correct to assume that the Government should not try to spread any particular religion, but it also be remembered that religious education cannot be equated with the deliberate campaigning for some particular religion. All that is required in religious education is that the educand should be taught the basic elements which are at the root of every religion, thus, developing the educand's faith in moral character, religious values and humanitarianism.

And, since India is also a democratic country, it has a great stake in the development of democratic values, which also depend upon religious education. Hence, religious education has its significance even in a secular state because it is the most powerful medium for developing democratic values. But religious education in a secular state must be carefully planned so as not to injure the sentiments of any particular sect of religionalists, and also to avoid giving undue importance to any one religion. Every educand must be given the freedom and opportunity to profess his own religion, but he should be accompanied by acquaintances with other religions, since this alone is the way to religious tolerance.

True religious feeling can be evolved in the educand by telling him about the lives of all the great religious leaders and founders. The subject matter of religious education should be designed to conform to the level of training and intelligence of the educands. A religious life is a life with a purpose, the same purpose which religious education has.

Moral Education

The aim of education is the complete development of the child a development in which moral development occupies an important place. Man's greatest characteristic is his character. Vivekananda has defined character as the sum total of an individual's instincts, the inclinations of his mind. Man is made by his thoughts. One finds that children develop characters according to the ideas presented to them during their growth. For this reason they should be initiated into the ideals of sacrifice, hard work and contemplation.

Good thoughts lead to a sound determination and this in turn puts the man on the path to good life, and he is filled with strength of soul which inspires him to adhere to this path. In order to form character, it is necessary to pay attention to subtle and small things, for character is manifested through habits. Character can, therefore, only be improved by the habits of the individual.

For this, both determination and courage are required. Vivekananda had said in a resonant voice that one must form one's character and express one's true nature, the enlightened pure element in oneself. One must also look for the same element in every other individual.

According to Sri Aurobindo, moral education is the education of the heart, without which no individual can be completely human. But this moral education cannot be imparted through lectures and textbooks because the basis of this education is proper feelings, proper conduct and the development of proper habits of thought, feeling and action.

The task of education is to guide, direct and suggest to the child, without interfering with his activities in any way. Teachers should present the highest ideals but must also remember that moral education is imparted through imitation and setting examples rather than through discipline. In ancient India, the child acquired moral education only by imitating his teacher. The modern teacher, therefore, must also have the highest ideals. In addition, moral education takes place through moral conversation and behaviour. Senior educands should be required to read literature which encourages the purest emotions in them and inspires them to attempt at the highest ideals. In order to give moral training to the child, the latter should be acquainted with the means of distinguishing between the right and the wrong. The various emotions of the child are not to be suppressed but sublimated.

Mahatma Gandhi, like Sri Aurobindo, believed that development of character is the aim of education, for which, in his opinion also, moral education is essential. Dayanand believed that education of any kind is impossible without the practice of abstinence.

Dr. S. Radhakrishnan also said that moral education is absolutely necessary for any education. In Indian culture, very great importance has always been attached to moral character. No education is complete without moral education, and this morality is the foundation of man's future and therefore the seed of this must be sown in the school.

Dr. S. Radhakrishnan said that we must create the proper social order but we must also keep in mind that the individual does not become complete only by achieving economic prosperity. In order to become a complete individual the pleasure and beauty of the soil is essential. This soul must be brimming with love, faith, and the willingness and ability to serve humanity re-born.

From the foregoing account of the opinions of various philosophers, it is evident that moral education is as much a part of education as religious education is.

In this connection, it is stated in the report of the Secondary Education Reorganization Committee for U.P., "That moral and humanistic education should form an integral part of our education; students should be taught the fundamental truth from all religious and ethical movements with a view to emphasizing their essential unit."

QUESTIONS FOR ANSWER

1. What is culture? Discuss its types.
2. Discuss the influence of culture on education.
3. Throw light on the influence of education on culture.
4. Write a note on 'religious education'.
5. Write a note on 'the effect on education of the principle of religious secularism'.
6. "Religion and education are natural allies." Discuss the implications of this statement and say what steps you would take to introduce religious education in Indian school system.
7. Point out the main issue involved in the problem of Religious Education and suggest a practical solution.
8. What should be the place of religion in the Educational Programme of Secular State?

25

Principle of Population Education

The increase of population in every nation the world over but in India in particular is of alarming nature which creates formidable problems. Therefore, educationists have thought it right to include population education as a principle area of study in education. Hereunder, some aspects of this problem, as thought fit, are being discussed.

One of the formidable problems which stare us in the face is our rapidly increasing population which offsets every endeavour, for development. Therefore, a need is being felt for imparting factual knowledge about population dynamics so that the younger generation may understand the nature and magnitude of the burden imposed by rapid population growth. Population education emphasises that what other agencies have failed to do. Let agencies imparting education come forward and develop values and attitudes among the young and enable them to make rational decisions on their own behaviour on population matters.

In India, it was Prof. Sloan Waylan of Columbia University, who gave concrete shape to the notion of 'population education'. According to him, we are concerned with the fact that the public policy on family planning and the desirability of family planning should be tagged to the system of formal education.

Burleson has conceived of population education as population awareness. In his view, the increase in population brings about an increase in the already increasing expenditure on education. Education can solve the problem by arousing population awareness among teachers and students. Population education, therefore, is the awareness of knowledge relating to population. Prof. Noel David Burleron who has given this significant term (of population education) further says, "Population education or population awareness refers to factual knowledge about population dynamics required to understand the nature and magnitude of the burden imposed by rapid population growth."

Another definition is, "It is an educational programme which provides for a study of the population situation in family, community, nation and the world, with the purpose of developing in the students rational and responsible attitudes and behaviour towards that situation."

The National Seminar on Population Education held in Bombay in 1959 gives a comprehensive definition of population education. It emphasises knowledge about the quantity and quality of population and the need to control them for happy human existence. According to this seminar, population education is essentially related to human resource development. It is not only concerned with population awareness but also with developing values and attitudes, which take care of the quality and quantity of population. It must explain to the students cause and effect relationship so as to enable them to make rational decision on their own behaviour on population matters.

According to Gopal Rao, "Population education may be defined as an educational programme which provides for a study of the population phenomenon so as to make the students to take rational decisions towards problems arising out of rapid population growth.

Viderman is of the opinion that the purpose of population education is to develop awareness and understanding of the relations between population growth and national development, both in short-and long-run and to develop an understanding of the consequences of individual decisions in the important area of reproduction behaviour.

An analysis of the views given above highlights that population education is an exploration of knowledge, and attitudes about population, family living, reproduction education and basic values. It means educating the students about large population of ever increasing population and the problems which this over-population creates.

Need and Importance of Population Education

Keeping in view the above-mentioned problems and the need to tackle them, the need and urgency of population education is self-evident. It is strongly felt that population education is essential as programmes like family planning will not give the desired results. Due to a number of reasons including superstition and orthodoxy, adults sometimes cannot appreciate the ideas of family planning. Children are always more open-minded, and therefore, it is felt that the younger generation be gripped with the new ideas about India's population problem.

Thus the idea of population education is based on the following major assumptions:

1. The unprecedented population growth is responsible for retarding economic progress of our country.
2. Over-population impairs the health and well-being of the younger generation.
3. The country is pledged to raise the standard of living of the masses since chronic poverty provides a constant stimulus to unrestrained population growth.
4. In order to affect any significant change in the rate of growth of over-population, we direct our attention to future parents and inculcate in them attitudes which favour small family norms.
5. Population education is not to be mixed with sex education or the methods of family planning. It is a motivational force for creating the right attitudes to family size.
6. Population is not only to be considered quantitatively but also qualitatively.
7. Population education is not a "once for all affair", rather, it should be a continuous process.

India is facing a population explosion. Simply family planning and providing incidental information is not sufficient. Moreover, as Dr. Gopal Rao has observed, about 45 per cent of our population is below 16 years of age. They will soon be adult. The reproductive behaviour of this critical mass is of crucial importance in controlling the rate of population growth. Hence, the need to develop population education programme.

Population Problem in India

The problem of population is alarming, almost everywhere in the world. Population explosion has made the sociologists worried about the future existence of man. It is one of the most fundamental human problems. It affects every aspect of man's life—individual, national and international. It affects health, wealth and happiness of individuals and families; it affects the prosperity and progress of nations; it affects the international security and peace. India being one of the most over-populated countries of the world, such problems are being felt even more actually.

The main problems regarding over-population in India may be summarised as under:

1. Rapid growth is a constant threat to our economic development. It is undoubtedly true that the greater the population, the less there is to distribute to the people. In India our entire economy is being eaten up by more rapid growth of population. Thus, the major part of our economy goes to the current consumption and there is little kept for fresh investment. This retards the economic progress of the country.

2. The second major problem arising out of the rapid growth of population is that of providing adequate food for more and more people. In our country after independence, food production has been sufficient but demands have been larger. Thus the food problem in our country is a continual issue and we have no hope to solve the problem keeping in view the rate of growth of population.

3. Over-population has effected the economic standards of the masses, who are underfed and illiterate and consequently inefficient and less productive. Poor productivity leads to further poverty.

4. Our population leads to certain other social problems including the problems of urbanization of population. Thus, environment problems and limited civic amenities affect the health and productivity of the people. Problems of transport, housing and pollution of water and air are also important which crop up because of over-population.

5. Educationally, over-crowded schools are the result of over population. Low quality of education and lack of training for productive occupations is evident in our schools. It is the aimless formal education which is responsible for this mass unemployment of the educated.

Aims of Population Education

Aims of population education are as follows:

1. To develop an understanding of some demographic concepts and processes.
2. To develop among the younger generation an understanding of the most important phenomenon of the modern world viz. rapid growth of population and its causes.
3. To develop an understanding of the influence of population trends on the various aspects of human life—political, social, cultural and economic.
4. To develop an understanding of the close interaction of population growth and developmental process, with special reference to the development programmes for raising the standard of living of the people.
5. To develop an understanding of the evil effects of over-population on the environment and the concomitant dangers from population.
6. To develop an understanding of biological factors and phenomenon of reproduction which are responsible for the continuation of the species.
7. To develop an appreciation of the small family norms as proper and desirable, the relation between population size and the quality of life, and the fact that family size is a matter of deliberate choice and

human regulation, rather than of accident of forces beyond human control.

8. To develop an appreciation of the relationship between the preservation of the health of mother, the welfare of children and small size of the family.
9. To develop an appreciation of the fact that the personal and national decisions concerning family size and population have long range consequences for the whole world.
10. To develop an awareness of the population policies and programmes of the country.

Contents of Population Education

After finalising the objectives of population education, the next question is as to what should be the contents or the curriculum of population education so that the avowed objectives are properly realised.

The N.C.E.R.T. organised a workshop on 'Population Education' at New Delhi in July, 1970. It suggested that the following five areas should form the curriculum of population education:

1. The Population Growth.
2. Economic Development and Population.
3. Social Development and Population.
4. Health, Nutrition and Population.
5. Biological factors, Family life and Population.

Dr. C.T. Fanenff suggested the following curriculum:

1. Birth rate, mortality rate and population.
2. Health and population.
3. Food production and population.
4. Family size and population.
5. Standard of living and population.

Dr. Gopal Rao suggests the following topics forming the contents or curriculum of population education :

1. The history of population growth—World in general, India in particular—Causes, trends and implications.

2. An introduction to demography with particular reference to India. Comments on population growth, population distribution and its composition.
3. Effects of rapid population growth on economic, social cultural and political aspects of national development.
4. Effects of rapid population growth on individual and family life—standard of living.
5. Effects of rapid population growth on the physical environment, food, natural resources and quality of life.
6. An elementary knowledge of the physiology of reproduction wherever feasible.
7. The population policies and programmes of the world in general.

Population Education at all Stages of Education

Population education should start from the early classes and should continue in the secondary and higher secondary stages. Thus, population education should be a constant process. It is desirable that small children even in the primary classes should be made conscious about the scarcity of means, and the vastness of demands. At the later stages, the idea may be developed and more details may be furnished, so that the students may accept this education in a natural manner.

Some educators are opposed to the idea of beginning population education at the school stage. They say that it has a definite relation with birth control and sex education. In the absence of these ideas, the idea of population control is not possible.

They argue that the knowledge of sex at this stage is definitely harmful. Also the idea of controlling the population will cause the immature students to get excited emotionally and they will be more and more curious to know about sex. This may lead to harmful results from social and moral point of view.

But, most of the educationists are in the favour of beginning population education from the school stage. They say that the situation regarding population is so alarming that it is absolutely essential to make the children conscious about the rate of increasing population, and school is the best place for giving this knowledge.

Moreover, new ideas can be assimilated only by the school children who are at the impressionable stage. In addition to this, it is only at the primary stage, that the maximum number of children can be given the ideas of population education.

At the secondary and higher stages of education, the number of students is meagre. If we teach these ideas only at the secondary and higher stages, large number of children will escape these ideas and the very purpose of population education will be shattered—Keeping in view the above arguments, population education should be started at the school stage.

In fact, it should be taught at all stages of education. Population education is a constant process. It is not an idea which is needed only for a few years. In the present set up of society, it is desirable that from the very beginning, that is, from the primary school, even small children are made conscious about the scarcity of means and vastness of demands.

In this way, when the present school going generation will develop as an elder generation, the required influence will be visible. Thus population education should be started from the very beginning and should be continued through all the stages of education.

QUESTIONS FOR ANSWER

1. What is the concept of "Population Education"? What are its long-term advantages?
2. What is the need and importance of Population Education in India? What efforts have been made to promote Population Education in the country?
3. What is Population Education? State its objectives.
4. What should be the content of Population Education? How can it be incorporated in the school curriculum?

26

Principle of Socially Useful Productive Work

Since school is a social institution, therefore, as a matter of principle it must aim at providing socially useful as well as productive educations. Hereunder, we will discuss this aspect in detail.

The National System of Education as conceived by our leaders during the national movement for freedom and as propounded by Mahatma Gandhi has its genesis in work-based education. Gandhiji was against education leading to the search for white-collared jobs. He was of the opinion that if education is based on Socially Useful Productive Work, it would be an instrument for personality development and social transformation.

After Independence, a number of committees and commissions have been appointed to recommend changes in the system of education. All of them have expressed their appreciation of the Gandhian philosophy of Basic Education as the best solution for our educational problems. It may be mentioned here that although few in number, some Gandhian voluntary organisations have successfully implemented educational programmes based on this philosophy. Tradition, however, dies hard and the system of education continues to be bookish in character and divorced from the needs of society. Socially Useful Productive Work must, therefore, be given a central place in the curriculum at all stages of school education and content of the academic subjects should be related to it, as far as possible.

The Concept

Socially Useful Productive Work may be described as purposive, meaningful, manual work resulting in either goods or services which are useful to the community. Purposive, productive work and services related to the needs of the child and the community will prove meaningful to the learner. Such work must not be performed mechanically, but must include planning, analysis and detailed preparation, at every stage, so that it is educational in essence. Adoption of improved tools and material, where available, and the adoption of modern techniques will lead to an appreciation of the needs of a progressive society, based on technology.

It will be recalled that programmes of Work Experience were introduced as a result of the recommendations of the Kothari Commission with the objective of relating education to productivity. These programmes, however, lacked the component of social usefulness and, in practice, were not even casually correlated to other subject areas.

The purpose of demarcating a distinct curricular area as Socially Useful Productive Work is to emphasise the principle that education should be work-centred, as the concept of Socially Useful Productive Work is to be developed in the light of the Gandhian Philosophy of Basic Education, and in through work.

The aim of this is to provide children with opportunities of participating in social and economic activities inside and outside the classroom, enabling them to understand scientific principles and processes involved in different types of work and in the setting in which they are found in the physical and social environment.

Criterion for Selection of Activities

The criterion for selection of activities should, thus, be that the work involved is productive, educative and socially useful. It is felt that if Socially Useful Productive Work is given a central and dominant place in curriculum the gap between work and education will be reduced, 'the school will not remain isolated from the community and the gulf that divides the affluent from the weaker and poorer sections of the community will be bridged. Such a scheme will provide equality of opportunity for working and learning to all children irrespective of caste, creed, sex and economic status.

It is unfortunate that those who receive education migrate from the villages to the towns, deserting the community which had nurtured them and spent money on their education. A cleavage is thus created between the so-called educated and the rural masses, resulting in lack of harmony, where previously there was community of outlook. Those who have been thus educated are soon disenchanted as education brings unemployment. A paradoxical situation arises in that national resources are spent on their education only to help them join the ranks of the unemployed.

Social Service

The component of Social Service in the curriculum is allied to Socially Useful Productive Work. For example, when children participate in an environmental cleanliness programme by way of social service, they can simultaneously prepare compost pits for manure. Similarly, if children conduct surveys of population, habitations or cattle, they can use the information for planning programmes for child-care and sanitation. During the harvesting season when the entire village is under pressure of intensive work, the schools, instead of remaining in isolation, can render valuable help.

Help from and to Other Agencies

Activities under Socially Useful Productive Work must not be confined to the four walls of the school, nor can they be provided by the teacher only. Programmes should, therefore, be so planned and implemented that the local community, community development organisation and governmental agencies participate in them and cooperate with the school. For example, no school can, by itself achieve effective results in the environmental cleanliness programme unless the village panchayat extends full cooperation and support to the school. In fact, many governmental and social organisation such as Khadi and Village Industries Commission, All India Handicrafts Board, Harijan Kalyan Samiti do render valuable help to the community. If their programmes can include participation by school children, they will be introduced to activities in which they will realise, that they are cooperating with adults.

Decentralisation

The planning for Socially Useful Productive Work should be decentralised as far as possible. The Central and State agencies should prepare model programmes which will serve as specimens for developing programmes by local institutions. District, taluqa and village level committees should be set up by including representatives from various departments and organisations. These committees should provide plans and programmes to the schools well in advance; these programmes should be reviewed from time to time. The committees should also consider feasibility of making provision for the supply of raw material and the sale of finished products.

Need of Core Programmes

Depending upon the needs and facilities available, the activities pertaining to Socially Useful Productive Work will differ from school to school.

But it should be possible to identify common core programmes, which should be undertaken by all schools. The overall programmes should be so designed to involve regular and universal participation of the children throughout the year.

Productive work and services, where possible, should result in remuneration in kind or cash where possible; this will develop attitudes of self-reliance.

Objectives

The objectives of Socially Useful Productive Work will be to:

(i) prepare pupils to practise and perform manual work individually and collectively;

(*ii*) acquaint children with the world of work and services of the community and develop in them a sense of respect for manual workers;

(*iii*) develop a desire to be useful members of society and contribute their best to the common good;

(*iv*) indicate positive attitudes of team work and socially desirable values like self-reliance, dignity of labour, tolerance, co-operation, sympathy and helpfulness;

(*v*) help in understanding the principles involved in the various forms of work; and

(*vi*) lead children to participate increasingly in productive work as they go from one stage of education to another and, thereby, enable them to earn while they learn.

Programme

In order to ensure that the educational objectives of this programme are achieved it is necessary to follow the problem solving approach. Children should be made aware of the problems related to their needs: they should be led lo arrive at solutions by discussing the material, tools and techniques necessary for performing such work and services. A built-in system of evaluation should be developed to enable them to improve their performance and to enable teachers to give a fair assessment of their work. As recommended later Socially Useful Productive Work must be given the status of a full-fledged subject in the final public examination taken at end of Class X.

Teaching-Learning Process: Three Phases

Children have a natural curiosity of explore their environment. They explore the world of work by observation, enquiry and manipulation of material and tools, they learn to work by imitation. They enjoy working together and enjoy helping adults in their work. Therefore, the teaching-learning process in Socially Useful Productive Work will have three phases:

- *(i)* study of the world of work through observation and enquiry;
- *(ii)* experimentation with material, tools and techniques; and
- *(iii)* work practice.

The first two are concerned with preparation for actual participation in productive work and services and the third may lead to remuneration.

Work Situations: Six Areas

Thus, productive manual work situations relating to production of goods and service will have to be drawn from the areas of:

- *(i)* health and hygiene;
- *(ii)* food;
- *(iii)* shelter:
- *(iv)* clothing;
- *(v)* culture and recreation; and
- *(vi)* community work and social service.

These work situations occur in the home, in the school and in the community. It has already been mentioned that such programmes will have two components:

- *(a)* a common core programme;
- *(b)* work practice.

The purpose of the common core programme will be to bring about attitudinal changes and to develop readiness for work practice.

The purpose of work practice is to give a vocational bias to the programme. It will, therefore, be repetitive in nature and, it is hoped remunerative in kind or cash.

Programmes by Classes

Such programmes will take the form of simple projects in classes III-VII/VIII and will include main and subsidiary crafts in classes VIII/IX and X.

The programme of Socially Useful Productive Work may be summarised as follows:

(a) *Classes I and II*
Helping in work situations in the home in the school and in the community; manipulating simple material with simple tools for creative self-expression.

(b) *Classes III-VII/VIII*
Common activities pertaining to the six areas mentioned earlier.

(i) *Health and Hygiene*
Dusting of furniture; cleaning of classrooms, school buildings, the school compound and its vicinity.

(ii) *Food*
Vegetable gardening or pot culture; cooking of meals.

(iii) *Shelter*
Construction with plastic, pliable and rigid material. Maintenance of articles of use.

(iv) *Clothing*
Spinning and simple hand weaving or knitting; washing of clothes; stitching; mending.

(v) *Culture and Recreation*
Decorating the classroom, school and home; flower gardening; preparation for important national days (including hoisting and saluting the National Flag), festivals and school functions.

(vi) *Community Work and Social Service*
Cleaning the neighbourhood; preparation, maintenance and use of a compost pit; planting and care of shade trees; running of cooperative stores; the school panchayat; helping adults in productive work.

In classes V/VI to VII/VIII activities as in the previous classes will be continued but they will be of an advanced type.

Work practice will be in the form of projects selected from the list given below:

Two projects at least be selected from the following illustrative activities in each class.

1. *Health and Hygiene*

Making of tooth powder; soap; disinfectants; detergent powder; hair oil; brooms; waste-paper baskets; dust bins; compost manure; first aid boxes; health posters; booklets on health and hygiene; keeping health records; keeping the neighbourhood clean; working at health centres.

2. *Food*

Growing of selected vegetables and ornamental plants in plots or pots, where possible for sale.

Seed collecting; soil testing; experimentation with different kinds of soil, different types of seeds, different kinds of manure; vegetative propagation by cutting; vegetative propagation by breeding; vegetative propagation by grafting; vegetative reproductivity; layering; soil conservation.

Making of jam; jelly; ketchup sauce; pickles; fruit juices; confectionery or bakery items.

Working in canteens or stalls for a specified period.

Packing of food material.

3. *Shelter*

Making articles of use with the help of any material, making stationery items; white washing; polishing doors, windows, and furniture; caning chairs; repairs of furniture; casual labour work in the school.

4. *Clothing*

Spinning, making school bags; school uniforms; handkerchiefs; table-clothes; pillowcases; knitting; making mats.

5. *Culture and Recreation*

Toy-making; artificial flowers; pottery painting; making games material; cards for festivals; fancy covers for books and bookbinding, fancy candle-making.

6. *Community Work and Allied Social Service*

Helping adults in their work as Projects, such as, keeping a specified area clean; helping in the care of the sick; first aid; helping at functions and during festivals; traffic control; helping in the literacy campaign.

(c) Classes VIII/IX-X
Greater emphasis should be placed on work practice in these classes. Work practice will include one main

craft or equivalent service and at least one subsidiary craft or equivalent service.

Main Areas of Activities

(i) *Health and Hygiene*
Growing medicinal plants; eradication of communicable diseases; paramedical service.

(ii) *Food*
Agro-industries; kitchen gardening; pot culture; crop and seed production; repair of farm implements; soil conservation and desert control; horticulture animal husbandry and dairying; bee-keeping; poultry farming; fish culture; bakery; confectionery; cooking.

(iii) *Shelter*
Pottery; masonry work; workshop practice (mechanical); workshop practice (electrical); workshop practice (electronics); cane and bamboo work; house craft; blacksmithy; foundry work; carpet weaving.

(iv) *Clothing*
Production of cotton, wool, silk and other fibres; weaving; dress making; knitting; hosiery work; embroidery work; dress designing leather work.

(v) *Culture and recreation*
Making toys and puppets; making and repairing musical instruments; making games material; printing; bookbinding; making stationery; photograph.

Subsidiary Areas of Activities

(i) *Health and Hygiene*
Cleanliness of the neighbourhood, well and pond and the disposal of garbage; construction of toilet facilities and compost pits; making tooth picks; tooth powder; soap; detergents; disinfectants; first aid boxes; construction of waste-paper baskets; dust bins; garbage cans; brooms: brushes; cob-web cleaners; dusters; mops; etc. detection of adulteration.

(ii) *Food*
Distribution of fertilisers and insecticides; processing and preservation of food; hydroponics; mushroom culture; khandsari gur and candy making; catering; making jam, jelly, squashes, pickles; bari and papad etc. packing food; marketing.

(iii) *Shelter*
Home, village and town planning. Lac culture. Renovation and effecting minor repairs in buildings, fittings, furniture and household articles. Decorating the home; gardening; surface decoration; interior decoration; construction of decorative pieces; plaster of pairs work; chalk and candle making; making limestone.

(iv) *Clothing*
Spinning of different fibres; dyeing and printing repair of garments; laundry work.

(v) *Culture and recreation*
Stage craft; making costumes; holding exhibitions.

Teachers

Importance of teachers

The provision of properly skilled teachers for the implementation of the programme of Socially Useful Productive Work is of the utmost importance. In order to give this area of work its proper place in the school programme it is recommended that:

(i) The professional status of teachers of Socially Useful Productive Work should be the same as that of other teachers;

(ii) There should be provision for the part-time employment of skilled personnel for different activities;

(iii) There should be cells for Socially Useful Productive Work in the State Department of Education and the State Institutes of Education to develop programmes of in service training;

(iv) a scheme of course content of Socially Useful Productive Work for Teacher Training Colleges should be produced. NCERT in collaboration with such other institutes which have included manual labour in their regular programmes.

Implementation

Committees

Coordinated efforts should be made for the implementation of the programme.

High level committees at the Central level and State level should be constituted by the respective Departments of Education so that the decisions made by them should invariably be accepted and implemented without delay. These Committees meet regularly to review the progress of work in these areas and remove difficulties in implementation and also create a climate of opinion in favour of this area of the curriculum.

(From Report of the Review Committee on the Curriculum for the 'Ten Year School—Government of India, Ministry of Education, 1977).

27

Principle of Nationalism (Education and Nation)

All human beings belong to society, similarly they also belong to a nation or state and thus alike social responsibility they have to perform some national duties. But according to some intellectuals, it hampers internationalism. Yet there are other intellectuals who say that unless someone is nationalist, he cannot be internationalist, therefore, this chapter is devoted to study the subject as a principle of education.

What is Nation

Nation can be defined as that human group which lives in an area with clearly defined geographical boundaries, united by common traditions, common interests and common sentiments, possessing a desire for unity and common political ambitions. Elements which go to make up the nation are of two kinds—the objective and the subjective. Among the six elements are—geographical unity, unity of language, unity of race, a common religion, political unity and independence.

According to Renan and Mill, it must also possess consciousness of a glorious past, feelings of pride and shame, happiness and pain, common experience and sacrifice, true glory, allied to this past. The chief among these emotive elements are common interests and traditions, common political ambitions, and most important of all, a community feeling, or we feeling.

Consciousness of Nationality

Community feeling or we feeling is such an important constituent of nationhood, that MacIver has defined nationality in terms of this feeling. He defines nationality as a kind of community feeling that has its origin in certain historical circumstances, and which is also strengthened by such strong common psychological factors. Oppenheimer has commented that consciousness of nationality makes the nation.

Nationality and Education

This consciousness of nationality is generated in the younger generation through education, and hence, there is a profound relationship between nationality and education. In India, when the revolt against the British government was awakened, all national leaders demanded the formation of a national educational programme.

They argued that the educational programme of the country should be modified to suit the requirements of the nation. In 1921, Mahatma Gandhi expressed his views on this subject in *Young India*. He demanded that the educational pattern must be modified to suit the demands of the nation. His reasons for adding manual work to education were sound.

Rabindra Nath Tagore conducted an experiment in Shantiniketan to produce a novel kind of human society in which the problems of the individual and the community, the nation and the world, could be solved simultaneously.

Swami Dayanand insisted upon reforming education to suit the educational pattern that existed in ancient times. On the other hand, Annie Besant's educational plan, which included the establishment of primary schools, lower middle schools, higher middle schools, high schools for general education, high schools for general science, commercial schools, technical high schools, agricultural high schools etc., was more directory in touch with the problems of contemporary India.

Madan Mohan Malviya established the Hindu University at Kashi in order to realise the ideals of education which prevailed in ancient India. Sri Aurobindo, Vivekanand, etc. also favoured the modification of the educational pattern in order to make it conform to ancient Indian values, ideas and thinking.

In more recent times, in his report of the Universities Commission, Dr. S. Radhakrishnan pointed out the defects of the existing pattern of education, and suggested that it should be refashioned to fulfil national needs. Everyone has stressed the need for education to be a character building process, because without this the future of the nation will always remain dark.

Dr. S. Radhakrishnan has said that the future of the nation is made by character. No country can be great if its inhabitants have low characters. If we want to create a great nation, we must educate our young men and women in such a manner that they should posses the force of character.

Stressing the need for an education for nationality the Kothari Education Commission has said that the objective of our system of education should be to develop national consciousness. For this we must develop the knowledge of our cultural heritage, but we must also submit this cultural heritage to revaluation. At the same time, we must have faith in the future towards which we are moving.

Development of Nationalism in the New Generation

Following suggestions can be given for generating nationalism in the younger generation; through proper education:

1. *Development of a national language.* The first prerequisite for developing nationalism is the development of a national language in the country. In India, this position can be occupied only by Hindi. When the succeeding generations learn Hindi and use it, the feeling will gradually take root that India is one nation.

2. *Development of a national literature.* Development of a national language will lead to the development of a national literature. With the propagation of Hindi in every part of the country, a new literature will be created, which will be read everywhere. Apart from encouraging national unity, it will also enable the people to create a literature which encourages national power and protects the cultural heritage of the country.

3. *National educational programme.* In India, the spread of education is the responsibility of both the central and the state governments but as yet, it has not been possible to formulate a national programme of education with the result that one can see considerable disparity in the various parts of the country.

In order to evolve a feeling of nationalism, the country should have unified educational programme which should be flexible enough to take within its purview the differences that exist between one region and another. This will lead to a certain similarity in the education in all parts, and make possible the application of a single curriculum through which national literature on the all India scale can be created.

4. *Observance of national festivals.* The feeling of nationalism can also be strengthened by enthusiastic observance of national festivals, independence day, republic day, children's day, teacher's day and the birthdays of all great men.

5. *Respect for national symbols.* Another way of fostering the feeling of nationalism is to generate and show respect for national symbols such as the national anthem, the national flag, the national bird, etc. Now-a-days the national anthem is played after every film show and people are required to stand at attention to show their respect for it. This also helps growth of national sentiment.

6. *Improvements of curriculum.* In order to help the development of the national sentiment, it is desirable that the teaching of history, civics, etc., should be conducted in such a way that it helps national sentiment. This can be done by preventing the publication of any material in text books and other media of publication which hurt national sentiments and pride. The government seizes all copies of such material and punishes the publishers and authors.

7. *Cooperation of political parties.* It is impossible to generate nationalism if the political parties fail to cooperate. Many political parties not only hinder the growth of this sentiment, but actively engage in activities calculated to harm the national interest. Such political parties owe their allegiance to other nations, show no respect for national symbols and spread anti-national feelings among the people. As far as

possible, political parties should be prevented from indulging in such activities.

8. Cooperation of teachers. Education for nationalism can never be really successful without the active co-operation of teachers. For this reason the educators must themselves possess this feeling, because then they can set an example for the educands. It will then be even easier to foster the national sentiment among the younger generation.

Synthesis of Nationalism and Internationalism

Now-a-days many thinkers object to the use of education for fostering the national sentiment because they have come across many bad effects of narrow nationalism in many countries and seen that education for nationalism has stood in the way of the growth of internationalism.

The education for nationalism that was given in Italy and Germany, for example, was completely opposed to internationalism. It is in connection with this one-sided education that Bernand Russell pointed out that children are taught to exhibit complete devotion and worship to the state of which they are citizens. The lesson taught to them is that worship of the state consists in doing as directed by the state.

For this, they are taught distorted versions of history, politics and economics so that they should not be critical of the blind national faith expected of them. They are acquainted with the evil actions of other nations but not of their own, although the truth is that each nation has been unjust to other nations. It is unquestionably true that if the facts of history are distorted in order to propagate the sentiment of nationalism it is undesirable. But this danger is not peculiar to nationalism alone.

It is true of almost all human relations that as they become deeper and stronger they also become narrower, and that they impede the growth of any liberal attitude. If, for example, an individual has intense love for his family, this may come in the way of his loving his nation, but this does not imply that love for nation can exist only at the cost of love for family.

Proper and healthy love for the family does not impede love for the nation, it helps it to grow. In the same way, healthy nationalism also does not preclude the possibility of internationalism.

As Dr. Louise has said that it is essential to strengthen one's love for one's motherland, but this does not make it proper to violate the cannons of humanity, for the external benefit of one's own nation. It is obvious, therefore, that education must not only propagate nationalism but must also encourage internationalism. The plan for national education presented by such eminent educationists as Mahatma Gandhi, Sri Aurobindo, Vivekanand, Rabindra Nath Tagore, etc. has kept this in view, that nationalism and internationalism should grow harmoniously.

That is the reason why Rabindra Nath Tagore's Shantiniketan turned into an ideal institution for education in internationalism. According to Tagore, the educand's aim is to reach the level at which there is no distinction between nationalism and internationalism.

Obstacles in the Development of Nationalism

The progress and growth of nationalism in India is being impeded by certain elements and obstacles, the more important ones among which are the following:

1. Casteism. Casteism is the most restricted form the narrow interests. As a result of this, not only the country but even Hindu society has been fragmented into small pieces, each one of which is concerned only with preserving its own interests, without caring for those of other groups.

1. Castesim
2. Regionalism
3. Communalism
4. Linguism
5. Classicism (economic and social classes)
6. Untouchability

The purpose behind recounting these obstacles to national sentiment is to point out that both negative and positive steps must be taken. Nationalism can be spread among the younger generation by following the suggestions given earlier and also by removing these hindrances. Mutual cooperation between the people, government and educators is of the essence. It is impossible to improve the country's future without increasing the sentiment of nationalism, irrespective of industrial and scientific progress. The future of the nation is dark unless a high national character of the people is formed.

QUESTIONS FOR ANSWER

1. Write short note on place of Nationalism in Education.
2. What is meant by 'national culture'? How can children imbibe it through various agencies of education? Answer the question with special references to the present day needs of India.

28

Principle of Emotional and Inter-Cultural Integration (Education for Emotional and Inter-Cultural Integration)

Emotions and culture guide most human actions, therefore, there is an urgent need for emotional and inter-cultural integration for the good of Indian society and nation because India is a land of cultural diversities, though we have a sense of unity in diversity. The principle of emotional and inter-cultural integration in education aims at infusing complete unity among younger people, through our system of education, a brief of which is given hereunder:

Meaning of Emotional Integration

Meaning of Emotional Integration—Emotional integration means that feeling which ties into one whole all the diverse castes, creeds and various groups of persons by raising them above narrow differences and divisions. It brings about an emotional synthesis of diverse elements. With the development of this national consciousness, all individuals pursue national ideals, contribute to national aspirations and solve all the national problems with all sincerity and devotion.

India is a nation and we all people, belonging to diverse religions, castes and groups, are its inhabitants. Thus it is our joint responsibility to defend the freedom of our nation. But this is possible only when all of us are fired with the flame of national love and are fully devoted to national integrity and prosperity.

Need of Emotional Integration

During the alien rule, the British people tried with all cunningness at their command, to divide the Indian people on lines of caste, religious creeds, regionalism and language diversities in order to consolidate their hold on India.

They succeeded in their nefarious attempt to a great extent. But ultimately they had to leave this country and now we are a free nation. This could be possible only when all the Indians got united under the spell of nationalism and struggled as one people against the alien rule.

It is really a matter of pity today that fissiparous tendencies and disintegrating forces namely casteism, communalism, regionalism and provincialism are raising their ugly heads again threatening the very existence of the nation.

Not only this, every now and then one hears a call of separate home land for this or that region or this or that section of population. This virus of communalism and sectarianism is developing into fends and conflicts endangering national integrity and prosperity. Such evil mentality has to be stopped because it is a very vital need of the times.

The recourse is to propagate ideals of national strength and national well-being. The slogan of essential unity in diversity should be our moto all over the country.

For this, we should develop a feeling of belongingness to the nation. This ardent devotion to national ideal will develop our national character which the country needs for its survival.

Education and Emotional Integration

If we want to change a nation, we should change the minds of that nation. In other words education is the only means to change the mentality of the people who constitute the nation. Thus if we wish to achieve true emotional integration in India, we should re-organize our system of education keeping into consideration the high ideal of emotional integration.

For this, our education should inculcate national and human values forming attitudes of respect for national culture, national history, national traditions, national language together with a sense of honour for national emblem.

In other words, our people should be moulded through education in such a way that they think, feel and act like one nation. Such education will foster emotional integration leading the nation to the pinnacle of national glory and prosperity.

Emotional Integration Committee

It is clear from the above discussion that education is a potent means to achieve emotional integration and national unity. As such the ministry of education at the centre appointed a committee in 1961 to suggest measures for meeting the fissiparous tendencies and promoting emotional affinity.

Dr. Sampurnanand, the chairman of this committee has rightly remarked—"This is unity in the country and it will remain united howsoever great may be the diversities in its inhabitants. But the demand made today for national and emotional integration is to do away with those fissiparous tendencies which want to sap the strength of the country."

Suggestions of Emotional Integration Committee

The emotional integration committee gave out the following suggestions for the purpose of attaining emotional integration:

(1) Reconstruction of Curriculum—The curriculum needs to be re-organized with a view to meet the following needs of the nation:

- *(a)* At the Primary Stage, national anthem, other songs, poems and stories of national feelings should be included in the curriculum.
- *(b)* At the Secondary Stage, social studies, language, literature, cultural, moral and religious instruction together with co-curricular activities should be included in the curriculum.
- *(c)* At the University Stage, comparative study of different languages, literatures, arts, cultural attainments and social sciences should be encouraged and insisted

upon. In addition, students and teachers should be provided proper facilities for country wide tours to different places in the country.

(2) *Co-curricular Activities*—At different levels of education, besides the above mentioned subjects, topics and items, other co-curricular activities fostering national outlook and national attitudes should be properly organized.

(3) *Text Books*—There should be a close scrutiny of all text books and general books which contain anti-national items and references. Such harmful things should be scrupulously removed from books and only such items and narrations should be allowed which foster emotional and national integration.

(4) *Language*—As to language, the committee advanced the following suggestions:

(*a*) In some areas, use of Roman script should be allowed. This will promote knowledge of Hindi language and literature.

(*b*) International numericals should be used in the whole country.

(*c*) In those areas where Hindi is not spoken or written, facility should be given to understand this language through their own regional languages.

(*d*) Dictionaries of Hindi and regional languages should be got prepared and standard books of Hindi be translated into regional languages.

(*e*) At the University level, greater attention should be paid to the teaching and study of Hindi and English. More and more facilities be provided for the same.

(*f*) In the formulation of national policy on language, proper attention should be given to the needs of the minorities.

(5) *Other Suggestions*—The committee gave some other suggestions about various items as under:

(*a*) Before the start of teaching work, there should be a common assembly of all students in a school and a common prayer be sung.

(*b*) For about ten minutes, the teachers, from school and learned persons from outside the school should be invited to speak about general morality and day-to-day living daily.

(*c*) Each and every child of the school should, once in a year, take a solemn pledge of national service.

Place of Teacher

For the development of emotional integration, the place of teacher is a matter of great importance. We need such teachers who are well imbued with the feelings of emotional affinity and fellow-feeling, lead their lives above caste, creed and regionalism and possess national outlook together with national interests above their own self interests or the interests of their community or group.

Meaning of Inter-Cultural Understanding

Inter-cultural understanding refers to the development of that insight and attitude in the individuals who, rising above their own selfish and narrow interests, find out the really valuable items in all the other cultures, besides their own. This leads to the synthesis of cultures which goes by the name of National Culture.

With such a developed all-embracing attitude and point of view, the individuals try to understand and appreciate the values, ideals and qualities in other religions, castes, customs, traditions, ways of living of other sections of Indian society.

This feeling avoids all kinds of conflicts and fends and promotes fellow feeling and Co-operative attitudes which eventually lead to national unity and in turn to international brotherhood also.

Need for Developing Inter-Cultural Understanding

Our country is a big one. People belonging to various communities and groups are its inhabitants The culture patterns of all these different communities and groups are different. In other words the ideals, values, customs, traditions, ways of living, eating and dressing of different communities and sections are different. Because of this diversity, these communities live in isolation from others.

This isolation and mutual tension, unfortunately, leads to

national disintegration. In other words, the goal of emotional integration and national unity is shattered under the stress and impact of such mutual tensions and conflicts.

Thus national progress stands still and the nasty process of decay and destruction sets in. Such state of affairs has to be checked up and all kinds of differences resolved by the promotion of liberal, tolerant and all embracing out-look in the citizens. Then only, cultural synthesis will take place which is so essential in our country.

A large number of minority people reside over here. They should be made to feel the sense of belongingness to one nation or one mother country. This feeling will develop in them when they have a sense of security and find respect, regard and appreciation for their religion, culture and traditions of social living. It should be remembered that this feeling of oneness is a must in all the citizens. Only then, our nation will march ahead on the road of progress avoiding all pitfalls of diversities.

Education and Development of Inter-Cultural Understanding

Education is a powerful medium to achieve the high ideal of inter-cultural understanding. It can mould an individual into any form we like. As such, we should provide such wholesome educational experiences and programmes which develop this understanding of other's cultural patterns, beliefs and ways of living. They will be able, then, to understand and also to appreciate the ideals and values of others.

Development of such understanding will promote co-operation and through a process of give and take, a cultural synthesis will take place. Such education will be able to achieve the high goal of national culture so essential to National unity and National Integration.

Teacher plays a very vital role in promoting the inter-cultural understanding. It should be noted that only those teachers can perform this noble task who are themselves full of such a noble sentiment of inter-cultural understanding.

They possess the requisite insight and knowledge of intricate values of the culture of others and have a word of appreciation for them. They lead a life above petty selfish interests, narrow attitudes and promote by their words and deeds the high ideal of cultural understanding and emotional integration.

Educational Programme

To promote inter-cultural understanding the following programmes are suggested:

(1) To implement all those suggestions given for National Integration and Emotional Integration.
(2) Children should be provided such experiences which promote their knowledge about other cultures.
(3) In the curriculum such subjects should be included which develop this understanding.
(4) National language should be made compulsory. This will lead to free exchange of thoughts and feelings among all the children of the country. This will also instill in them a sense that they belong to the nation and thus they will begin to love and admire their own Bhartiya culture.
(5) National and international celebrities should be invited for lectures and discussions in schools. This will add to the knowledge of other people and their cultures.
(6) Symposiums and seminars on different cultures should be organized in all schools.
(7) School should not impart knowledge of any specific religion.
(8) Teachers, writers, artists and cultural groups should be encouraged to travel in all parts of the country.

QUESTIONS FOR ANSWER

1. Define emotional integration and write a note on the impediments in its attainment.
2. Explain inter-cultural understanding and define how it can be developed through the system of education.

29

Principle of National Integration (Education for National Integration)

Emotional and inter-cultural integration is a social aspect of national unity, whereas national integration is a political proposition for the good of the nation, which is a must for the present day political set up in India—the land of unity in diversity.

It is a well-established fact that in spite of various stresses and strains over the ages, there has been remarkable cultural continuity in the history of the Indian nation.

Meaning of National Integration

Politically, India is one, united and integrated. But National Integration is much more than mere political unity. It includes the feelings and sentiments of its citizens which govern their political and public behaviour. A nation is said to be integrated if its citizens, maybe belonging to any caste, community, religion, language and state, have feeling of oneness, share each others joys and sorrows, smiles and tears and have an interest in the welfare of the nation as a whole.

The citizens of an integrated nation have mutual understanding, tolerance, and respect for the culture, traditions and ways of life of the different sections of people in their country. They have common national ideals, common objectives, common interests and above all a profound confidence in the future of the nation. National integration is the end whereas emotional integration is the means to achieve that end.

India—Unity in Diversity

India is a country with many diversities. People belonging to different religions, castes, creeds, languages and cultures live here. But this is no problem in itself. The main trouble is that Indian people are narrow minded. They have local, regional, linguistic, religious and other sectional or parochial loyalties. They take pride in calling themselves Punjabis, Bengalis, South Indians rather than Indians or Hindustanis. They think in terms of Hindus, Sikhs, Muslims, Christians etc. Many a time, Indians have forgotten warning of Pt. Jawaharlal Neheru, who said:

> "We should not become parochial, narrow-minded, provincial, communal and caste-minded, because we have a great mission to perform. Let us stand up right, with straight backs and look up at the skies, keeping our feet completely and firmly planted on the ground and bring about this synthesis, this integration of the Indian people."

Now the question arises whether the country can make progress when people are torn apart among themselves; when there is disunity in their ranks and files; when there are narrow religious, linguistic and provincial loyalties; when there is no love and sympathy between man and man, when there is no national consciousness, and when selfishness, greed and lust for power reign supreme all round. The answer is a big "No". Then what remedy is there for all these ills? Only "National Integration."

Importance of National Integration

The view of C.D. Deshmukh. Feelings of belonging to one nation are essential for the progress of the country. It is especially needed for the success of democracy. As Sh. C.D. Deshmukh has observed, "National Integration is the incalculable prerequisite for the fulfilment of our democracy."

Pt. Nehru's View. In the words of our late Prime Minister Pt. Nehru, "Political integration has already taken place to some extent, but what I am after is something much deeper than this—an emotional integration of the Indian people so that we might be welded into one, and made into one strong national unit, maintaining at the same time all our wonderful diversity".

Mahajan's View. Shri Mehar Chand Mahajan, Late Chief Justice of Supreme Court of India warned us, saying. "Unless steps are taken to create an emotional upsurge amongst the people for national unity, the fissiparous tendencies in the population may lead to serious consequences".

It is, thus, clear that the great need of the hour is emotional and national integration in our country, which is not a small geographical unit, but as big as a continent. On the one hand, we have to banish from our rank and file the enemies of national integration like casteism, communalism, linguism and regionalism, and on the other hand we have to remove the class conflict and emotional divorce between the educated classes and the illiterate masses.

Hurdles in the Way of National Integration

The following are the major hurdles in the way of national integration:

1. *Communalism.* Communalism is a great obstacle to national integration. There are many communities in India. The British accentuated the problem of communalism by their policy of 'Divide and Rule'. As a result of this policy, India was partitioned. It is natural for different communities to look after their own selfish interests but it should not be at the cost of other communities. A non-communal atmosphere should be built up and maintained in India.

2. *Religious Prejudices.* Religious Prejudice is related to communalism and casteism. Every community is free to develop its religion but not at the cost of other religions. Religious prejudice and communal narrowness have partitioned India and they are still prevalent in one shape or the other.

India is a secular state but still there are sudden outbreaks of violence in the name of religion. Religious feelings are also aroused and exploited in elections. This endangers national integration.

3. *Casteism.* Caste system hampers the progress of national integration. Casteism causes bitterness among the people. It prevents people from getting a reasonable opportunity in all fields only because of accident of birth. The system widens the gulf between the people of different castes and prevents their coming closer.

4. *Linguism.* Language, which is considered to be a great uniting force, has become a disruptive factor in India. Some people make language a cloak for their ambitious designs particularly in politics and employment.

One can understand the desire of linguistic minorities to provide education to their children in their mother tongue. But when this question is mixed up with other matters it becomes a disruptive factor.

5. *Regionalism.* Another force hindering integration is the feeling of regionalism. Two factors have given rise to this feeling. The first is the urge of the people speaking a simple language to form distinct linguistic state. Another is the urge of economic development.

Then, there is the dangerous disruptive ideology, propounded by certain political parties regarding the question of North and South. This ideology should be met strongly and the vested interests of the persons who want a separate Southern State should be exposed.

6. *Provincialism.* Provincialism is another obstacle in the way of national integration. People think themselves as Gujarati, Marathi, Bengali, Punjabi etc. but they don't think themselves to be Indians. Some states do not even admit students from other states in their institutions of higher learning. This tendency of provisionalism should be curbed because it tends to disintegrate our country.

7. *Defective Education System.* Our defective education system is also responsible for lack of national and emotional integration. System of Education should have been changed after independence, but, practically nothing has been done. On January 1978, Indira Gandhi, stated in Gandhigram, "One of

the biggest mistakes we made when we gained independence was not to have overhauled thoroughly our educational system and structure.

Several features of our present educational system give promotion to divisive tendencies. Kothari Education Commission has clearly stated, "Instead of promoting social and national integration and making an active effort to promote national consciousness, several features of the educational system promote divisive tendencies".

8. Foreign Language as a Medium of Instruction. Importance of English as an international language and its rich literature can't be denied but to adopt it as medium of instruction and expression has resulted in disintegration of people to some extent. This hampered the development of Indian languages and consequently the people of different states could not come close to one another.

Similarly, English as medium of instruction has created the gap between the educated and the uneducated people. The educated people, particularly through the medium of English, think themselves superior. It is needed that English as a medium of instruction should be replaced by Indian languages as early as possible.

9. Economic Conditions. Economic conditions affect integration. Frustration felt by educated young people, who do not find employment makes them prone to indiscipline and easy victims to anti-social and anti-national ideas.

The provision of employment opportunities to those young men shall prove helpful to national integration. A better co-relation between country's needs and the supply of trained personnel should be brought about.

Education and National Integration

Kothari Commission links National Integration with Education as follows:

View of Indian Education Commission (1964-66). According to Kothari Education Commission, national integration means:

(*i*) Confidence in Nation's future.
(*ii*) Continuous rise in the standard of living of masses.

(*iii*) Reduction in unemployment.
(*iv*) Provision of equal opportunities for social, economic and political development.
(*v*) A deep sense of obligation of citizenship.
(*vi*) Identification of the people not with sectional loyalties but with nation as a whole.
(*vii*) Good and impartial administration.
(*viii*) Respect for cultural traditions and ways of life of different communities of the people and mutual understanding.

Dr. Radhahrishnan's View. In the words of Dr. Radhakrishnan, "National Integration cannot be built by brick and mortar or with chisel and hammer. It has to grow silently in the minds and hearts of men and the process by which it can be achieved is Education".

A matter of feeling and attitude. National Integration is a matter of feelings; it is a matter of attitude with the individual feelings and attitudes developed during the impressionable period of one's life, continue to influence his life upto the last breath. Child spends this period of life in schools. So schools can play an important role in inculcating feeling of patriotism, unity and love for mankind.

Dr. Shrimali's View. Dr. K. L. Shrimali at the inaugural meeting of National Integration Committee, observed, "If we are convinced that in the present state of our development we must make a deliberate effort to develop national consciousness among our people it is a legitimate demand that our educational system should be geared to fulfil this purpose.

Educational policies and practices are determined largely by national needs and requirements and our greatest need today is the development of national consciousness among our youth. Schools must become the instruments for the realisation of national ideals. They must give to the youth a feeling of common interest and a sense of belongingness to a worthy national community, which had a great past and the present full of hopes and dreams merging into a glorious future.

Education must make the growing youth realise that they are indissolubly bound to the nation and its destiny, its tragedies, joys, its conflicts and settlements, its failures and achievements, its mistakes and wisdom and they should come to regard it with pride and with love and the impelling desire to serve it wholeheartedly.

The View of Secondary Education Commission. This very point was emphasised by the Secondary Education Commission in 1953 when it said, "If Education does not strengthen the forces of national cohesion and solidarity, we are afraid that our freedom, our national unity as well as our future progress will be seriously imperiled".

National Integration Through Education

As we have noted above, education can definitely play a vital role in strengthening national integration. By its deliberately planned programme, education can develop all aspects of a student's personality by broadening his outlook, fostering a feeling of oneness and nationalism so that his narrow group interests be submerged in the larger interests of the country. This programme can be undertaken by adopting the following measures.

1. *Restating the Aims of Education.* Education should aim at creating a feeling among rising generations that the country and her resources belong to them. Education should also aim at encouraging all those studies and activities which lead to greater understanding between different communities and different states thus fostering a feeling of national unity.

2. *National System of Education.* We have not succeeded during the last thirty five years in evolving a national system of education. The central and state governments do not pull together in the implementation of the educational policies, particularly where these policies have national approach. Effective co-ordination between the centre and the states is absolutely necessary to evolve an effective national policy of education.

(*a*) There should be common pattern of education throughout the country. The recommendations of the Education Commission (1964-66) are important in this respect.

(*b*) The Central Government should assume a great responsibility in this regard in the interest of national unity.

(*c*) There need not be a uniform syllabus for schools all over the country but only the broad framework.

(*d*) Similar opportunities for education with similar standards all over the country are necessary for emotional integration.

3. *The Teaching of Languages*. India is a country with a variety of languages. In different states, different languages are taught upto Secondary and University levels and these are also the media of instruction. It is really a pity that even after more than two decades of India's independence we could not so far decide about a common language for the whole of the country.

Our youth festivals, inter-state and inter-University competitions in soprts, debates, dramas and music, our all India organisations like Boy-Scouts, Girl-Guides and the like, will, no doubt, go a long way in fostering national integration.

But better, quicker and permanent integration of different communities in different states will be possible only if one common language is studied compulsorily by every student at the secondary stage throughout India.

4. *Methods of Teaching*. The methods of teaching in schools should aim not merely at the imparting of knowledge but also at inculcating desirable values and proper attitudes in the students. Students should be given adequate opportunities to work in groups and to carry out group projects so that the qualities which are most essential for group life and cooperative work are developed in them.

5. *Courses of Study*. The text-books are not written from the national point of view. They do not give the idea of a nation. Rather, they give the idea of a state. These text-books should include folk tales collected from different parts of India, biographies of all national heroes, human geography of each region, an account of the heritage of each region in art, industry and literature.

Map reading should be made compulsory so that the pupils become familiar with whole of the country. These will help to inculcate national outlook in our children.

6. Educational tours and Trips. Educational tours and trips are very useful for national integration. These help the students to have first hand knowledge about their country. They come to know about the type of life lived by their countrymen in different areas like the hilly areas or the areas near the sea shore, their ways of eating and drinking, their religious and cultural ceremonies and their occupations. Thus educational tours must be encouraged in our schools for achieving national integration.

7. Co-curricular Activities. An extensive programme of co-curricular activities can help to inculcate national feelings in our students. Such activities should include:

(*a*) Singing of National Anthem and national songs.
(*b*) Saluting the Nation Flag.
(*c*) Celebration of National Days and birth anniversaries of national leaders.
(*d*) Inter-school debates and declamations on topics concerning national integration.
(*e*) Arranging talks on topics dealing with the unity and oneness of the country.
(*f*) Conducting Social Service Programmes.
(*g*) Display of films of national importance.
(*h*) Celebrating festivals of other communities.
(*i*) Students' participation in dramas depicting glorious events in our Indian history or the life of great national heroes.
(*j*) N.C.C. etc.

It is suggested that these activities and many more should be made compulsory for national integration. It is generally observed that many of the institutions in less developed areas do not celebrate even the national days. Such days are taken merely in terms of holidays.

8. Exchange Programmes. The government should arrange that some teachers and students from one state in the North go and study in another state in the South and vice-versa. It will held our teachers and students of one part of the country to live in another part of the country and appreciate the ways of life of that area. Their acquaintances and friendship in that area will help to bring national integration. It is quite satisfying to note that the government is doing a lot in this direction through its scheme of scholarships. The Conference of State education Secretaries held in October 1968 recommended exchange of studies, teachers and educational administrators at the secondary and University level to promote national integration.

9. *Moral and Religious Education.* People of different religions and faiths live in our country. India is a secular state and everyone is free to have faith in his religion, enrich it and propagate its principles. Narrow religious feelings, many times bring the people of different religion into clash and the result is communal riots. The riots endanger life and property. The main thing required is the right approach, right attitude, open-mindedness, religious toleration and mutual understanding. This can be achieved through a programme of religious and moral teaching. This programme should include the fundamental principles of all religions. The best talent available in the country should be drawn for the preparation of this programme so that the essential values of each religion are included without getting involved in theological doctrines.

10. *Projects for Improving Knowledge about Other States.* Knowledge about their states is essential for national integration. The Committee on Emotional Integration (1963) suggested that "schools may conduct several projects which improve their students' general knowledge of country". For example, a 'know your country' project can be undertaken during which children may share in collection of information about a state in India other than their own.

11. *Encouraging Inter-State Pen-friendship.* Inter-state Pen-friendship among both teachers and students should be encouraged in every educational institution. Every school should have addresses of teachers and students living in different states of the country. These will facilitate exchange of letters among teachers and students living in different parts of the country. This exchange will help them in many ways. First, it will help them to increase their knowledge about the country. Secondly, it will facilitate travelling as they are likely to receive invitations to visit their friends. Such activities will develop interest and love for the nation and promote understanding among students and teachers living in different parts of the country.

12. Organising National Integration Camps. It is heartening to note that the Union Ministry of Education has started the organization of National Integration camps in the country. This is a step in the right direction and it will prove quite useful in inculcating feelings of oneness among the students and teachers. Everyday the participants in the camp are enabled to pick up simple conversational skill in the language of the camp mates, the campers are acquainted with special religious and social customs of their camp mates. They also give lectures on the contribution of their respective states to the national life and economy. The main object of such camps is to enable school students understand and appreciate the social and cultural life of people in different states of India.

13. Role of the Teacher. Children are the most sensitive section of the community. They look to us for guidance and imitate our ways of life. This takes place imperceptibly. Millions of children's eyes are focussed on us and there are no eyes more observant, keen and preceptive than the eyes of a child. So if we really wish our children to be good, honest brave, national minded and patriotic, we will have to get our own example before them. Let teachers act up to brotherhood among his pupils.

National Integration Committee

The Government of India appointed two committees—one for Emotional Integration and the other for National Integration. Dr. Sampurna Nand became the chairman of the committee for emotional integration in 1961 and Mrs. Indira Gandhi presided over the committee for national integration in 1967.

Here we are discussing about the national integration committee. The first meeting of this committee was held in June 1968 at Sri Nagar (Kashmir) where it delebrated upon and expounded the main aims of national development and discussed about the various problems that beset this all important task. It appointed a sub-committee to tackle the various problems allied with the task.

The first was concerned with the problem of achieving communal harmony, the other concerned itself with the problems of regionalism and the third tackled the task of re-organizing the educational system to achieve unity in the diversities which beset the nation.

All the three sub-committees put forward weighty suggestions before the national integration committee which accepted all the recommendations made by three sub-committees.

The national integration committee while giving valuable suggestions for the work of national consolidation, also exhorted in clear terms that this very essential tast can not be tackled by government alone. The responsibility to help in the achievement of this great ideal lies on the shoulders of each and every citizen. Thus it appealed to every citizen to do the best in achieving this most sacred and vital task of national consolidation.

Suggestions of National Integration Committee

The national integration committee while recommending measures for national integration, also laid out important aims of education to attain. They are as under:

(1) All children should be made familiar with all the various aspects of national life.

(2) All children should be given knowledge about the important events and happenings of national movement for national independence.

(3) That education should be organised and those educational programmes be structured which teach the essential unity in the diversities of national life, and which try to inculcate in the children qualities of communal harmony and human fellow feeling.

Suggestions for Educational Programmes for National Integration

The committee prescribed the following measures for national unity:

(i) Scrutiny of the books, taught in schools, should be made.

(ii) Items which spoil national outlook and preach antinational things should be removed from those books.

(iii) People of different castes and religions should willingly participate in national fairs and festivals.
(iv) Dramas and discussions advocating national harmony should be organised all over the country.
(v) Motion pictures Radio, Television and newspaper should be harnessed to achieve national unity.
(vi) Special films should be made to demolish antinational tendencies.
(vii) All government services should be thrown open to all without any consideration of caste, creed, colour, sex, region and province.
(viii) National views and attitudes of the candidates should be tested and given due credit while recruiting them for higher posts and services.

Programme of Education for Developing National Integration

Keeping into consideration the above recommendations, the programme of education in schools should be organised in such a way that they foster a spirit of ardent nationalism and national unity. We are throwing light on the educational programme to be organized at different levels in the following lines:

(1) Primary Stage—At this stage the following programmes should be organised:

(i) Children should learn about National Flag, National Song, National Emblem, National Flower, National Bird and other national objects.
(ii) Independence day and Republic day should be celebrated as national festivals by all people of the land.
(iii) Children's day, Teacher's day and birth days of great personalities should be celebrated with interest and enthusiasm.
(iv) Children should be made to know about the life stories of great Indian saints.
(v) Folk songs and folk lores should form an important part of curriculum.
(vi) Stories about the various areas of the country should be told to children.

(vii) A general description regarding the society of India should be given to children.

(viii) Human geography of all areas should be taught to all children in a general way.

(2) *Secondary Stage*—At this stage the following programmes are prescribed:

(i) Children should be taught about the social and cultural history of the nation.

(ii) They should learn about the social conditions and cultural traditions of different regions of the country.

(iii) Children should learn about the economic development of India.

(iv) National consciousness should be inculcated and stimulated.

(v) Lectures by leaders, discussions, debates, symposia about national consolidation and national unity should be organised in all schools.

(vi) More and more use of national language should be encouraged in all spheres of national life.

(3) *University Stage*—The following programmes are suggested at the university stage:

(i) Children should be afforded more and more opportunities to do comparative study of various religions, regional cultures and languages with all seriousness and sincerity.

(ii) Youth festivals and other similar programmes should be organised throughout the country.

(iii) Study circles, symposia, discussions and debates should be organised for youths to participate and speak about topics of national importance at various places in the country from time to time.

QUESTIONS FOR ANSWER

1. What do you understand by 'National Integration'? What are the hurdles in the way of National Integration?
2. Why is National Integration important for us?

3. Emotional integration is the way to national integration. How can education help in training the emotions of young people?
4. "National integration is vital for India's survival". What educational programme do you suggest to bring about national and emotional integration?
5. Discuss the role of the school in promoting national integration.
6. What is education for National Integration? What programmes of education do you suggest for promoting National Integration.
7. Write a note on the efforts made by the government of India to foster national integration.
8. Write a note on the suggestions for educational programme for national integration.

30

Principle of International Understanding (Education for International Understanding)

The concept of international understanding in Indian philosophy is as old as the concept of mother and child relationship in human civilization. Ancient Indian philosophy teaches us that for larger human good all people must consider the whole world as family and follow the principle of universal brotherhood. The concept of international understanding is just a political concept and by and large the product of 20th century. Hereunder we will discuss this concept as a principle of education for the good of humanity.

Meaning and Definition

International understanding means in a sense world citizenship. This sense emphasizes that all human beings are fellows and members of the world family. As such, this feeling is concerned with international good will and contributes to the good of the whole humanity. In other words, international understanding indicates love, sympathy and co-operation among all the people of all the nations of the world.

International understanding implies mutual understanding, faith and respect among the various nations or countries of the world. With the development of the supersonic means of transportation and communication, all the countries of the world have come closer to each other.

Consequently, no country can remain aloof and unconcerned from other countries, because whatever is happening in one country, inevitably has its repercussions felt in other countries as well. This has necessitated mutually good and cordial relation amongst the countries of the world, which is termed as international understanding.

International understanding implies respect for human rights and dignity, as sense of the solidarity of mankind, international cooperation and to live together in peace with one another. Thus, international understanding is equated with world citizenship.

International Understanding Defined

1. *Oliver Goldsmith*: "International understanding or Internationalism is a feeling that the individual is not only a member of his state, but a member of the world".

2. *Dr. Walter H.C. Lewis*: "International understanding is the ability to observe critically and objectively, and appraise the conduct of man everywhere to each other, irrespective of the nationality or culture to which they may belong. To do this, one must be able to detach oneself from one's own particular cultural and national prejudices and to observe means of all nationalities, cultures and races as equally important varieties of human beings, inhabiting this earth".

3. *Dr. Atmananda Mishra*: "International understanding refers to friendship and harmony amongst different nations of the world and also includes co-operation amongst them—each one maintaining its identity and sovereignty as usual".

In the words of Dr. Radhakrishnan, "The world, once divided by oceans and continents, is united physically today, but there are still suspicions and misunderstandings. It is essential for us not to live apart but to live together, understanding one another's fears and anxieties, aspirations and thoughts, that is what we are expected to do. We must not claim a racial extermination, enslavement or segregation, but work for racial harmony. We may be German, we may be American, we may be Russian, but we are essentially human beings. Let us not overlook that fundamental fact. Let us learn to live in a world community".

Internationalism is one idea of the twentieth century. It came into prominence after the Second World War when it was realised that the world cannot afford another world war as its consequences may be extremely destructive.

The modern destructive weapons have necessitated in maintenance of everlasting peace. But peace, these days, does not mean peace between one particular community and the other, or between two or three particular nations. It means peace on international level—peace between man and man and narrow nationalism has no place in the present day circumstances of the world.

Differences of caste, colour, race and religion must not stand between man and man. The last two world wars have made it quite clear that force cannot solve our international disputes, such disputes can only be solved through negotiations, discussions, mutual understanding and amicable settlement in a peaceful atmosphere.

This is exactly what we mean by the term internationalism or 'international understanding'. Thus international understanding may be defined as, "Informed consciousness of the place of one's own nation in the world society and the contribution that it can make to world society, whose survival depends upon maintenance of peace and relief from war".

Need for International Understanding

Romain Rolland has rightly said—"The two global wars, with their terribly devastating results, have at least established the fact that the narrow bonds of sordid and aggressive nationalism must be smashed through and an unwalled unhedged federation of mankind should be brought into being for fostering human relations on the plane of love, pity and sympathy".

Arguments for Developing International Understanding

The following arguments are adduced in favour of international understanding:

(1) In this world, there are nations having different colours races and religions, but the inner soul or spirit is the same in all. The only difference is that people living in Germany are called Germans and people residing in Japan are known as Japanese. Much in the same way people belonging to America and Russia are designated as Americans and Russians respectively.

The real fact is that whole human race is one and the whole world is also one unit. To promote this feeling of oneness, the development of international understanding is essential.

(2) In the modern world, all nations have come so close to one another that events and occurrences in one nation have their direct impact upon the life of other nations also. Under such circumstances, if the emotion of fear will remain developing in all against the onslaughts of the other, each nation will prepare feverishly for defence or offence.

Thus more and more money and other resources will be diverted towards military preparations. Not only this, science will be exploited for human destruction. Hence a sense of international understanding should be developed in all people of the world so that each nation uses its resources for the welfare of humanity.

(3) Modern scientific researches like radio, T. V., wireless and jet planes etc., have annihilated the formidable barriers of time and place. No nation, howsoever protected by natural barriers, can feel secure in isolation today. All high mountains and deep oceans have been scaled and encompassed by human beings.

In other words, on account of a rapid rise in the means of transport and communication the whole world appears to have shrunk and become small in comparison with previous times. This closeness and nearness is increasing day-by-day. Hence our thinking should also change.

Prof. K. G. Saiyidain has rightly remarked—"A war starts in Europe and three millions die of famine in Bengal and millions more find themselves uprooted from their homes, cutoff from their normal occupations and deprived of all that makes life pleasant, gracious and meaningful".

(4) In the modern world of today, no nation can boast of its self-sufficiency and self-reliance. All the nations of the world depend upon each other economically, politically and culturally. In the field of industry, the success of a nation depends upon the raw material imported from other nations.

In the field of politics, every small nation tries to form an alliance with one of the big ones. Even the so-called neutral nations have their own block of nations dependent upon one another and upon others of different blocks. Not only this, the cultural bonds are also bringing all the nations of the world nearer and nearer with the result that no nation can boast of its own culture as pure.

We observe that the culture of a nation invades the culture of other nations. Hence it penetrates, changes and grows. As a result, a synthesis of all cultures is going on and a world culture is gradually coming into being today. All this clearly proves that the dire need is interdependence based upon strong bonds of international brotherhood and fellow feeling.

(5) As said above, all nations belong to one world. Thus all nations, backward or advanced belong to one family —The world family.

Just as all the members of a family have a duty and moral obligation for each other, much in the same way all nations of the world should feel dutiful and morally obliged for promoting the welfare of all others, may they be week, backward or advanced.

The affluent and developed nations should try to improve the conditions of poor, weekend backward nations. This will develop mutual love and friendship between all the nations resulting in peace and prosperity throughout the world.

(6) Each human being has certain desirable qualities namely—love, sympathy, co-operation and friendship. Geographical boundries can not delimit these human qualities. It is just possible that the political ideologies of citizens of different nations may differ but the essential milk of humanity is the same everywhere in all nations at all times. This fact should lead us towards international fellow-feeling and international understanding.

(7) In democracy, the thoughts, feelings and will of the people receive due consideration. To achieve success in this connection, education of the people is essential so that, before

expressing his point of view, each citizen thinks and plans properly with broad points of view. As such, the development of international understanding is essential.

(8) The development of international understanding has an immense value in our country. The chief reason of this fact is that India has recently attained its freedom. Now we have to develop our nation in all spheres.

For this, we need peace in the world. Pt. Jawahar Lal Nehru has rightly remarked—"Isolation means backwardness and decay. The world has changed and old barriers are breaking down, life becomes more international. We have to play one part in this coming internationalism".

Modern scientific means of rapid communication like the radio, the television, the telephone, etc., have conquered both time and space. There is more interdependence and intimate relationship in the world today.

The problem of international understanding is becoming increasingly important because with the modern scientific weapons for destruction another war may mean the end of the present civilization and humanity.

The painful recollections of the fate of Nagasaki and Hirshima are still vivid in the memory of the present generation. If peace and prosperity are to be created in our country, it becomes necessary to create good living conditions all over the world.

Therefore, the idea of internationalism must be inculcated in the minds of men. In the words of Pandit Jawahar Lal Nehru, "Isolation means backwardness, and decay. The world has changed and old barriers are breaking down; life becomes more international. We have to play our part in this coming internationalism".

To sum up, international understanding is needed because of the following reasons:

- *(a)* To prevent world wars,
- *(b)* To maintain one's sovereignty,
- *(c)* To strengthen democratic principles,
- *(d)* To develop backward nations,
- *(e)* To develop contacts with other countries,
- *(f)* To promote human welfare.

Now-a-days science and technology have completely removed the barriers of time and distance. The entire world has become one indivisible unit. Things have now come to such a pass that events in one country must affect other parts of the world.

After the removal of geographical barriers among the nations of the world, there is found a strong desire among them to have greater collaboration and co-operation with one another. The urgency of this collaboration and co-operation has greatly increased on account of the economic factors. All the countries of the world are economically interdependent upon each other.

Principles of International Understanding as Recommended by UNESCO

The UNESCO's programme or principles for international understanding are as follows:

1. Make it clear that unless steps are taken to educate mankind for the world-community, it will be impossible to create an international society conceived in the spirits of the Charter of the United Nations.
2. Make clear that States, whatever their differences of creeds and ways of life, have both a duty to cooperate in international organisations and an interest in so doing.
3. Make clear that civilization results from the cultivation of many nations and that all nations depend very much on each other.
4. Make clear the underlying reasons which account for the changing ways of life of different peoples, their past and present, their traditions, their characteristics, their problems and the ways in which they have been resolved.
5. Make clear that throughout the ages, moral, intellectual and technical progress has gradually grown to constitute a common heritage for mankind. Although the world is still divided by conflicting political interests and tensions, the interdependence

of people becomes daily more evident on every side. A world international organisation is necessary and it is now also possible.

6. Make clear that engagements freely entered into by the member states of international organisations have force only in so far as they are actively and effectively supported by those peoples.
7. Arouse in the minds, particularly of young people, a sense of responsibility to this world-community and to peace.
8. Encourage the development of healthy social attitudes in children so as to lay the foundations of improved international understanding and co-operation.

Education for International Understanding

All philosophers, educationists, politicians, scientists and social reformers of the world agree that while on the one hand United Nation Organization and other similar world organizations are striving to develop international good will in children, it is essential on the other hand that citizens of each nation should realize and appreciate the difficulties of the citizens of other nations and appreciate their good achievements.

Education is the only important and effective agency to develop such type of international understanding. The reason of this is that school has a special environment which includes the essential attributes of highest truth, beauty and goodness.

This fact has been confirmed in 'Towards World Understanding' (UNESCO) which lays "School may, and generally do represent the best elements in the surrounding culture. They should be and they generally are, above the average level of the community in their regard for truth and honesty and fair dealing. They contrive to raise appreciably the standards and values of people".

Because all the philosophers and educationists of the world have accepted education as the only effective agency to develop international understanding, therefore according to all of them the aim of education in all the nations of the world should be the promotion of international understanding.

To achieve this aim a number of questions may arise. For example, what should be the principles of education, what should be the nature of curriculum, what should be the teaching methods for the presentation of curriculum, what should be the role of teachers and what kind of books should be prepared to achieve this aim. The following discussion will try to meet the above queries—

Principles of Education for International Understanding

Education for international understanding should be based on the following principles:

1. *Developing the capacity of independent thinking.* The first and foremost principle on which education for international understanding should be based is the developing and cultivation of the power and capacity of independent thinking in our young men and women so that they may be able to understand that above all, the world needs peace today.

Peace leads to progress and happiness while war leads to destruction and misery. With their capacity for independent thinking, the youth will not be led by false propaganda. They will refuse to be misled by warmongers. They will be able to judge the statements of others before accepting them. They will be able to distinguish between truth and propaganda. They will also understand the importance of living in peace.

2. *Belief in Universal Freedom.* The time of imperialism, colonialism and capitalism has gone. No nation can now be allowed to subjugate and exploit other nations, politically or economically. This is the age of democracy which believes that freedom is the birthright of everybody. "Live and let live" should be our motto, and we should have firm belief in the brotherhood of man and fatherhood of God.

3. *Emphasising correct values.* Education for international understanding should be based on the principle of emphasising correct values. Democratic values, group-responsibility, cooperation, toleration and mutual understanding should be stressed and impressed upon the students. We should impress upon the students that they belong to the entire world.

In other words, we should create faith in humanity in their minds. Humanity is the true religion of human beings, while all the great religions are only in different forms. It should be impressed upon the students that man is the most beautiful creation of the universe and basically we like goodness and peace.

4. *Inculcate Corporate Responsibility.* Prof. K. G. Saiyidain is of the opinion that education for internationalism should be based on the principle of corporate responsibility. Our children should be taught to believe that they are citizens of the world which is one and indivisible.

If there is anything bad or ugly in the world, they are all equally responsible for it. All of us shall have to work together for the achievement of common aims. Let our education make us realise that we are all brethren and as such we must help one another, in times of difficulty and distress.

5. *Practical use of knowledge.* Mere theoretical knowledge is not enough. All high-sounding principles of international understanding will be useless and futile if they are not translated into action. Of course, it must be properly understood that knowledge and action are the two wheels of the chariot of human progress. One without the other would be lame.

Hence, we should train and educate our young men to use the theoretical knowledge of principles of international understanding for doing something practical in the service of international unity and friendship. This will go a long way in promoting international understanding.

6. *Developing tolerance and mutual co-operation.* 'Live and let live, should be the one great principle that all nations of the world should follow in their everyday relationship with others. Once that is accomplished, an important cause of war, i.e., mutual distrust and suspicion will vanish. Lack of mutual understanding leads to frictions in the international sphere. Therefore, the idea of cooperation and toleration should be stressed through proper education.

7. *Interdependence should be stressed.* Education for international understanding should stress the idea of interdependence of nations. No country in the modern world can afford to live in isolation. Each country has to depend

upon others for the satisfaction of its physical, social and economic needs. The prosperity of one country is linked with that of other countries. Thus, the needs of all nations can be better satisfied if there is international cooperation and understanding.

8. Redefining Patriotism in the modern context. The term 'patriotism' should not be conceived in its narrow sense, as the narrow concept of the term patriotism is very dangerous for the world-peace. The slogan "My country first—right or wrong", stands nowhere in the present day world. The love of one's own country should not stand in the way of the wider loyalty to humanity. Therefore, the term 'patriotism' should be redefined and reinterpreted so that it is wide enough and consistent with internationalism.

9. Elimination of Fear. Fear is the basis of mutual suspicion of nations which leads to a race for armaments. Being afraid and suspicious of one another, the nations prepare themselves for war.

Fear can be removed through proper training and education by stressing the principle of "Live and let live". In the words of Bertand Russel, "The universal apprehension is itself a potent cause of war". Hence, fear should be eliminated from individual and national life.

Education for International Understanding

The UNESCO beautifully remarked, "Since war begins in the minds of men, it is in the minds of men that the defence of peace must be constructed".

Education is a powerful force in developing internationalism. In the words of Bertrand Russel, education may not bring internationalism from political point of view but education is the only agency through which it is possible to develop the feeling of internationalism.

Therefore, education should be so organised and formulated that it may promote international understanding. The following are some of the ways and means of organising education for promoting the feelings and thoughts of internationalism:

1. Reorienting Curriculum and Text Books. For promoting the feelings of internationalism, the first step should be the reorientation of the educational curriculum and the text books. It is through the right type of curriculum and textbooks that the children's mind can be reoriented in the direction of peace and international understanding.

Hence while redesigning the curriculum, the aim of developing international understanding among students must be kept in view. The redesigned curriculum should enable the students to acquire the following knowledge:

(a) Knowledge of interdependence of different countries of the world.
(b) Knowledge of the similarities of ideas and moral ideals propagated by different religions of the world.
(c) Knowledge of various cultures of the world.
(d) Knowledge of the entire world, its countries and people, their ways of living and thinking.
(e) Knowledge of the struggle of mankind for the establishment of peace.

Thus, all the school subjects like history, geography, sciences and literature should initiate the students into the wider world of which they are the members. The children of today are the citizens of tomorrow.

Sri C. D. Deshmukh writes in his book, 'Education for International Understanding', "It is in their minds that must take root ideas, leading to the realization of the common heritage of man, an understanding and appreciation of differences among peoples a recognition of the basic human dignity which must be respected and safeguarded, an awareness of the interdependence of nations and the consequent need for international cooperation

Therefore, the teaching of different school subjects should be remodelled in such a way that the students may develop a wider and cosmopolitan outlook, realising this basic unity of the world. The whole curriculum should be reoriented with the object of promoting international understanding

2. Proper Co-curricular Activities. International understanding can also be promoted through various types of co-curricular activities. These activities should include the celebration of birthdays of great men and women belonging to different countries and religions, like Gautam Buddha, Lord Christ, Mohammad, Guru Nanak, Lord Krishna, Newton, Marcony, Edison, Washington, Rousseau, Lenin, Gandhi, Tagore, etc.

The celebration of international days like the U.N.O. Day, the Human Right Day, the World Health Day etc. The organisation of Pen-friend Clubs and other international clubs. Lectures by foreign scholars may be arranged from time to time.

The school should also keep the students informed of the latest developments in the world through newspapers, magazines, journals, lectures and discussions. Lastly, the school should try to cultivate world mindedness among students by co-operating with the UNESCO in all its activities.

Thus, the various types of co-curricular activities organised in the school can considerably promote and cultivate the ideas and feelings of international understanding in the minds of the students.

3. *Cultural Exchange.* Schools should co-operate and actively participate in the programme of sending cultural missions, consisting of teachers, students, scholars, poets, artists, and writers, etc., to different countries of the world. Such cultural tours to other countries can be frequently arranged. We can also invite foreigners to visit our country.

The face to face contact will be of much help. It will rectify wrong notions and will create sympathy and affection for the people of other countries. This will also broaden the mental outlook of the people and will help in establishing cultural ties among various nations.

In the words of Dr. C.D. Deshmukh, "One important means of furthering international understanding is international exchange of persons directed not only with a view to facilitating the transmission of knowledge, skills and experiences, but also to encourage free and frank discussion of differences in such a way as to minimize the area of misunderstanding and to maximize that of cooperation. The programme in this behalf should lay stress on living together and benefiting from direct contacts".

Role of the School

Undoubtedly the mass media like radio, T.V., wireless and press try to develop international understanding, but school has a special importance in this connection. Hence schools should be places for co-operative work instead of competitive activities. Co-operative planning and working will develop in children social feeling, mutual adjustment and tolerance.

Schools should also organize such schemes which develop in children healthy attitudes and goodwill towards other religious, social and cultural groups.

Thus the entire environment of school should develop a sense of brotherhood, corporate responsibility for the good and welfare of all and above all an all embracing sense of oneness in children.

As discussed above the curriculum should be informative about all people, their attitudes and behaviour, their needs and model of living and their achievements in all fields of human activities.

There should be international gatherings, seminars, symposia and exchange of teachers and students between various countries of the world. Not only this, international organisations like United Nations Organization, World Health Organisation, UNESCO and other organizations should become subjects of discussion and discourses in the students.

Persons of international repute should also be invited to deliver lectures on international topics. Since the centre of all these formative educational activities is the school, it should organize with full sincerity and zest the U. N. O. Day, World Peace Day and events of international importance.

Role of the Teacher

To develop international understanding in children, the role of the teacher is very important. It is the personal qualities of a teacher which make the whole process of education successful or unsuccessful. It should be noted that a teacher imbued with a high mission can infuse high ideals in children and inspire them to strive for international fellow feeling and good will. Thus he should himself be fired by high ideals, then only he will be able io inculcate them in children.

A teacher of liberal and wide outlook can convince children that differences of caste, creed and religion can never divide human race. It is only the personal feelings which keep away one individual from the other.

He can easily inculcate in the minds of children that world is a unit and his nation is only an integral part of the same.

Thus if a nation does not develop itself with other developing or already developed nations, it may prove a terrible problem to the whole world. As members of a family are, individual nations are also morally bound to help and co-operate in the development of all especially the weaker, the poorer and the backward ones. Then only, the concept of World Family will materialize.

The teacher can further convince children, that culture is not the personal possession of a particular person or group but is a result of the co-operative efforts done by all the nations of the world.

A teacher inspired by a sense of international goodwill does not remain satisfied by teaching his subject alone but tries to develop the sense of international understanding in children by organizing various activities namely—international get together and international conferences etc.

Role of UNESCO

Establishment of UNESCO—After the two global wars, it was seriously thought by eminent leaders of the world that the dire need of the time was to develop goodwill and co-operation between different nations and regions of the world. Till then discord, differences and disbelief among different nations will not be removed and this will explode into wars every now and then.

To establish peace in the world, an international organization was established. This goes by the name as United Nations. Organization. As a subsidiary body of this U.N.O. another organization was also established to promote good will among the various nations of the world.

As a matter of fact the credit for this organization—UNESCO, goes to scientists, artists, thinkers and educationists of about three dozen countries who thought that international goodwill and co-operation could not be achieved by mere political and economic treaties, plans and such other programmes. They were of opinion that the problem of war was less political than psychological.

Hence to solve this problem, some other programmes were essential than mere political treaties and economic alliances The need is of social, cultural and educational programmes which bring different countries together and promote understanding and appreciation of another's ideals, values and behaviour patterns.

Such programmes should be of cultural, artistic, literary and scientific nature. UNESCO plans and executes these programmes with the help of member nations. Let us study its purpose and mode of working.

Preamble of UNESCO—"Since wars begin in the minds of men it is in the minds of men that the defence of peace must be constructed...the wide diffusion of culture and the education of humanity for justice and peace are indispensable to the dignity of man and constitute a sacred duty...a peace, based exclusively upon the political and economic arrangements of Governments would not be a peace which could secure the unanimous lasting and sincere support of the people of the world and it must, therefore, be founded, if it is not to fail, upon the intellectual and moral solidarity of mankind".

The above preamble of UNESCO clearly asserts that if a stable peace is to be established in the world; then all nations must rise above differences and co-operate in the fields of art, science, culture and education to the development of all by the efforts of all. Thinkers, scientists, artists and educationists of different nations of the world should come together from time to time and devise plans for such world wide co-operation and help.

Aim of UNESCO

The main aim of UNESCO (United Nations of Educational Scientific and Cultural Organization) is to promote in international good will through education to establish a lasting world peace. It organizes such programmes of education, in different countries and regions, which educate the minds of people psychologically and intellectually so that they form strong attitudes against conflict and war and promote international amity and brotherhood.

Functions of UNESCO

To achieve its aim UNESCO is doing to the following activities:

(1) It tries to remove fear and disbelief in the nations by promoting fellow-feeling and good will among them.
(2) It tries to remove illiteracy and ignorance from the backward nations of the world.
(3) It brings culture, art, science and literature of one country within the reach of other countries for the benefit of both and all others.
(4) It gives financial aid to research scholars to promote research work as far as possible.
(5) It carries out teachers, scientists and thinkers to exchange programmes among various countries so that they are able to discuss individual and common problems and devise solutions for them.
(6) It gives financial aid for opening schools in poor and backward countries.
(7) It devises nations about scrutiny and preparation of books, reorganization of curriculum and promoting translation of higher standard books for the use of those who need these translations.
(8) It organizes exhibitions of periodicals, magazines, books and art creations on an international scale, the purpose being to promote international understanding.
(9) It encourages international tours of students to stimulate good will and fellow feeling among students of different nations.
(10) It tries to propagate the ideals of fellow feeling and brotherhood among the different nations of the world through T.V, press, wireless and other published material.

QUESTIONS FOR ANSWER

1. "International understanding is the vital need of the present day war-torn world". Discuss. How can education help in this direction?
2. What is Education for International Understanding? What is the role of education in promoting international understanding?
3. How can education for nationalism and education for internationalism be reconciled ? What is the role of the teacher in this regard?
4. What changes should be incorporated in the school curriculum to make it suitable for promoting international understanding?
5. What do you mean by international understanding? Education is the only means to develop this feeling. Why? Discuss in detail.
6. What should be the principles of developing international understanding?
7. What do you understand by UNESCO? Discuss its aim and functions.

31

Principle of Democratic Polity (Education and Democracy)

We are living in democratic era of civilization. Our country is democratic republic. Democracy is a way of life and unless people accept democratic philosophy fully and act accordingly, the democracy can not succeed. Educated citizens make democracy to function well, therefore, educators are of the view that principles of democratic polity must find place in the educational set up of the nation. Hereunder, we will discuss concept concerning this aspect.

Meaning of Democracy

Before discussing the relationship between democracy and education, it is essential to understand the meaning of democracy. The word democracy has been derived from two Greek roots—'Demons' and 'Cratic' which mean 'Power' and 'Public' respectively. Hence etymologically democracy means power of the people as a whole. The former president of America, Abraham Lincon defined democracy as—"Democracy is a government of the people, by the people and for the people". It may be borne in mind that this concept of democracy means only political democracy, though in essence it is a way of living and organization of community that has unity in its political, economic and social aspects. In other words democracy is not merely a political arrangement but a complete social philosophy. It is a way of life and covers all the aspects of our life—political, economic, social and religious.

Definition of Democracy

To make the concept of democracy more clear, following definitions are being adduced:

(1) "A government by the many." —*Aristotle*

(2) "Democracy is the form of government in which the ruling power of the state is legally vested not in any particular individual or class but in the members of the community as a whole".

(3) "Democracy is a way of life and not a mere political arrangement. It is based on the principle of equal freedom and equal rights for all regardless of race, religion, sex or economic status".

—*Radha Krishna University Education Commission*

(4) "Democracy is a government in which everybody has to share". —*Seely*

(5) "Democracy is a way of life and a way of life means a determining influence in every area of life". —*Bode*

(6) True democracy refers to—"The progress of all, through all under the leadership of the wisest and the best".

—*Mazzine*

Basic Principles and Values of Democracy

The success of democracy is not judged and evaluated by the establishment of legislative bodies and other constitutional and legal agencies of administration, but by the application of democratic principles and democratic values in human life and in all areas of human activity. Basic principles of democracy are—Freedom, Equality, Faternity and Justice, while values of democracy are—Respect of the Individual Tolerance—liberty leads to tolerance, Faith in change, change through persuasion, service, individual and social progress etc.

Need of Education for Democracy

It is only in recent times that democratic principles and values have entered the field of education. The credit of this revolutionary change goes to the American educationist John Dewey. He emphasized that in a democratic society, educational planning should be done in such a way that each individual member is made capable to shoulder social responsibilities efficiently and discharge them effectively and profitably.

According to him education should inculcate in the individuals the sense to welcome needful changes in the social structure and reoriented one's behaviour smoothly to the ever changing social mileau. The impact of this philosophy has brought about revolutionary changes in the thinking about educational planning and schemes of public education have begun to emphasize the provisions of the education of the masses so that general people become conscious about their rights and duties, about their individual and social responsibilities and about their national and international obligations.

As the democratic rule is by the people, for the people, they should be made to understand their obligations and to discharge their duties intelligently. Hence in all democratically ruled countries, more and more emphasis is being laid upon free, compulsory and universal education.

Democratic Tendency in Education

The impact of democratic tendency in education is evident on the working of the following elements:

(1) Provision of Equal Opportunities and Recognition of Individual Differences—In a democratic set up, each child is a sacred and valuable entity of society. As such, equal opportunities are made available to one and all for their fullest development.

In this connection the principle of individual differences is given proper recognition and therefore each child receives proper support according to his interests, aptitudes and capacities to develop his individuality to the fullest extent.

(2) Universal and Compulsory Education—In democracy, the reigns of government remain in the hands of the people. Hence common people must be so educated that they develop them-

selves as responsible and dynamic citizens conscious of their rights and duties, fully conversant with their national and international obligations, well aware with the government procedures and administrative processes. This is possible when one and all are brought under the schemes and plans of universal and compulsory education.

(3) Free Education—The principle of universal and compulsory education involves free education to all irrespective of their social or monetary status. Hence education is now regarded as the birth right of each child irrespective of colour, caste, creed and sex.

In almost all democratic countries, education has been made free upto a certain standard. In addition, education of the physically and mentally handicapped is also receiving proper and increasingly effective attention.

(4) Importance of Individual Attention—As discussed above, each child receives individual attention. His family background, his own interests, likes and dislikes, his needs and capacities are fully taken care off in all plans of educational development, the purpose being to achieve the maximum development of personality.

(5) Social Activities—Bookish and academic activities are not over emphasized in schools now-a-days. Proper attention is paid to social, cultural and co-curricular activities, so that children develop in a wholesome way and gain more and more social experience.

(6) Student Unions—Student unions and student welfare associations are formed in institutions to promote student welfare in all spheres with the aim of achieving balanced, dynamic, efficient and socially motivated personalities.

(7) Provision of Adult Education—Under the influence of democratic tendency, in different countries, emphasis is being laid upon adult education, women education and education of the mentally retarded and physically handicapped.

Schemes are under operation in our country also for the effective education of the adults who constitute a bulk of our entire population. Night-schools, short-term courses, one day schools and other schemes are being launched to solve this stupendous problem.

(8) Child Centred Education—Democratic way thinking emphasizes the importance of each child as a sacred individuality. Hence educational schemes and plans are so structured that each child receives full attention and full facilities to develop his individuality to the fullest extent.

(9) Methods of Teaching—Under the impact of democratic tendency, methods of teaching are undergoing revolutionary changes. Old, traditional and mass education methods are being gradually replaced by individual attention methods. Nothing is now enforced or thrust in by force.

Self-learning devices are encouraged and such methods are promoted which motivate children to pay attention and learn by their own efforts. Such wholesome and welcome environment is created wherein children search for truth, gain knowledge by their own efforts and learn by their own experiences.

(10) Physical Health of Children—To promote physical well-being of children, facilities for games and sports, gymnasia, medical tests and medical help are being provided freely and on an increasing scale. Medical check up, advice and medicines are now provided to the needy.

(11) School—School is now regarded as a centre of promoting national consciousness and international understanding. Education for dynamic citizenship is associated with education for national and international understanding, amity and fellow-feeling. Thus schools is now regarded as a miniature to society.

(12) Co-operation between all Agencies of Education—In a democratic set up, all the agencies of education co-operate actively for the development of children. Hence under the influence of democratic tendency, schemes are being formulated now-a-days to establish co-operation between all the agencies of education namely—family, school, community, church and state.

(13) Respect of Teacher's Personality—Democratic philosophy respects teacher as a very dynamic and effective agency of social change for social progress. Thus teachers are now made to participate more and more in curriculum construction and educational planning.

Side by side, they are allowed to experiment freely in respect to methods, techniques and devices of teaching as well as materials which aid teaching procedures and processes. Not only this, more and more plans are being laid and worked out for increasing the professional competency of teachers.

(14) School Administration—To inculcate in children the sense of self-discipline and self-administration, their association with school administration is being welcomed. Such schemes are being formulated in various institutions where student participation in actual educational and school administration is a fact.

(15) Intelligence Tests—Schemes of intelligence tests are under operation in various institutions all over the world to evaluate the mental capacity, growth and achievement of children. Diagnostic tests are proving very useful for this purpose.

Aims of Education in Democracy

(1) Development of Democratic Values—The success of democracy does not depend upon Legislative buildings and massive structures of Parliament houses, but it rests upon the quality of the citizens devoted to democratic values. As such, the prime aim of democratic education is to promote in children a sense of devotion to democratic values.

No book teaching can achieve this aim unless children are provided with opportunities to practise democratic norms and standards of behaviour. In fact, a child learns to live democratically by living democratically. Hence the whole educational set up of a school should reflect the values of democratic philosophy.

(2) Development of Worthy Interests—The second aim of democratic education is to develop useful and worthy interests in children. Interests form character and enrich a child's life. Hence the famous educationist Herbart has insisted upon the fullest development of diverse interests.

To achieve this aim, children should be provided with various and varied opportunities to participate in diverse activities and programmes in all fields of human life. If a large number of worthy interests are developed in children, they will be happy, well balanced and efficient as citizens.

(3) Development of Social Outlook—Development of social outlook is the sixth important aim of democratic education. This aim emphasizes upon the fact that children should be imbued with the sense that they are the integral parts of society, the welfare of which should be their ideal.

Not only this, they should learn to live and die for the nation. Education should develop this sense of service and sacrifice making them learn the sacredness of obligations and duties for the welfare of the nation to which they belong.

(4) Development of Harmonious Personality—The seventh aim of democratic education is to develop the individuality of a child into balanced and harmonious personality. In the modern world of strife, stress and strain, a balanced and harmonious personality can only seek and find adjustment with the surroundings.

Hence education should develop character, dynamism and social outlook for this purpose. Prof. Humayun Kabir has rightly said—"Education should cater to all aspects of man's nature and give equal importance to the humanities, the sciences and technology, to that it can fit a man to perform justly and magnanimously to all the offices".

(5) Development of Vocational Efficiency—For the success of a democratic set up, economic contentment of citizens is a must. An indigent and poor person can be a victim of all kinds of allurements, inducements and exploitation by the resourceful and the powerful. Hence the third aim of democratic education is to develop vocational efficiency in children, so that they are able to become self-reliant and serve the nation as much as possible.

(6) Development of Sound Habits—The fourth aim of democratic education is to develop sound habits in children. Habits are the sources of good or bad conduct. Hence education should develop good habits in children from the very beginning to make democracy a successful venture.

(7) Development of Thinking Power—The fifth aim of democratic education is to develop thinking power of children. In fact children of today are citizens of tomorrow when they will be confronted with all kinds of problems in political, social and economic fields. Education should develop in children the capacity to think clearly and take decisions confidently.

(8) Training for Citizenship—Democratic education should impart to children training in dynamic and healthy citizenship. For this, education should instil in children—(1) Capacity to understand and solve the diverse problems of the country, (2) Capacity to distinguish between propaganda and reality, (3) Capacity to think and decide about issues, (4) Economic efficiency, (5) Consciousness of one's rights and duties, (6) Capacity to shoulder responsibility, (7) Development of diverse interests, (8) Sense of service and sacrifice, (9) Good use of leisure Hour, (10) Development of human qualities as love, sympathy, fellow-feeling, co-operation, sense of nationalism and internationalism, (11) Healthy and dynamic outlook about problems, good behaviour and respect for moral values.

(9) Development of Leadership—The eighth aim of democratic education is to develop leadership qualities in children. For this, education should instil in children the leadership qualities from the very beginning. They are the future citizens who will have to shoulder the multifarious duties and responsibilities of their nation in all areas. Their character, strength of will, insight, courage of convictions, clarity of thinking and decision-making will be the foundations on which the national edifice will go up and up.

(10) Development of National and International Feelings—For the success of democracy, the ninth aim of democratic education is to develop in children the sense of ardent nationalism and devotion to international brotherhood. It may be noted that the two are not contradictory. On the other hand they are mutually complementary and supplementary. In fact a nation can not exist in isolation. All the nations of the world are mutually in interdependent. Hence education should foster the sense of interdependence, international good-will and fellow feeling.

Curriculum and Democratic Values

In a democratic country curriculum construction is done with the purpose of realizing democratic values. Hence those subjects, activities and programmes are included in the curriculum which instil and promote healthy attitudes, dynamic habits, insight and understanding so that children are able to lead successful lives as happy citizens. The bases of such a curriculum are as under:

(1) Diversified—Democratic curriculum is diversified to suit the needs of all children with basic differences of interests and aptitudes. Class room activities, games, sports and other co-curricular activities bear an imprint of variety to suit various needs of children.

(2) Achievement of Social Aims—While constructing a democratic curriculum emphasis is laid upon social aims and values. In other words, development of social sense in children is kept in view. As such, student activities, associations, corporate programmes and fellowship programmes are liberally provided.

(3) Flexibility—Democratic curriculum is flexible to accommodate various needs and requirements which are in a state of constant change. A portion of it is made compulsory in the form of co-curriculum and diversified subjects are made optional for children to choose according to their interests and aptitudes.

(4) Emphasis on Local Needs—Democratic curriculum is constructed on the bases of local needs and available resources. It may be changed according to the needs of time, place and local requirements.

(5) Provision of Vocational Needs—Democratic curriculum very well meets the needs of vocations, professions and economic requirements of a region or the whole country. This enables the country to develop economically.

(6) Emphasis on Activity—Democratic curriculum is laid on the foundation of an important principle known as learning by doing. It is through practical work and activities that development of mind and intelligence is fostered. Instead of enforcing and compelling cut and dried ready made concepts into the minds of children, they are allowed to search for truth through their own experiment and experiences. This is real learning, develops confidence, foresight and farsight, the three important ingredients of wisdom.

(7) Place for Leisure Hour Activities—Democratic curriculum also contains such relevant and useful activities in which an individual can profitably indulge during leisure time. Thus it ensures the total development of personality.

Methods of Teaching

Democratic ideals and values exert a powerful influence upon the methods of teaching also. Since the individuality of a child is regarded as a sacred legacy in a democratic set up, all methods of teaching are child centred. We are throwing light on some important democratic methods as under:

(1) The fundamental principle of democracy is activity and progress. Hence the old, traditional and inactive methods of teaching are discarded and new, dynamic and progressive methods are adopted at all stages of teaching.

(2) Freedom is the soul of democracy. Hence all democratic methods give full freedom to children to learn by their own efforts, experiments and experiences. Montessori method, Dalton plan, Heuristic method, Laboratory plan and Experimental method are such democratic methods in popular use all over the world. Teacher's role in these methods is that of a friend, philosopher and guide. Children are free to plan and structure their own learning activities. These methods of teaching make children investigators, researchers and speakers of truth.

(3) Democratic methods of teaching foster and develop the intelligence of children in all its aspects and to the fullest extent. They are assigned problems which are increasingly difficult and require on the part of children to exercise their thinking power and capacity to conclude. The progressive development of this capacity makes children confident, self-reliant, possessed of keen insight, and foresight. In later life this capacity makes them able to solve national and even international problems in all areas and in all spheres of life.

School Discipline

Discipline is the cornerstone of democracy. But democratic discipline does not believe in repression or compulsion. It advocates self-discipline. In schools where democratic set up is in vogue, the following ideas are emphasized for fostering and developing self-discipline-

(1) In democratic schools the headmasters, the teachers and the administrators are not despots or police officers. Instead, they are friends, philosophers and guides. Through

their friendly and affectionate behaviour, they mould the behaviour of children and thus promote self-discipline by creating a congenial and cordial atmosphere.

(2) In democratic schools, such activities and progammes are structured which cater to the interests and needs of children. This develops self-discipline among children.

(3) In the administration of a democratic school, children participate actively, discuss problems and decide them freely. They, thus, feel their integral and intimate relationship with the school and feel internal kinship with its progress and development. Thus the sense of self-discipline is kindled and fostered.

(4) In democratic schools full freedom is given and opportunities provided for each child to develop his individuality to the fullest extent. Hence no problem of indiscipline arises at any time.

(5) In democratic schools, student unions, students parliaments and all kinds of student organizations are encouraged for the benefit and development of children. They learn self-government, co-operation, fellow-feeling and other human qualities together with qualities of self-discipline and leadership.

(6) In democratic schools, the sense of rights and duties is instilled in children. They, thus learn self-control through social service and social consciousness. Nothing is imposed on them from above. They discuss, decidc and carry out the decision with perfect co-operation and cordiality. Thus they learn that self-discipline is essential for their own betterment and development of personality.

Role of the Teacher

In a democratic set up a teacher is a friend, philosopher and guide. He often works as a social reformer. Such teachers possess the following qualities—

(1) The teacher is devoted whole heartedly to the ideals and values of democracy. Hence he tries to impart the same faith to children through gentle persuasion and affectionate rapport.

(2) The teacher regards every child as a sacred legacy to society. Hence, believing in the principle of individual differences he allows every child to develop his individuality to the fullest extent according to his own interests, aptitudes and capacities.

(3) In a democratic set up, a teacher lays greater stress upon environment rather than on heredity. Hence he tries to structure such a wholesome environment for the child that fullest development is naturally achieved.

(4) The teacher tries to solicit maximum co-operation from the guardians, parents and other social agencies for the greatest possible development of children as dynamic and socially oriented citizens of the future.

(5) In a democratic set up, each teacher is fully conscious of his rights and duties towards society. Hence he tries to instil the same sense of responsibility in children also to make them capable and intelligent citizens of tomorrow.

(6) Each teacher is well-versed in knowledge of his subject and has full academic competency to make children develop physically, mentally, morally and spiritually so that they are able to shoulder national and even international responsibilities in times to come.

School Administration

In democracy, school administration is based upon democratic principles and democratic values. Such a democratic administration develops children into capable and responsible citizens on the one hand, and, on the other hand, trains them as future leaders in all spheres of human activities. Thus the national development and welfare goes on as a continuous process. The following elements predominate in the democratic set up of school administration—

(1) School organization is based upon democratic spirit. The headmaster, the staff, the students and the clerical staff all work as a team to run and develop the school to higher and higher levels. The headmaster and the teachers discuss, decide and plan all school activities and carry them out into practice as one group of dedicated workers.

(2) The headmaster and the management strive to develop the initiative of teachers who receive constant appreciation and reward for their good and devoted work.

(3) Supervisors, higher administrative officers and management personnel criticise the work of teachers in a constructive spirit of cordiality and beneficial evaluation, so that teachers strive to do better and thus develop their competency more and more.

(4) The headmaster does not impose his plans upon teachers. Instead, everything is discussed and decided in the group and carried out with full co-operation of all.

(5) Mutual relations of teachers, supervisors, parents, guardians and social workers are based upon democratic philosophy.

From the above discussion it is clear that the whole administration of the school runs on solid foundations of democratic philosophy.

QUESTIONS FOR ANSWER

1. What do you understand by education for democracy. Discuss special features of such education.
2. Write short notes on the following:
   (a) Role of teacher in democracy.
   (b) Discipline in democracy.
   (c) Aims of education in democracy.
   (d) Democratic tendencies in education.

32

Principle of Modernization

Development, growth and increase in knowledge is the source of modernization, therefore, the nations and societies which fail to keep pace with it remain undeveloped and are over powered, in one way or the other, by the better developed and most developed nations. Hence, educators advocate that education must follow the principle of modernization in its educational system, which we discuss hereunder, in brief.

In the words of S.N. Eisenstadt, "Historically modernization is the process of change towards those types of social, economic and political systems that have developed in Western Europe and North America from the seventeenth century to the nineteenth and have been spread to other European countries and in the nineteenth and twentieth centuries to the south American, Asian and African continents." Modernization is the characteristic feature of modern society, which aims at greater social welfare.

Characteristics of Modernization

The process of modernization becomes evident from its characteristics. Following are its chief characteristics:

1. *Social mobilization.* Social mobilization is that process by which the old social, economic and psychological elements are transformed and new social values of human conduct are set up. The social mobilization is a peculiarity of modernization.

2. *Social differentiation.* Another feature of modernization is social differentiation. In this process there is increase in the complexity in social, political and economic activities and there is progress in the activities of individuals in various fields. Industrialization is a result of modernization.

As a result of modernization new trends in philosophy, religion, science and literature become visible. Briefly, an increase in modernization leads to a progress in social, economic, political and cultural fields.

3. *Structural differentiation and change.* Another characteristic of modernization is structural differentiation and continuous change. In the social and economic fields, old organizations break up yielding place to new. In political field new parties emerge. The cottage industries are replaced by big industries. The new means of production develop. Many new professions develop. The production becomes more complex.

4. *Change in organizational and status system.* A feature of modern society is the emergence of a number of specialized organizations. Secondly, there is greater division of labour. Thirdly the organizations based on close kinship lose in importance. With the acceleration in the speed of change the status of individuals and families undergoes change. New classes emerge in society. From the cultural and economic viewpoint, there come into being three classes, namely: upper, middle and lower.

5. *Urbanization.* The phenomena of urbanization and modernization are inter-linked, one leads to the other.

6. *Social and political movements.* An important feature of modernization is the emergence of new social and political movements which aim at the transformation of society. This transformation becomes imperative in order to make man adjust to fast changing conditions. These movements also aim at casting off orthodoxy and paving the ground for change to modernity. In order to attain the new aims, a change of outlook becomes imperative.

7. *Comprehensive and multi-sided education.* An important aim of modernization is the spread of education. In modern society it is tried that all should be educated. Besides academic education under modernization, the need for technical and professional education becomes acute; therefore, many technical and professional institutes spring up to meet this demand.

8. Development of international cooperation. Lastly, the development of international cooperation is the aim of modernization. The national movements gave birth to many nations. For the development of mutual relations among nations, a league of Nations and later U.N.O. came into existence.

Means of Modernization

After discussing the characteristics of modernization, the means of modernization are as follows:

1. Industrialization
2. Urbanization
3. Secularization
4. Rise of new social class
5. Social change
6. Westernization
7. Democratization.

Education and Modernization

S.N. Eisenstadt has rightly pointed out, "Perhaps the best starting point for the analysis of the characteristics in the educational institutions in modern societies is the pattern of demands for and the supply of educational services that tended to develop with modernization".

In the words of Yogendra Singh, "...education has been one of the most influential instruments of modernization in India. It has led to the mobilization of people's aspiration for nationalism, liberalism and freedom. It alone has been responsible for the growth of an enlightened intelligentsia which carried forward not only a movements for independence but also a relentless struggle for social and cultural reforms".

The most important function of education is modernization. Modernization is a comprehensive concept aimed at capturing, describing and evaluating profound qualitative and quantitative changes in society. It stands for progress beyond tradition.

Modernization according to some sociologists is based upon European and American models. As compared to urbanization, industrialization, westernization and

Europeanization, modernization presents a more complex process and a more complex result. In the intellectual sphere, it is an awareness that it is possible to see a rational explanation of physical and social phenomena.

Thus, it is represented by positivism and empiricism and rationalism. In the field of religion it is expressed in secularism. In philosophy it is expressed in humanist thought. It includes social mobilization and differentiation and specialization in individual and institutional activities.

In political field it stands for democratization. In ecology it is characterised by advancing degree of urbanization. But the most important feature of modernization as related to education is cultural. In cultural sphere its symptoms have been pointed out by A.K. Desai as follows:

1. Growing differentiation of the major elements of cultural systems, "The spread of literacy and secular education: a more complex intellectual and institutional system for the cultivation and advancement of specialized roles based on intellectual disciplines".

2. Emergence of a new cultural outlook characterised by emphasis on progress and improvement, on happiness and spontaneous expression of abilities and feelings, on the development of individuality as a value, and efficiency.

3. Emergence of a new personality orientation, traits and characteristics revealed in greater ability to adjust to the broadening societal horizons: some ego-flexibility; widening spheres of interests; growing potential empathy with other people and situations; a growing evaluation of self-advancement and mobility; a growing emphasis on the present as the meaningful temporal dimension of human existence; a growing awareness of dignity of others and an increased disposition to respect them; a growing awareness in the individual that "this world is calculable, that other people and institutions around him can be relied on to fulfil their delegation and responsibilities", growing faith in sciences and technology and a growing awareness that, "rewards should be according to contribution and not according to either whim or special properties of person not relating to his contribution".

4. Finally, modernization implies, "the ability of society to develop an institutional structure capable of adjusting to

continually changing problems and demands". The emergence of such a flexibility constitutes, according to Prof. Eisenstadt, the central issue and challenge of modernization.

Education is the most important instrument of modernization, and modernization includes:

1. Directed change in the system of attitudes, beliefs, and values, and also in the institutional complex, to enhance the acceptability of modern technology and its organizational and operational framework.

2. Growth of the infrastructure essential to the adaptation to technology of foreign origin to specific national needs; and

3. Laying the foundations of institutions and organizations which could, in time, assume responsibility for independent innovation and technological growth to the country's needs and problems.

In view of the above mentioned changes required by modernization the functions of education in this direction may be achieved by the following:

1. By enlarging the congnitive map of those exposed to it, education suggests alternatives to tradition, brings into focus the rewards implicit in them, and indicates—roughly at least—the paths through which the new goals with their attendant regards can be achieved. It broadens mental horizons, raises expectations and predisposes people to make experiments.

2. As an instrument of socialization it can project new images and values. Purposively used, it can be helpful in obliterating attitudes and behaviour patterns that are dysfunctional to programmes of modernization.

3. By providing ideological articulation it can promote the development of national consciousness and can help people see their needs and their problems in a national perspective. This can stimulate the creation of a national consensus at least on major issues.

4. Education provides a highway to elite status on the educated. The educated provide a reference model to the masses, who, in imitation of the former, take the first step away from tradition. Modernizing elites are almost always the products of modern or semi-modern school/university systems.

5. Problems-solving leadership—scientists and technicians, management experts and administration—with the requisite knowledge and skills, can only be expected to emerge out of

the educational system. Large-scale programmes of modernization demand specialists of several types at different levels, and look to the educational system for a steady flow of technocrates, planners and managers to operate them.

6. Education is a mobility multiplier. Although its impact is on the immobility of thought—ways, in the long-run it does alter rigid forms of social stratification. Modernization requires both types of mobility.

In sum, with proper planning and under efficient direction, education can make a meaningful contribution to the attainment of modernization.

Modernization and Institutional Education

Researches have been conducted in West and India about the role of educational institution in bringing about modernization. Most of them have shown a positive correlation between the two. However, Saunders in his study *Education and Modernization* in Brazil has found that it undermines modernity.

He remarks: "Brazilian schools, especially at the primary level where their impact on personality development is greatest, tend to stiffle rather than develop the personality traits on which modernization depends, and from which the society must draw its innovators".

This has been collaborated by S. L. Sharma in his work *Modernizing Effects of University Education* published by Indian Council of Social Science Research in 1979. This conclusion has been again supported by articles in a special number of *International Journal of Comparative Sociology* (1974, XIV, 3-4). In this special number, researches conducted independently in various parts of the world, showed remarkable uniformity in concluding that schooling promotes attitudinal modernity in developing societies.

Besides the relation of schooling and modernization researches have been conducted about the effect of higher education on modernity. Williamson studying university students in United States, Germany, Japan and Columbia concluded that while Americans and Colombians are at the conservative end, Japanese are on the other end of the scale of rationalism-traditionalism developed by Kahl.

M.S. Gore, I.P. Desai and Suma Chitnis found encouraging evidence of the relation between education and modernization. According to them, "The state, sex and educational level of the respondents were all important variables in determining the modernity of student sample".

Similar conclusion was reached by Malik and Marquette in their study *Changing Social Values of College Students in the Punjab.* They concluded that, "...an overwhelming majority of Punjab youth favours the abolition of such traditional institutions and caste and untouchability and strongly approves of a general social revolution in India".

In his book *Education in Social Change* Sullivan found that, "Factors other than experience at a particular training college appears to be operative in changing the students outlook towards traditional social practices".

The latest study in this connection was however made by Dr. S. L. Sharma published by ICSSR (1979) under the title *Modernizing Effects of University Education.* On that basis of a study of 3437 students in the 34 teaching departments of Punjab University during the academic year 1973-74, Dr. Sharma reached the following important conclusions concerning the relationships of modernization and education:

1. The level of higher education is of no consequence as an explanatory variable of student modernity.
2. There is the lowest percentage of moderns in the humanities, followed by social sciences and professionals with the highest percentage in the science faculty.
3. Males are more modern than females.
4. High status students are more modern than low status students.
5. There is a significant and positive correspondence between level of student modernity and that of their reference teachers, provided the latter preferred character-building role, over other roles, favoured no social distance in their relations with students and reported greater interpersonal interaction with students.

6. There is a weak though positive relationship between years of hostel exposure and modernity's course.
7. Age is found to be inversely related to student modernity. Boys out scored girls in modernity.
8. Caste has no bearing on modernity.
9. A significantly larger percentage of high modernity cases hails from medium size families with 4 to 6 numbers.
10. Family type has no association with modernity.
11. Socio-economic status of the family has significant though weak positive relationship with modernity.
12. Father's education and occupation are only weakly related to student modernity.
13. Father's income has moderately strong positive association with modernity.
14. There is no relationship between parental modernity and student modernity.
15. Students with early urban background are not more modern than those with rural background.
16. Those who have lived longer in urban setting are more modern than those with fewer years of urban dwelling.
17. The initial exposure to cosmopolitan city like Chandigarh makes not much difference in modernity.
18. Duration of urban exposure is positively associated with modernity.
19. Early residential background and modernism of the city have no influence on student modernity.
20. There is a significant and positive relationship between media exposure and modernity.
21. There is a strong positive relationship between extent of exposure to other cultures and level of modernity.
22. Constant exposure to other cultures significantly increases the negative effect of education on modernity.
23. The convent and/or public school educated students are more modern than the government/and/or aided school educated.
24. The type of schooling is the best predictor of modernity with the convent or public school educated being most modern.

25. Early socialization variables account for greater variance in student modernity than the later socialisation variables.
26. Developmental variables are more powerful than structural variables in explaining student modernity.
27. Educational variables, particularly schooling background, tops the list of explanatory variables.

On the basis of the above conclusions Dr. S. L. Sharma points out inverse relationship between the level of higher education and the student modernity. He gives the following reasons for this surprising fact:

1. The present higher education stresses mere transmission of information to the neglect of inculcating ability to think for one self. It stresses mere skill acquisition to the neglect of generating this position, for skill formation. It neglects character training and stresses mere certification for white collar jobs.

2. The system of higher education in India lacks an articulate social ideal.

3. The present educational system has not changed in the life of goals set by the Constitution of free India.

4. The present system of education is not a source of characterological transformation.

5. The course content of the present higher education does not lead to modernisation.

6. The cognitive and value content in conjunction with the social context of the present higher education is not relevant to the cultivation of modernity.

7. Our teachers are not so modern as to influence the student. They are not interested in character building and social training. They are unsure of what the community expects from them. The persistent authoritarian orientation limits the power of teachers to act as agents of student modernity.

8. The objective conditions in our educational institutions such as overcrowded classes, low teacher-pupil ratio, impersonal character of teacher-taught relationship, render the task of change orientation on the part of the teacher the more difficult. Small classes are better for such influence than large and unwieldy classes.

9. The lack of freedom for the teacher to design his own courses restricts considerably his potential for induction for

social changes. In the words of Dr. S. L. Sharma, "Our teachers thus presented a case of double failure as socializers of student modernity; first, they lacked strong modernity orientation, and second, they failed to modify their role orientations so as to bring them in line with modern norms".

10. The extra academic component of campus climate restricts its relevance to modernity.

11. Routinization of educational experience is a possible reason for the failure of higher education as a modernizer.

12. The overgrown structural format of higher education is a significant reason for its failure to modernize.

13. The built-in traits of present higher education such as under emphasis on the value element in its course content, are responsible for its poor performance.

Dr. Sharma suggests the following three objectives as the aims of higher education to make it a better instrument of modernization:

1. To prepare skilled manpower for a developing economy;
2. To re-socialize people in the values conducive to socio-economic development; and
3. To inculcate in man a creative self-awareness, an ability to think for himself and a sense of critical judgement.

He suggests that three areas should be particularly modernized: the reorientation of the content, the recasting of the teaching-learning nexus, and improving the quality of education. The quality of early education should be improved. Group extra-curricular activities should be encouraged. A secular-relational and egalitarian man should be created.

To conclude, "Besides providing the highly skilled manpower to a technico-industrial economy, higher education in our view can lay down the foundation of socio-economic development in the following ways: (1) by imparting to the younger generation the requisite psychological dispositions which are regarded as helpful for development; and (2) by instilling in students a reflective ability and a capacity to make rational decisions".

Two Patterns of Modernization

In his paper *'Social Change and Educational Policy'* published in

The Sociology of Education in India (NCERT, 1967), Professor A.K. Desai accepts two patterns of modernization of a traditional society pointed out by Don Martindale—exogenous and endogenous. He defines these two patterns by pointing out that, "An exogenous factor is one arising outside the social system, and endogenous is one arising internal to the social system".

Both these factors initiate and shape social change. They determine the nature of leadership and its basic aim. These in their turn determine the objectives of education, the structure of the machinery of education, technical and other means of spread, the allocation of finances of education and the nature to personnel executing it.

QUESTIONS FOR ANSWER

1. What is modernization? Discuss its characteristics.
2. Explain the impact of modernization on educational institutions.
3. Describe modernization through education in India after independence.

33

Principle of Mass Education (Universalization of Primary Education)

Wisdom and knowledge are the greatest assets and wealth of human being, hence education has always been and will always be the prime need of every individual, society and nation. Since democracy is the government of the people, for the people and by the people, therefore in democracy education is of vital importance. It has rightly been said that education shapes the fate and future of the nation, hence, most intellectuals consider education as the most productive investment and, therefore, educators consider mass education as one of vital principle of education in democracy.

Introduction

India is a democratic country today. Adult franchise has been granted to every citizen irrespective of caste, creed, religion and sex. Unless the people of India grow in enlightened judgment and character, the democratic ideal cannot be made a living reality. In that case, the new-found power is going to prove, ultimately, a menace to themselves .and to the larger human interests, since no government can rise higher than its source. Here, indeed, is a "race between education and catastrophe".

India has been a land of learning throughout the ages, not in the sense that education has been universal, but in the sense that learning has always been very highly valued. It is interesting to watch the pageant of Indian education move from ancient forest schools to the modem and fully equipped schools of today.

"Education in India", remarks Howell, "under the British government was first ignored, then violently and successfully opposed, then conducted in a system now universally admitted to be erroneous and finally placed on its present footing". It is against this background that every problem of education—primary, secondary or higher education—must be studied.

Primary Education: Background

Following the introduction of English System of education in India by Lord Macaulay in 1835, the educational situation was reviewed first by Charles Wood in 1854 and then by the Hunter Commission 1882. The Hunter Commission made as many as 36 recommendations on Primary Education but, unfortunately, there was not even a distant indication of the possibility of universal primary education.

How amusing, if not ironical, does it seem that the Commission recommended: "Strenuous efforts of State should now be directed to primary education in a still larger measure than hereafter". What to talk of 'strenuous efforts', even the bare minimum requirements were not met with and the 19th century ended in an educational deadlock.

While the rest of the world was going full steam ahead in the educational field during the early decades of the present country, the policy in India continued to be characterised by the same fatal gradualness as before. In 1904, a resolution of Indian Education Policy was conceived and published by Lord Curzon, in which the Government of India went as far as to "fully accept the proposition that the active extension of primary education is one of the most important duties of the State".

In order to give expression to the seriousness of their purpose, the government grant for education in all the provinces was raised from forty to seventy lakhs of rupees.

However, the first definite and vocal demand for the introduction of compulsory primary education was made by Mr. G.K. Gokhale, in the imperial legislative council during 1910 and 1911, but the Government ruled that low funds prevented the adoption of such a course.

The kind Emperor, at the Culcutta Darbar in 1912, announced, "It is my wish that there may be spread over the land a net work of schools and colleges, from which will go forth loyal, manly and useful citizens.... It is through education that my wish will be fulfilled, and the cause of education in India will ever be very close to my heart". Gokhale's bill failed to achieve its end; but it did stimed up public imagination and created a flutter in government circles.

The first world war of 1914-18 disrupted all efforts to achieve the goal of compulsory primary education. Following the close of the wars various provincial governments passed a crop of primary education acts. Unfortunately these acts failed to solve the problem of mass education.

In spite of the best of recommendations of a number of committees as well as Gandhiji's scheme of Basic Education which provided for 7 or 8 years of compulsory primary education, the dream of universal primary education could not be realized in pre-independent India.

Primary Education in Free India

The Constitution of Independent India provides for free and compulsory education for all children upto the age of 14 years. Article 45 of the Directive Principles of State Policy lays down:

"The State shall endeavour to provide, within ten years of the commencement of this constitution, for free and compulsory education for all children until they attain the age of 14 years."

This constitutional directive has not been realised till today. The greatest tragedy of the Indian educational policy has been its lack of vision and farsightedness, a failure to realize that no palliative measures but a tremendous nation-wide crusade alone can meet the situation.

The problem of universal, compulsory primary education requires:

1. Universal provision of school facilities;
2. Universal enrolment of pupils;
3. Universal retention of the enrolled children till they complete the prescribed course; and, above all ;
4. Qualitative improvement of education.

1. The Problem of Universal Provision of Schools: Universal provision of schools implies that school facilities should be provided to all the children within the easy walking distance from the home of the child. This requires bringing every home and every village on the educational map.

To provide this facility, primary schools have set up in all the villages, howsoever small they may be. Much ground has been covered during the past five year plans, but much still remains to be done. There are still some backward and remote areas where efforts to open schools are under way.

We can hope that cent per cent universalization in this respect will be achieved in the near future. It should, however, be noted that with the increase in population, there is corresponding need of more and more primary schools to be opened to meet the additional demand.

2. The Problem of Universal Enrolment: Universal enrolment of pupils means that once provision of school facilities have been made, all children in the desired age-group should be enrolled by one or the other school. In order to achieve this end, states have brought into force compulsory primary education acts. It is a sad commentary on our social system that the desired targets have not yet been achieved.

The problem of universal enrolment in rural areas is more complicated. The following factors push back the pace of progress:

(i) Ignorance and illiteracy among adults;
(ii) Lack of cooperation between the school and local community;
(iii) Indifferent attitude of authorities towards the desired enrolment;
(iv) Financial difficulties.

3. The Problem of Universal Retention: Universal retention means that after going the school, the child should remain there till he completes his primary school course.

Again, in primary education, the main objective is the attainment of stable literacy through a minimum of five-year schooling. If a child entering the school leaves it or is withdrawn from school before completing class V, leads to wastage in education. And, this creates another serious problem.

It has been estimated that at the higher primary stage educational wastage is 24 per cent among boys and 34 per cent among girls. Unless this huge wastage is eliminated and the children are retained in schools, the purpose of providing compulsory education stands completely defeated.

4. *The Problem of Quality Improvement*: Universalisation of compulsory primary education has failed to catch up with the desired targets because quality control of primary education has not been maintained. No doubt some praiseworthy work has been done in the field of expansion of primary education, but the standards have deteriorated.

The curricula at the primary level remains dull, the primary school teacher is non-serious about his work, his methodology is out-dated and inadequate to meet with the demands of time, there is total chaos in rural schools on account of maladministration, there is lack of ancillary services and adequate facilities for research work on various problems of primary education are hardly available. All this makes confusion whose confounded.

No doubt primary education is one of the costliest social service, it is, at the same time, the foundation of economic, social and cultural development of a nation. It is essential that efforts should be made both by the government and the voluntary organisations to give serious consideration to the quantitative expansion and qualitative improvement of the foundation education.

Measures for Successful Universalisation of Primary Education

A few measures are suggested below for making universalisation of primary education in the country successful.

1. *Universal legislation is essential*: The mere framing of an ambitious programme is no *ipso facto* guarantee of its

practicability. It does not offer any solution of the financial and administrative difficulties.

Universalisation of primary education must be a part of a much greater movement. The country must utilise its freedom for fashioning a society based on social justice and planning its economic and industrial life on rational lines. That alone can stimulate the enthusiasm and guarantee the men and the money, the spirit and the sacrifice necessary for this stupendous task.

2. *Primary Education to be free*: It must be realized that to make compulsory education a success, it is absolutely necessary to make it entirely free. It should not only be free but there should be provision for a number of additional facilities like mid-day meals for children, free books, free medical service, scholarship on generous scale and, in special cases, even maintenance allowance for parents.

If education is fundamental civic and human right, and basic to the health of body funds must be found for the purpose whatever the cost of the scheme.

3. *Equalization of educational opportunities* : If we believe in democracy, it is necessary that it must be an educated democracy. One of the most important social objectives of education, is to equalise opportunities. This will enable the backward and underprivileged mass of people to use education as a lever for the improvement of their condition. For removing the inequality of opportunity in education in India, the Indian Education Commission has suggested:

(i) abolition of tuition fee at the primary stage and provision of tuition free education to all needy and deserving students;
(ii) supply of free text-books and writing materials;
(iii) adequate number of text-books to be kept in school libraries;
(iv) development of an elaborate programme of scholarships.

4. *Harnessing wastage and stagnation*: The problem of wastage and stagnation at the primary stage of education gives a major set back to its universalisation. Adequate steps should be taken to overcome this phenomenon or, at least, to minimise the incidence of wastage.

5. *Education of girls*: In spite of all efforts to provide for equality of educational opportunities, there is still a disparity in the education of boys and girls, and it increases as one moves up the educational ladder. Universal provision of girls' education would be a major step forward to the attainment of universal compulsory primary education.

Special funds should be provided for its development in the years to come. Councils for the welfare of women and children both at the centre and state levels should contribute their best efforts in this direction. It is necessary to develop special programmes for bringing about rapid expansion in the education of girls. The most important of these are the preparation and employment of women teachers, and provision of all ancillary services for girls in all areas.

Approach for Universalisation of Primary Education

The approach to universalisation of the elementary education will cover:

1. Intensified use of existing facilities, including the adjustment of schooling hours, according to local needs and conditions;
2. Provision of new facilities which would not be economically viable and educationally relevant; and
3. Promotion of non-formal system of learning.

Programmes of Non-formal Learning

Under the Plan programmes for universalisation of primary education, non-formal learning would be organised and oriented towards target groups and decentralised in regard to their contents, course duration, place and hours of learning and pattern of instruction.

Basic Minimum Package

There would be a basic minimum package of inputs identified by the public educational authorities which would have correspondence to the formal system of education. In both formal and non-formal systems, the emphasis would be on retention of students and effective delivery of services of children.

Appropriate Incentives

It is essential to ensure appropriate incentives like free mid-day meals, supply of uniforms and learning materials, and compensation to the families of scheduled caste girls towards the opportunity cost involved.

Wastage and Stagnation

Efforts should be made by state governments to introduce measures with a view to eliminate wastage and reduce drop-out in elementary education.

Wastage and Stagnation

The problem of wastage and stagnation is an age old one in our system of education. But as a result of quick expansion, it has been highly aggravated. At the primary stage, out of one hundred children that enter into class I, only 55 come out successful. Out of these 55, taking admission into class V only 38 reach class VIII. This alarming drop-off, due whether to premature withdrawal or to retardation, involves, not only a large wastage of public expenditure, but also great loss of income and energy of the children. This has continued to be a persistent feature of education at the elementary stage ever since the present system had been established.

What is Wastage ?

Wastage means premature withdrawal of children from school, at any stage, before the completion of primary course. If a child leaves the school after class I or Class II, it amounts to wastage.

What is Stagnation ?

When a child fails in a certain class of primary stage and he is required to study again in that very class, it amounts to stagnation. According to Hartog Committee:

"Stagnation is the detention of a child in the lower class for period of more than one year."

Causes of Wastage and Stagnation

Causes of wastage and strong nation may be listed as follows:

1. *Economic Causes*

The parents can't afford the expenses of education of their children. Moreover, their children at the age of 9 or 10 lend a helping hand in their occupation. They become a source of income. Thus the poverty of the people causes wastage and stagnation.

2. *Social Causes*

1. Some of the parents are illiterate and as such do not understand the importance of education. They are prejudiced and steeped deep in ignorance. They do not realise that their education is of vital importance.
2. There are some backward classes, like the scheduled or tribal people, who do not take interest in the education of their children. They do not enjoy adequate social facilities because of their social set-up they show reluctance in keeping their children in schools.
3. Some people are orthodox and do not like girls' education. Such people withdraw their daughters from the school at an early age.
4. Girls help heir mothers at home. Therefore, they are generally withdrawn from school without the completion of primary education to assist their mothers in domestic affairs.
5. Most of the primary schools are co-educational institutions. Orthodox people do not like their daughters to study in these schools. So as soon as they are a little grown up, they are withdrawn.

6. Early marriage system is another hurdle. The girls are married early, therefore, they can't continue their education even at primary stage.

3. *Educational Causes*

Present primary education is not worth-while both for the children and the parents. The following are some of the educational causes which lead to wastage and stagnation:

1. Because of heterogenous group of students in a class, the students of higher age group can't adjust properly. So they are compelled by the problem of adjustment. They leave the school.
2. The curriculum of primary education is not in accordance with the real life of the children.
3. The environment of primary schools does not meet the psychological needs of children. So they play truant.
4. Admission in class I continues throughout the year. The children who join late can't pass the examination. Their failure leads to stagnation and wastage.
5. Teachers of primary schools don't take interest in their job. Neither they attend to their duties regularly, nor do they pay heed to the difficulties and problems of the children.
6. Teaching methods adopted in primary schools are dull and boring.
7. Ours is an examination-ridden education. Fear of examination always remains in the mind of children. Because of this fear they develop repulsive attitude towards education.
8. Punishment inflicted upon the children is so severe that they cease to take interest.
9. Some of the existting schools are incomplete, i.e., these schools provide instruction up to third or fourth standard.
10. The provision of instructional material in primary schools is not adequate.
11. Individual attention is not paid to the children.

12. There is lack of healthy contact between parents and teachers.
13. Most of parents feel that education imparted to their children is useless. It does not train them for better work. On the contrary it isolates the children from habit of work. So they think it better to withdraw their children from the school.
14. Primary schools do not provide basic facilities like medical facilities, text books, writing material, mid-day meals etc.

The Causes of Wastage and Stagnation as Mentioned by Kothari Commission

Kothari Commission has mentioned the following causes of wastage and stagnation:

(i) The heterogeneity of the age composition of students in the first class.
(ii) The practice of making fresh admission throughout the year.
(iii) Irregularity of attendance.
(iv) Lack of educational equipment in the school as well as with the children.
(v) Over-crowded classes.
(vi) Unsuitable curricula.
(vii) Inability of the teacher to use play-way techniques which can assist in initiating the children pleasantly to school life.
(viii) Poor teaching.
(ix) Inadequately prepared-teachers.
(x) A wrong system of examination.

Remedial Measures Recommended by Kothari Commission

For minimising wastage and stagnation, Kothari Commission has made the following recommendations:

(a) Examinations at the end of class I should be abolished and first two classes (and where possible, even class I to IV) should be regarded as one unit.

(b) Introducing a year of pre-school education.
(c) Providing part time education for poor children so that they can work as well as learn.
(d) Adoption of play-way techniques in class I.
(e) Providing "Literacy classes" for a period of one year at least to all children in the age-group 11-14 who are not attending schools.
(f) Providing similar facilities of part-time education for children who have completed the lower primary stage and desire to study further.

In addition to the above recommendations made by Kothari Commission, the suggestions given ahead can also be of great use for minimising wastage and stagnation:

(i) Curricula of Primary-education should be made activity-centred.
(ii) Right type of trained teachers should be appointed. Lady teachers have proved better in handling young children.
(iii) The school should be properly equipped with teaching material, furniture, building etc.
(iv) Medical facilities, free books to poor students and mid-day meals be given.
(v) Admission should be restricted to certain months, especially in the beginning of the year.
(vi) Class I should be made a homogeneous unit of age group 6-7 years.
(vii) Educational system should be made realistic.
(viii) No failure at this stage.
(ix) Provision for adult education be made so as to create parents' consciousness and interest in the education of their wards.

QUESTIONS FOR ANSWER

1. Trace the historical background of universal, compulsory, primary education.
2. What is meant by universal, compulsory education at the primary level?

3. What, steps should be taken to make primary education universal and compulsory?
4. What is meant by 'wastage' and 'stagnation'? What are the possible causes of wastage and stagnation?
5. What remedial measures should be taken to reduce the incidence of wastage and stagnation in primary education?
6. Discuss the problem of wastage and stagnation in about 300 words.
7. What steps have been taken so far in your state to achieve universalisation of primary education?
8. What programme of universalisation of elementary education has been envisaged in the Sixth Five Year Plan?

34

Principle of Scientific Attitude (Education and Science)

Mudalliar Commission report (1952-53) has rightly stated as follows:

"To be effective, a democratic citizen should have the understanding and the intellectual integrity to sift truth from falsehood, facts from propaganda and to reject the dangerous appeal of fanaticism and prejudice. He must develop a scientific attitude of mind to think objectively and base his conclusions on tested data."

Introduction

Democracy and education are the two supreme powers of modern age. As a matter of fact, both are complementary mutually. During the 15th and 16 centuries, scientific researches and astonishing inventions in the realm of science started the vogue of teaching science in the 17th century to children in place of mere theoretical and academic learning. The purpose behind this was to achieve effective, complete and well-adjusted living in the ever-changing circumstances and situations of society.

Due to the industrial revolution of the 18th century and under the impact of newer and newer scientific inventions and researches in technology, human life changed to new patterns of beliefs and behaviour as individuals and as social beings.

The result was that in England, Germany, France, America, and other progressive countries scientific subjects were added to the curriculum placing them in prominent positions replacing much of the dead wood of mere academic learning. Now, we see that in this age of science it has become greatly essential to impart scientific education to all children of society. Therefore, one of the principles of education is scientific attitude.

Meaning of Science

Knowledge of science is superior to all other types of knowledge. While ordinary knowledge generally does not reflect attributes of validity and reliability, scientific knowledge possesses these qualities. It is open to testing and real life experiences. It is a logically related and clearly arranged knowledge of items about which any one can experiment and apply tests for validity and reliability. Science is the systematic knowledge of a particular thing.

The principles of science are clear, definite, broad-based, valid, pure, real and reliable in all respects. The following steps are gone through as logically related steps of scientific analysis, interpretation and conclusions:

(1) Formulation of hypothesis.
(2) Collection of data.
(3) Analysis of data.
(4) Classification of data.
(5) Observation of relationship between facts and events.
(6) Establishing relationship between cause and effect.
(7) Evaluation of hypothesis.
(8) Establishing a principle.

Science and Education

Before eighteenth century science had not developed so much. Today scientific investigations and researches are being made with such fast speed that their knowledge needs a complete knowledge of science.

Science has become an integral part of human life. All our means of communication, radio, television, foodgrains, clothes and medicines depend upon the development of science.

As soon as we are deprived of any of these scientific investigations and researches even for a short period of time, we feel unhappy.

Advantages of Scienctific Education

Following are the advantages of scientific education:

(1) Thinking and memory develops.
(2) Principles are formulated.
(3) Self-confidence and self-reliance develop.
(4) Love for truth enhances.
(5) Confidence regarding unity in diversity increases.
(6) Devotion towards nature increases.
(7) Avenues open for newer and newer vocations.
(8) Science has become the basis of our cultural heritage and social progress.
(9) Like other disciplines, education is placed in the Faculty of Science. Education is not only an art but also Science.
(10) Most of the principles of modern education are scientific. Almost all the strategies, tactics and techniques of teaching are scientific in nature.

Scientific Attitude

Scientific attitude includes the following elements:

(1) Identifying causes of the problem.
(2) Establishing relationship between cause and effect.
(3) Believing in intellectual integrity.
(4) Raising above blind beliefs and dogmas.
(5) Having full faith in truth irrespective of one's own likes and dislikes.
(6) Developing the capacity of clear thinking and receptivity to new ideas.
(7) Accepting the authentic ideas even with caution.
(8) Possessing a critical and constructive attitude while solving a challenging problem.
(9) Arriving at no conclusion at all on the availability of incomplete or false data.

(10) Basing conclusions on tested data only.
(11) Keeping certain exceptions into consideration while determining a principle.

Scientific Education in India

Ours is an age of science. It is essential for every individual to have a correct knowledge of this scientific age. Education should be organised in such a way that each child is inspired to participate actively in the economic reconstruction of society.

They should understand that development of modern society depends upon the development of science and technology. They should try to develop themselves technologically so that technological efficiency and high level competence is developed in them and they are able to enjoy maximum advantages of science in their daily life.

Though scientific education in India started in the beginning of 20th century, yet real advancement in this area was achieved during the second half of this century. Gradually newer and newer industries started growing. When India attained independence in 1947, national leaders thought of industrial growth side by side with the growth of agriculture and allied vocations.

Demand for engineers and technicians began to grow and more and more children began to receive scientific and technical education. Opening of more and more institutions of this type of education was undertaken by the central as well as state governments. But soon thousands of engineers together with technicians began to swell the ranks of the unemployed.

Lack of practical training in workshops and inefficiency of teachers contributed to these chaotic conditions. To improve this type of education. National Council of Educational Research and Training sponsored by the National Government at the Centre re-organized and re-planned the education of science in all areas and fields.

NCERT launched various schemes through its extension services for the improvement of scientific education at all levels and in all fields of human work. Some of its working schemes are as follows:

1. *Schemes of teaching science.* Various schemes have been launched to stimulate the urge for scientific education among school children. Class-room teaching is augmented with independent investigations and research at all levels of school and college teaching by providing guidance and equipment for experimental work.

2. *Promotion of science clubs.* Establishment of science clubs is promoted to popularise scientific education among common people. These clubs are provided with adequate equipment and facilities for experimental and practical work.

3. *Organisation of science fairs, seminars and symposiums.* Through newspapers, teachers of science are encouraged more and more to develop their knowledge of the subject matter and adopt the most up-to-date devices and techniques of teaching.

4. *Selection for science education.* Through examinations, talented and gifted children in the field of science are selected and encouraged by the award of scholarships, stipends and appreciations in various ways.

5. *Central science workshop.* On the advice and under the guidance of talented and learned members of UNESCO, science council has established a central science workshop for imparting effective instruction to science teachers in practical investigations, workshop methods together with techniques of work and instruction.

After such experience and training, teachers as well as students are encouraged to prepare designs, models and scientific instruments for laboratories. The central workshop also tries to improve models and designs prepared by Indian schools besides modifying foreign equipments to suit Indian needs and conditions.

6. *Training of science teachers.* For laboratory and workshop, techniques, a part time curriculum for teacher training has been organized at various important places in the country to prepare efficient science teachers for effective teaching and productive guidance. It is expected that participants will be able to set right the instruments, models and machines lying useless in schools and colleges. Huge wastage of resources will be saved through these schemes and part time courses to teachers, students, laboratory workers and technicians.

Technological Advancement and Education

In modern age progress in the field of production science has been attained only through researches in methods and techniques of production. The supreme gift of science to modern age is technology of various types. Technology is the application of science to satisfy the daily needs and requirements of human beings. Technology is the practical or applied use of scientific knowledge. This scientific knowledge is being applied to all areas and fields of human activity.

Technological advancement opens new vistas of progress in all fields of development in a country. The USA, Great Britain, Russia and Japan have achieved great heights of prosperity because of advanced technology in all areas of human activity.

In India, the use of technology in the areas of industry, agriculture and commerce has revolutionized our productive capacity so that we are in a position to export various consumer articles, goods and even machines to other countries.

Scientific and Technical Research Bureau, Atomic Energy Bureau and National Security Scientific Laboratories have promoted science education to a considerable extent. Central and State Governments have established centres of advanced research in almost all the universities where ample facilities have been provided for higher researches and investigation in various fields of science and technology.

This has promoted industrial, agricultural and technological advancement to a very great extent, its pace is increasing day by day.

Hard work, understanding and insight are greatly essential for technological progress. Following suggestions have been given to promote this capacity:

(1) Technological knowledge which includes application of known technology and provision of further research in the field is essential.
(2) National prosperity and conducive atmosphere are required.
(3) Political and administrative encouragement is a must.
(4) Adequate capital, resources and other material for technological research and progress are needed.

(5) Provision of markets must be made for goods produced.
(6) Efficiency of planning and execution of plans must be taken into consideration.
(7) Education of workers to improve their efficiency must be imparted.
(8) Various efficient agencies are required to run the industries efficiently. A nation which can fulfil all these conditions and pool all its available resources will march ahead on the road of progress and prosperity.

In India, more and more industries are being established in various fields of productive work. But these industries are not being run as efficiently and profitably as they should due to the incapacity of our working and executive personnel. To increase the efficiency of workers and organizing personnel, we need the re-organization of our whole system of education and pattern of giving practical experiences in all aspects of technology.

Our national system of education should be linked with productive workshop experiences so that trained persons work efficiently and intelligently to achieve higher and higher targets of production of all kinds of goods and materials. Technical education should be integrally correlated with practical workshop experiences and most recent techniques of production.

An essential need of our modern education in science and technology is to re-orientate and reorganise it on sound and effective lines. Only then, India will be able to stand in the ranks of the developed and prosperous nations of the world.

QUESTIONS FOR ANSWER

1. What is science? Throw light on the relationship of science and education.
2. How can education promote scientific attitude in children?
3. Discussing the progress of scientific education in India, throw light as to how such type of education can promote technological advancement in the country.

35

Principle of Vocational Education (Vocational and Technical Education)

India as developing nation faces the problem of poverty whereas its population is increasing day by day, hence, we must keep pace with scientific and technological advancement taking place in the developed world and inculcate in our people an urge for technical know how which is a must for socio-economic growth of the nation. This is only possible through education. Therefore, educators opted to accept the principle of vocational education in our system of education. Hereunder, we will discuss various aspects concerning this concept.

In the present age of science and technology, social good and welfare as well as upliftment of the society and the nation depends upon vocational and technical education, because our main problem is poverty. Therefore under social compulsion, Government has to plan comprehensive development of industry and for doing so had to provide liberal vocational technical education. Let us see where do we stand today in this field.

Before the country had become independent, it had already witnessed the establishment of the Mines Institute in Dhanbad, the Cloth Institute at Kanpur, the Engineering College in Bombay, Engineering and Technical College in Jadavpur, Tata Institute in Jamshedpur, Téchnical College at the Banaras

University, the Polytechnic in Delhi, and many other similar institutions.

In 1947, there were 38 technical institutions in the country which provided 2,940 trained persons every year. At the same time there were 53 polytechnic schools in the country from which 3,670 students obtained their diplomas annually. On the 30th November, 1945, the Government of India established the All Indian Technical Education Board.

In 1947, the Scientific Manpower Research Committee came into existence. This Committee conducted a survey and discovered that by 1947 the country required 54,000 engineers and some 20,000 technicians.

After independence, the attention of the Government was soon drawn to the need for vocational and technical education as an essential means of progress and development in the country. Many programmes for this kind of education were put forward in the five year plans. In more recent years, the effort has been stepped up, and now both the Central and the State Governments are concerned with progress in this direction.

The Central Government makes provisions for technological advance in every part of the country, and provide financial aid to the universities and institutions providing the highest technical education. The Central Ministry of Education is concerned with care of these institutes of higher learning in the field of technical education, although the actual work is done by the All India Board for Technical Education.

This Board also has formed regional committees concerned with the organization of the board of study, the national diploma course, short-term courses and postgraduate programmes. In the case of the State Government, the responsibility is primarily one of advancing the cause of technical education through its department of technical education. A Board consisting of 17 members, under the Chairmanship of the Education Minister, makes provision for technical education in the State.

Institutes of Technical Education

In India, the various institutes for technical education can be divided into the following three categories:

1. *Degree and postgraduate institutions.* Such institutes provide education and facilities for research in such spheres as mines, industry, metallurgy, dam building, road, industry, irrigation, land reclamation, instrumentation, production engineering, chemical engineering, electronics and telecommunications, petroleum research, clothes, architecture, etc.

2. *Diploma course institutions.* Polytechnic institutes for girls and boys provide training in various technical subjects for periods ranging from one to three years, depending upon the curriculum. The successful candidates are awarded diplomas.

3. *Institutes for training in specific vocations.* Institutions belonging to this category provide training for many handicrafts and cottage industries such as weaving, printing, sculpture, leather work, carpentry, jeweller's work, the work of the blacksmith, etc. In addition to this many schools and colleges strain individuals to make them skilled and semi-skilled technicians. But such people must be literate.

In 1947, the country had 38 such colleges and 53 schools in which 3,670 students received diplomas and 2,940 received degrees. But over the last three plan periods, the number of technical education institutions has increased manifold. In addition to Warangal, Mangalore, Nagpur, Bhopal, Durgapur, Jamshedpur, Allahabad, Delhi and Srinagar, many other towns also have regional engineering colleges. The Indian Institute of Science at Bangalore provides special facilities for research.

The Kharagpur institute also performs the same function. Indian Institute of Technology have been established in Bombay, Madras, Delhi, Kanpur and Kharagpur. In addition to these, the Government is also establishing centres for training in urban and rural planning, printing, industrial organization, etc.

With the assistance of the Ministry for Community Development, the Education Ministry established 48 science temples in various parts of the country in 1964 in which educands were provided scientific information.

In 1950-51, the number of vocational and technical institutions in the country was 2,339 in which 11,568 educators taught 1,87,194 students. On these students, the Government spend some Rs. 3.69 crores. In 1965-66, the number of such institutions was 2,776 in which 2,47,910 students underwent training. It must be remembered that in 1960-61 the number of schools was 4,145 in which 4,01,274 students were being taught. In this manner there was a downfall in technical education in 1965-66.

In the same period the schools providing training in music, dancing and other arts and social services were 5,939 in which some 23,46,279 students were studying. In 1969, the number of institutions for higher training in engineering and technology in the country was 135, from which 17,800 students obtained degrees while 27,900 students obtained diplomas. In 1968, when unemployment spread to the technically trained sphere, the admission to these institutions was generally reduced. This reduction was to the tune of 30 per cent.

Since independence till date the government is patronising vocational and technical education and facilities of these studies at present is available to very large number of students.

Problems of Vocational and Technical Education

It is evident from the brief history of vocational and technical education given above that it faces certain special problems in the country. Some of these problems are as the following:

1. *Unemployment among trained individuals.* In the recent past, there were loud complaints from many sections of society that there were not enough institutions for technical and vocational training in the country. Even today, there are some demands to open more such institutions in certain parts of the country, but at the same time people are aware that there is widespread unemployment among technically trained graduates and technicians.

Besides, many of the people apparently employed are only inadequately or improperly employed. This has created a very redoubtable situation which suggests that there was no correlation between the increase in technical training and actual industrial progress. It has already been pointed out that all modern progressive nations carry out surveys to determine the number of trained people required in each sphere of industry before entering on a programme of providing institutions for their training.

These institutions are used to fulfil this demand for technical training. Although this idea was accepted in principle in India also, in actual practice no relation was maintained between the demand and supply of technically trained personnel.

In the Fourth Five Year Plan, the Government had decided to provide employment to such people and also to control admission to all such colleges as well as colleges providing general education.

2. *Shortage of technicians at the lower level.* On the one hand, one finds a large number of qualified engineers without employment while on the other there is an acute shortage of trained technicians at comparatively lower levels of work. Most of the craftsmen and mechanics are not trained individuals. Even today, one finds acute shortage of properly trained mechanics for maintenance work in motor vehicles, small machines, electrical appliances, etc.

3. *Absence of co-operation between the State, industry and education.* At the root of both the above problems is the lack of coordination and planning between the Government, industry and education, because this imbalance of demand and supply is clear evidence of lack of planning.

If technical education is to be really useful to nation, it is essential that there should be co-ordination between these three sectors so that education should train the right number and right kind of individuals for which there is a demand in industry. The Government can then really accept responsibility for finding employment for these trained personnel.

4. *Defects of administration.* To a considerable extent, the difficulties and problems of technical and vocational education in this country are enhanced by the administration, where sometimes one finds one man doing the job of three while at other times one finds two or more people engaged on a task which can easily be performed by one person.

In both these conditions, the quality and quantity of work suffer, apart from the unpleasant experiences which the trained individual has to suffer. Many times politicians interfere in the work of highly skilled technicians and specialists, and as a result one finds many industrial and technical programmes suffering unimaginable losses. This also leads to dissatisfaction among the workers. Unless these problems of administration are solved, it will not be possible to create a climate conducive to the trained individuals.

5. *Narrow curriculum.* As far as possible, the curriculum for technical education should also include teaching of several subjects keeping in mind that the technician is also a human being. In recent years, attention has been paid to this aspect, and one finds that the syllabi of most engineering colleges and technological institutes includes studies of social sciences and the humanities.

6. *Problem of the medium of education.* It is essential that the mother tongue should be the medium of education at the lower and middle level of technical education because educands coming in at this level do not have sufficient linguistic skill to study through the medium of English. But unfortunately, even today, there is little or no technical literature available in Hindi or any regional language, with the result that it has been impossible to use them as media of technical education.

The Government is engaged in the task of creating a vocabulary of technical terms in Hindi and other regional languages, which encourages one of the hope that it will be possible to grant technical training through this medium in the near future.

7. *Shortage of trained teachers.* In the sphere of vocational and technical education there is an acute shortage of trained educators. In order to overcome this difficulty, it is necessary to make the profession more attractive by offering high salaries to the staff of institutions engaged in this kind of education.

The possible people may find it more attractive and profitable to stay in the country than to settle abroad. Under the existing circumstances, a very high percentage of the trained talent migrates to foreign countries where the prospects are much better.

8. *Education after leaving school.* Another difficulty is that fairly soon after leaving school and taking up some job the trained individual finds that he is lagging far behind knowledge because he cannot keep up with more recent advances in knowledge and technology. It is, therefore, desirable that some

arrangement for refresher courses for these people should bemade so that they can keep up with the growing knowledge.

9. Lack of practice in laboratories. Generally speaking, there is definitely a shortage of good laboratories and workshops in the country, but even where they are available they are not put to sufficient use. Most of the education imparted to the educand is of a theoretical nature, with much less emphasis upon practical work and practice.

But research laboratories can only be increased when the industrialists co-operate with the government. Another aspect of this problem is that such laboratories should make use of the equipment manufactured within the country instead of depending exclusively upon exports.

10. Insufficient research. Compared to the more progressive nations, India spends far less on research in technology. In Russia and America an amount spent on research is 2.8 per cent of the national income while in India the amount invested in research is only 0.2 per cent of the national income.

In the absence of continuous research and new inventions, both technical education and industrial progress suffer.

Hence, there is every need for encouraging research on the materials available in the country.

There is no doubt that some attention is being paid to the solution of these difficulties of technical and vocational education in the country, but undue interference by politicians and the Government's inherent lethargy have only aggravated the situation. If anything positive is to be achieved, co-operation between the Government, industrialists and directors of education is unavoidable.

Unless some co-ordination is reached in the thinking of these three parties, there is no hope of progress in vocational and technical education. Neither will there be any chance of the trained people finding sufficient and proper employment. The one ray of hope is that the Government has professed a keen interest in the problem of the trained unemployed and has promised some relief.

The future of the country inevitably depends upon producing a large number of technically proficient individuals and upon the proper utilization of their talents in the industrial sphere.

QUESTIONS FOR ANSWER

1. Point out the significance of vocational and technical education. What are the chief sources of such education?
2. Write short note on Vocational Education.
3. What is meant by technological change? Discuss the influence of technology on human attitudes and activities.

Bibliography

1. Abbott, T.K., *Kant's Theory of Ethics,* London, Longmans Green, 1909.
2. Adams, Sir John, *The Evolution of Educational Theory,* London, Macmillan, 1912.
3. Aiyar, S.P., *"Education and the Traditional Society in India,"* General Education Quarterly (Vol. III, No. 1), October, 1965.
4. Altekar, A.S., *Education in Ancient India,* Nawal Kishore & Bros., Varanasi, 1957.
5. Bagley, W.C., *Determinism in Education,* Baltimore, Warwick and York, 1925.
6. Bagley, W.C., *Educational Values,* New York, Macmillan, 1911.
7. Barnet, P.A., *Common Sense in Teaching.*
8. Battle, Jean Allen, *Culture and Education for the Contemporary World,* Columbus, Ohio, C.F. Merrill Publishing Co., 1969.
9. Biddle, Brue J., *et al., Essay on the Social System of Education,* Columbia, Missouri, University of Missouri, 1966.
10. Brookover, W.B., *A Sociology of Education,* New York, American Book Co., 1955.
11. Broughton, H., *The Open Air School.*
12. Buch, M.B. and Santhanam, M.R., *Communication in Classroom.*
13. Chamber Lain, A.F., *The Child.*
14. Coleman, J.S., (Ed.) *Education and Political Development,* Princeton, Princeton University Press, 1965.
15. Crotean, J. M., *Non-verbal Communication Education.*
16. Curtis, S.J. and Boultwood, M.E.A., *A Short History of Educational Ideas,* London, University Tutorial Press Ltd., 1948.
17. Deighton, L. C., *Encyclopedia of Education.*

18. Desai, A.R., *Essays on Modernization of Underdeveloped Societies* (Ed.) Vol. I, Thacker & Co., Bombay, 1971.
19. Deway, John, *Human Nature and Conduct*, New York, Halt, 1922, p. 128
20. Dewey, John, *Democracy and Education*, New York, Macmillan Co., 1916, p. 144.
21. Dewey, John, *The School and Society*, Revised ed. Chicago, 1916. See further Sir Fred Clarke, *op. cit.* (note 4 in Chapter 1).
22. Ebel, R.L., *Encyclopedia of Education.*
23. Elkin, Frederick, *The Child and Society*, New York, Random House, 1960.
24. Erikson, E.H., *Childhood and Society*, London, Imago, N.d.
25. Findlay, J.J., *Principles of Class Teaching.*
26. Fitch, J.G., *Educational Aims and Methods.*
26. Fox, C., *Education Psychology.*
27. Goel, B.S., *"Caste and Class Tensions in Indian Education"*, *Conspectus* (New Delhi, Indian International Centre, Vol No. 4), 1966.
28. Government to India, *Emotional Integration Committee: Preliminary Report*, New Delhi, Ministry of Education, 1962.
29. Harris, P.E., *Changing Conceptions of School Discipline*, New York, Macmillan Co., 1928.
30. Hartog, P.J., *Examinations and their Bearing on National Efficiency.*
31. Hill, W.K., *Furniture, Apparatus and Appliances.*
32. Horne, H.H., *The Democratic Philosophy of Education*, New York, Macmillan Co., 1932.
33. India, *Education and National Development Report of the Commission* (1964-66), New Delhi, Ministry of Education, Government of India, 1966.
34. John Adams, *Evolution of Education Theory.*
35. Kabir, Humayun, *The Indian Heritage*, London, Asia Publishing House, 1962.
36. Klages, L., *The Science of Character*, Allen & Unwine, 1929.
37. Kothari, D. S., *Education Commission Report (1964-66).*
38. Laurie, S.S., *Institutes of Education.*
39. Mason, C.M., *Home Education.*
40. Mead, C.H., *Mind, Self and Society*, Chicago, University of Chicago Press, 1934.

41. Moore E.C., *What is Education.*
42. Munshi, K.M., *Foundations of Indian Culture,* Bombay, Bharatiya Vidya Bhawan, 1962.
43. Nunn T. P., *Education: Its Data and First Principles.*
44. Nunn, Sir Percy, *Education: Its Data and First Principles,* London, Edward Arnold, 1930, p. 9.
45. Radha Kumud Mukherji, *Ancient Indian Education,* Delhi, Motilal Banarsidas, 1951.
46. Rai, Lala Lajpat, *The Problems of National Education in India,* Delhi, Publications Division, 1968.
47. Ramanathan, G., *Education Planning and National Integration,* Bombay, Asia Publishing House, 1965.
48. Richmond, W.K., *The Permanent Value in Education,* London, Society for the Promotion of Christian Knowledge, 1920.
49. Ross, J.S. *et al., Sociological Foundations of Education,* New York, Thomas J. Crowell Co., 1942.
50. Saiyidain, K.G., *The Humanist Tradition in Indian Educational Thought,* Bombay, Asia Publishing House, 1960.
51. Shah, A.B., *Planning for Democracy and Other Essays,* Bombay, Manktalas, 1967.
52. Sharma, R.N., *Philosophy of Education,* Delhi, Atlantic, 1996.
53. Sharma, R.N., *Problems of Education,* Delhi, Atlantic, 1996.
54. Sharma, S.L., *Modernizing Effects of University Education,* ICSSR, New Delhi, 1979.
55. Sharma, S.P., *Teacher Education Principles, Theories and Practices.*
56. Sharma, Y.K., (1) *Fundamental Aspects of Educational Technology.*
    (2) *Sociological Philosophy of Education.*
    (3) *History and Problems of Education.*
57. Stanley, William O., *Education and Social Integration,* New York, Columbia University, Teacher's College, 1953.
58. T. Raymont, *The Principles of Education.*
59. Tompkis, Arnold, *The Principles of Teaching.*
60. Welton, J., *Logical Bases of Teaching.*
61. Whitehead, A.N., *Aims of Education.*

Index